AF544935

KENNETH S. NORRIS

Naturalist, Cetologist, & Conservationist

1924-1988

An Oral History Biography

Interviewed by Randall Jarrell and Irene Reti

Edited by Randall Jarrell

Published by University Library, UC Santa Cruz

Distributed in Association with University of California Press

Berkeley Los Angeles London

2010

Manufactured in the United States of America.

Library of Congress cataloging: QH31.N67 J37 1999

Cover illustration by Jenny Wardrip Keller. Granite Mountains in the Mojave Desert, looking northeast toward the Providence Mountains with male chuckwalla (*Sauromalus obesus*) in foreground. Black and white lizard illustration is also by Jenny Wardrip Keller.

ISBN 978-0-9723343-3-4

Acknowledgements

Many have contributed to the making of this book. The project was started at the request of Roger Samuelsen, Director Emeritus of UC's Natural Reserve System and Larry Ford, Vice President of the Institute for Sustainable Development; they got the project off the ground and through their fund-raising efforts we were able to inaugurate and complete this project on an accelerated timetable. The generous donors who made this possible include the Kenneth S. Norris Fund; Gary Griggs, director of the Long Marine Laboratory and Institute of Marine Sciences; Alexander A. Glazer, director of UC's Natural Reserve System; UCSC's Environmental Studies Department; Tom Morrish; Seeley W. Mudd, II; and an anonymous donor.

My gratitude to Ken Norris, who was so generous in spending time with me as he shared many aspects of his life; he was joyous, introspective, humorous, spontaneous, and despite his weakened condition, he gave these interviews his all. I will always appreciate that we completed together as much as we did. I also experienced what so many have said about Ken: that he made each person feel unique and appreciated. He was *sui generis*.

Ken's colleagues and friends made themselves available for interviews on short notice during a difficult time. Their recollections and insights into Norris's life and work have made this book possible.

Irene Reti, the Assistant Editor of the Regional History Project, has been my indefatigable colleague and partner in interviewing, research, endless fact-checking, typographical decisions, design, and layout, and the mechanics of bookmaking. Her enthusiasm, hard work, discriminating eye, and devotion have made this a joyous endeavor from beginning to end. Larry Ford, a walking encyclopedia of Norris's work at the NRS, in the Natural History Field Quarter, and in the Environmental Field Program, has been a constant inspiration; he wrote me numerous e-mails answering dozens of questions and assisted in fact-checking countless dates, names, and details. His abiding support and help throughout have been invaluable. Guy Oliver provided energy, suggestions, and enthusiasm throughout the project, providing me with much information as I conducted research and selected interviewees. My thanks to Daniel P. Costa for his permission to include his bibliography of Norris's publications in this volume. Phylly Norris graciously answered numerous questions so we could get all the details right. Paul Rich generously shared with me his insights into Ken Norris's evolution as a scientist and the nature of his creativity. Many thanks as well to Carol Howard and Susan Rumsey for their assistance in loaning and locating photographs for this book. When we were feeling helpless with computer problems, Raymund Ramos gave emergency computer assistance on many occasions, as did Susan Kramer. And thanks as well to Sharon Call, for her patient assistance and eagle-eye in keeping track of the numerous financial details of this project.

The Regional History Project is supported administratively by Alan Ritch, the head of Collection Planning, and University Librarian Allan J. Dyson, both of whom have been enthusiastic and appreciative colleagues in this endeavor.

Lorie Cahn (L) & Shoo Shoo Salasky (R) with Ken Norris, 1978. Photo by Tom O'Leary

"I think of Ken Norris often—when I admire a grand expanse of wildland, when I have a new insight into why a plant grows where it grows, when I spent time with students eager for discovery, when I share companionship and laughter and song, when I sit with discipline to write at my computer, when I gaze at a clear running stream and try to embrace all of the connections in the universe in my own small way. Ken will always be an important part of my life."

—*Paul Rich*

Photo by Donald J. Usner

Contents

Robert M. Norris

Lawrence D. Ford

Donald J. Usner

Bill Mayhew (left) and Ken Norris served together for many years on the University-wide NRS Advisory Committee. Here they are shown surveying a potential NRS site near UC Santa Cruz in the early 1980s. Photo courtesy of the UC Natural Reserve System.

Introduction

The Regional History Project conducted a series of interviews with Kenneth S. Norris, UCSC Professor of Natural History Emeritus, in the spring and summer of 1998. Halfway through the interviews, Norris, who had been in poor health, was hospitalized unexpectedly and died on August 16, 1998. Rather than publish an incomplete set of his edited interviews, I reconceived the project and selected a group of his colleagues and former students to interview, who could discuss many of the topics I had not had an opportunity to discuss with him. These additional interviews include recollections of Norris's myriad research interests (desert biology, herpetology, marine mammalogy) and his scientific legacy; his teaching philosophy and how it was so creatively manifested for almost two decades in the celebrated Natural History Field Quarter class; and his founding role in the creation in 1965 of UC's Natural Reserve System.

On October 24, 1998, at the Norris Memorial, held at UCSC, celebrating his life and work, many of his far-flung students and colleagues gathered together from around the country. During that weekend my colleague Irene Reti conducted interviews with Stephen R. Gliessman, Donald J. Usner, and Shannon M. Brownlee, for their recollections of the Natural History Field Quarter. I conducted interviews with Robert M. Norris, William N. McFarland, William F. Perrin, and later, with Roger J. Samuelsen, and Lawrence D. Ford, who discussed the genesis of the NRS and Norris as scientist and naturalist.

Norris was born August 11, 1924 in Los Angeles when Southern California was still a rural place with easy access to wild things. His mother and father relished the outdoors and were unusually encouraging of their boys' naturalist interests. They took Ken and his older brother Robert on many family camping trips and hiking in the mountains and by the time he was about ten, Ken's taste for natural history and collecting was already well developed.

Norris graduated from Van Nuys High School in 1942 and entered UCLA. He served in the U.S. Navy from 1944 until 1948, when he returned to UCLA, and earned his bachelor's degree in biology in 1948, after having almost completed his degree in geology. When he was a senior he met up with Raymond B. Cowles, who had a transformative influence on the direction of his life. Norris wrote of Cowles:

*[he] turned my career around just as I was becoming a senior. I went along on one of Cowles's trips to the Mojave Desert. He seemed to know everything, and he carried a romantic explorer's air about him. Born in South Africa of missionary parents, he spoke Zulu, and we got him to speak a few phrases in that curious clacking tongue. . . But his allure was much more than these momentary revelations. He was obviously buoyed by my questions, and when he answered me he led me down the paths of his own mind. His answers did not come from books. They were instead sharings of his life, his curiosities, his syntheses. And he was amazingly synthetic. He led me down dozens of intellectual trails I had never even thought existed. For him, always, the living thing-in-nature, was central. 'The specimen is the authority,' he said. If one wanted to learn about nature, one had to block out preconceptions and contrive to look directly at nature's life processes, without injection of any personal bias. That view is utterly central today to all I do. It was he who taught me to see in nature.**

Norris earned a master's degree in desert zoogeography at UCLA in 1951, with Ray Cowles as his major professor when he wrote his thesis, "The Evolution of the Iguanid, genus *Uma*." He moved from the desert to the sea when he began work towards his Ph.D. under the legendary Carl L. Hubbs, at the Scripps Institution of Oceanography in La Jolla. Two years into his doctoral work Norris was hired as the founding curator at the country's second oceanarium, Marineland of the Pacific in Palos Verdes, California, where he began his pioneering work with marine mammals during the period 1953 to 1960. He continued working on his dissertation on the opaleye, named after its lovely bluegreen eyes, a perch-like fish of the sea chub family *Kyphosidae*, in which he investigated the effect of water temperatures on this intertidal

*Peter G. Beidler, ed., *Distinguished Teachers on Effective Teaching*, (San Francisco: Josey-Bass Inc., Publishers, 1986 p.11.).

fish. For the groundbreaking ecological approach he developed in this dissertation, "The Functions of Temperature in the Percoid Fish, *Girella nigricans* (Ayres)," he received the Mercer Award of the Ecological Society of America for the best study by a young scholar in 1963.

He received his Ph.D. from Scripps in 1959 and in the same year Norris returned to UCLA where he was hired as Ray Cowles's successor and taught biology and herpetology and continued his research on desert reptiles. He was at UCLA until 1972, where he advanced to full professor of Natural History (the only professor of natural history in the UC system). In 1965, due to his efforts, UC's Natural Reserve System was established under UC President Clark Kerr. While continuing at UCLA on a part-time basis, he became the founding director of the Oceanic Institute in Hawaii, from 1968 until 1971. In 1972, he moved north when he was appointed at UCSC and founded Long Marine Laboratory and the Institute of Marine Sciences. He was Professor of Natural History until he retired in 1990 after eighteen years at UC Santa Cruz.

In these interviews Norris and his colleagues discussed the unusually varied range of his scientific discoveries and conservation activities. At UCLA his work as a desert herpetologist and ecologist led to his discoveries of the function of color changes in amphibians and reptiles and of circadian rhythms in snakes. His pioneering investigations in marine mammalogy confirmed dolphin echolocation skills in a series of elegant experiments. Much of what is now known about whales and dolphins, specifically their social and familial interactions is due to his work. His expertise in marine mammalogy also resulted in his strong influence on public policy in the crafting of the Marine Mammal Protection Act in 1972. His leadership and research were also instrumental in the national campaign to reduce the dolphin kill in tuna fishing. Norris was the author of over a hundred scientific papers and several books on dolphins and porpoises.

The tape-recorded interviews in this book were transcribed verbatim, edited for continuity and clarity and the text organized into chapters. Copies of this book are on deposit in Bancroft Library at the University of California, Berkeley, and at the UCSC Library.

—Randall Jarrell, June 20, 1999,
Santa Cruz, California

Part I.

Kenneth S. Norris: In His Own Voice

Kelso Dunes, Near the Sweeney Granite Mountains Desert Research Center at the Dedication of the Kenneth S. Norris Camp and Teaching Area and the Sibyl and Al A. Allanson Library and Center, April 21, 1996. Photo by Susan Gee Rumsey.

Photo by Donald J. Usner

Family Life and Early History

Jarrell: To start, Ken, when and where were you born?

Norris: August 11, 1924. I was born in Hollywood. I specify Hollywood because there's a slice of unincorporated land in the Los Angeles area on which the Presbyterian Hospital sits. That's where I was born.

Jarrell: Where had your mother and father come from? Had they grown up in Los Angeles, or had they come from somewhere else and settled there?

Norris: Well, let's see. My father came from Ohio. His father was a nursery importer and a very successful nurseryman. My father worked with him to some degree, and then he went to the University of Michigan and took an engineering degree, and from there he wandered through a lot of jobs during the Depression. It was a very hard time for him in that— He had a dreamy coefficient about him which came down unalloyed to me. It meant that he was always doing visionary projects that were going to take ten years to develop and then they would have made a lot of money, but in the intervening ten years in the middle of the Depression it was not a good time to do that. So he sort of drifted between being a nurseryman and being an engineer.

Jarrell: Was he sort of an inventor?

Norris: Yes, he was an inventor, as a matter of fact. He was a dreamer of schemes, a great outdoorsman. But he was a dreamer of these schemes which never worked because they were always before their time.

My mother was born on 4th and B streets in San Diego and was wonderful, steadfast, smart, ebullient. She was a beautiful young girl. She was just brighter than anybody and she knew how to do everything. She was the one who took over the books and the finances and so forth, through a lot of trials. It was not an easy time in the Depression. We lived through a series of houses in Los Angeles; we moved from place to place and ended up in the San Fernando Valley when it was [still] farm country. It was a wonderful place for a young kid to grow up, particularly one with leanings toward the wild world, which, by the way, came [to me] from both my parents. My mother was an artist. She made every rug in this house; she made a thousand rugs in her life. By doing this and by carefully getting herself allied with interior decorators she brought us through the Depression significantly, which was a really tough time. She had people in her employ and she was a real artist. That too came down to me; I'm an artist as well.

So I'm an amalgam of my parents. Both of my parents were lovers of the outdoors and of wild things and that has always been my ruling passion. It's been at the center of me forever, since I was a tiny little kid looking at tadpoles. So I've never wavered at all from being a naturalist and my father's dreamy side came through to me as something very useful in natural science, that is to say, imagining patterns way out in front of most people. That's been my stock in trade as a scientist. And I've gotten to such a degree of doing that sort of thing that I have to watch my step or else I'll speak too far out in front and then the rank-and-file will tell me to go jump. Which is a real possibility that happens to a lot of people. There's a very wavery line there between predicting how things work and being airy-fairy. I've always been close to that line but I've been very aware of it.

I have managed to get the reputation of somebody who sees things that other people don't see, but they don't know why. So they all say, well, let Norris play. He's usually right. That's been a true thing throughout, especially in the latter part of my career when some of the fetters come off of your mind and you say, oh damn it, I'm going to say this. I know it's right so I'm going to say it. That's where my reputation as a scientist has come from. I have been right about a lot of things that people have been surprised at often, I think. I've been way ahead of my time on some things.

Then the other thing that has propelled my career forward is that I love to work. I've always been at work. Ever since I started, I've been working. I've always worked with joy: if it isn't fun I don't do it. So I've had a wonderful, joyous career in which by some political sense, probably from my mother, I was able to balance that difficult conceptual line and get away with it.

Jarrell: Where did you go to high school?

Norris: I went to Van Nuys High School out in the San Fernando Valley. I was in Marilyn Monroe's class.

Jarrell: No kidding.

Norris: It gives you an idea about how antique Marilyn would be. Norma Jean Baker. She was a little dishwater blond who went with the football guys. I was kind of scared of her.

Jarrell: What kind of a student were you in high school?

Norris: I was a very good student when I wanted to be, and then sometimes I had trouble with some things. I was a lousy mathematician; that came very hard for me. But science in general was very easy for me, and full of pleasure and excitement which, I think, has been a hallmark of everything I've done. It's an excitement and pleasure and going full speed. I've never slowed down. Even now I'm busy dictating a book in the back room.

Jarrell: When did you graduate from high school?

Norris: 1942.

World War II

Jarrell: Where were you during World War II?

Norris: Oh, my mother said to both my brother and me that the place for us to be safest in the middle of a war like this was in the navy.

Jarrell: That's what your mother said? (laughter)

Norris: She directly stated that.

Jarrell: Where did you serve in the navy?

Norris: I was on a troop transport. I was an ensign, the lowest thing in the navy. I went through training at UCLA. We used to march everyday up to UCLA and take our classes. Then I was in the Navy ROTC which was supposed to be one level above the ninety-day-wonder officers. So I shipped out and we went across the Pacific sixteen times in a troop transport and once around the world. The around-the-world trip was after the war and it was to take the refugees back who had come to the United States. So the whole ship was full of missionaries and other people. We started taking them to the Philippines and then went to Singapore and up into India, up the Hooghly River to Calcutta. God, what an awful place. Then we went up the Red Sea through the Suez Canal to Port Said and then to wicked Alexandria, and then through the Mediterranean, the straits of Gibraltar, which I saw at 5:30 in the morning. Then through to Boston where the ship was decommissioned. Decommissioning was total chaos. What they did was simply to throw everything onto the dock. So I got one of these metal ammunition boxes and collected that stuff and sent it home. Amongst the things I sent home was a record player, a PA system, and during my first years after that at the university I played records at dances. I was a disk jockey. I had a microphone and it was my special pleasure to play dreadful Spike Jones records at midnight when everybody was dancing about a mile an hour which affected my saleability as a disk jockey. I couldn't restrain myself.

Jarrell: After the war when you returned to UCLA, did you have any idea what you wanted to do?

Norris: Oh, yes.

Jarrell: How had that been fermenting?

Norris: It had been fermenting all during the war. Part of my time in training I had been taking geology and I was very close to graduating as a geologist. So I looked at the world through that lens as we went around it and across it.

Raymond B. Cowles

Norris: I was very close to graduating but there was something missing. What was missing was life.

Jarrell: Do you mean in terms of your field?

Norris: Yes. My colleagues would walk right past a lizard on a rock. And God, I wanted to look at that lizard!

Jarrell: They were looking at the rocks?

Norris: Yes, they were looking at the rocks. Many of them were sucking on oranges into which they had poured bourbon. So they were walking across the landscape getting slightly smashed while I was chasing lizards and trying to learn the plants and so on.

A friend of mine at UCLA, Bob Lindberg, came to me and said, "you've got to go out in the desert with this naturalist I'm working with—Ray Cowles. He's your kind of guy; I just know you would make a connection with him." So I went out on a field trip with Cowles in his natural history of California course and it was the changing of my career.

He knew everything; he knew all the little things that I wanted to know. Cowles was originally from Kenya and when he was out in the field it was his habit to always carry a pistol and a snake stick with him. Once he picked up a rattlesnake, a Mojave green, the most dangerous rattlesnake in North America by three-fold. It has neurotoxic venom, instead of hemotoxic, which causes the red blood cells to blow up but leaves you mostly with big bruises. But the neurotoxic venom kills you; you simply subside and die.

The class was full of premeds and most of them didn't give a damn; they were just out there to fill a requirement. On the other hand, I was just swept away by this guy. Cowles saw that I was keen. One time he came over to me and said, "Ken, you seem to be interested in everything, including the plants.

Here's something I think you would like to see." He always wore these field jackets with deep pockets. He fished into his pocket, dug out a Joshua tree pod and broke open the capsule. "Look at these seeds." They were like little poker chips all stacked up. He said, "Look, there are going to be about thirty percent that have holes in them and that's from a moth that pollinates the Joshua tree." So I looked and it was thirty percent. What the moth does is take its tithe from the seed and then the organisms sprout. But the moth doesn't take everything. So both species persist and yet they are totally tied to each other. The moth doesn't pollinate anything else. It comes out in the flesh in the spring. If either one of them breaks the fragile equilibrium for any reason, both species will disappear. So I thought about that and about lives tied together and the story became more fascinating; I realized that with that tying-together, both species became fragile and it is no minor event when two species assist each other in that kind of way. That really shook me, just the thought of that kind of an arrangement; I was just swept away that there were two lives locked together in this obviously long evolutionary history that they built such a relationship. How could that be? How did the processes work that did that?

I went on from there and switched over from geology into biology, even though I was all but graduated in geology. It was total commitment, absolute total commitment. And oh Lord, this excitement just went on and on, that I'd found home. I knew right where I belonged. So that is the story of how I got into biology as a senior.

I got very excited about evolutionary process and was on the fringes of the work of the greats at UCLA. We went to an old botanist who turned out to be a real player in the maze of the unfolding of the theory of evolution.

Jarrell: Who was this?

Norris: Carl Epling, an authority on sages. Around him gathered the greats in the field. We went out in the field together and we got to see that these people were just people and they worked because of excitement and because they were uncovering how the world worked. It was a very exciting time for me.

Jarrell: So your encounter with Cowles was life-changing?

Norris: Yes, I had been within an ace of graduation. I even had a job with an oil company which would have been an awful thing to do.

Jarrell: As a petroleum geologist.

Norris: Anyway, I went into biology and I was a hog-head. I mean, oh my Lord, I was so excited. Every day was an adventure. I lived in Ray Cowles's lab, along with a couple of other students—[Richard G.] Zweifel, who became the curator at the American Museum, and Charlie [Charles H.] Lowe who became a professor of biology at Arizona. The three of us—we practically lived there. We cooked hot dogs in beakers and argued incessantly with each other and set up experiments and they couldn't get rid of us. It was total commitment. I knew I was home.

Jarrell: How exciting that must have been for you!

Norris: Oh, my Lord.

Jarrell: To discover this blissful niche in the world.

Norris: I knew I was home. That's where I belonged. That's who I was.

Jarrell: So, I was reading this entry on you that said you got your master's degree from UCLA in 1951, then your Ph.D. in 1959.

Norris: Yes, there was a long interregnum there. I started at Scripps Institution of Oceanography at La Jolla. I changed from the desert to the sea; that was a wonderful move because it let me enclose the whole world in my conceptions about how things worked.

I went to some seminars down the hall from Cowles run by a marvelous guy, Boyd [W.] Walker, who had been a captain in the army and boy did he know how to run people around. He was a wonderful guide for us as graduate students. He took us all over Mexico collecting fishes and I became much involved in doing the fishes of the Gulf of California with him. That seminar had some pretty amazing people. There was George [C.] Williams who became one of the great theorists of evolution at New York University; Bill [William N.] McFarland; who became one of the great authorities on light and the environment, and the reactions of fishes and so on; and Dick [Richard H.] Rosenblatt; who became the curator of fishes at Scripps. There was quite a list. I was in the middle of some real thinkers such as George Williams, who became a professor at [UC] Berkeley. It was a hothouse of ideas, and God I loved it! Boyd Walker sent me to Scripps under the great Carl [L.] Hubbs, the greatest figure in American ichthyology at the time. He turned out to be an incredibly hard worker but a person with only modest ideas, I thought, at the end.

Early Research Interests:

Opaleye Perch, *Girella nigricans*

Norris: So that's where I began my work. I walked down the beach and found a tidepool series with fishes going back and forth and then observed them as I usually would do and I found that they were incredibly wary. I had to get down behind rocks and look through cracks to ge't them to come out into the pools. I found that they were migrating up and down that intertidal zone on a map and I uncovered a whole lot of things about the lives of that animal.

Jarrell: What was its name?

Norris: The opaleye perch, Ultimately I wrote a paper on that which won the Mercer Award of the Ecological Society of America, an award that's given every two years to the best work by young scientists in America, in ecology, which totally amazed me. Anyway, that was Scripps which was an amazing place to be. We sleuthed around among the great there.

Jarrell: Were you working on your dissertation on the opaleye perch when you were there?*

Marineland of the Pacific

Norris: Yes, but I didn't finish it. Before I finished Boyd Walker pointed me to a job assembling the exhibit at a new oceanarium, Marineland at Palos Verdes, which was the second such exhibit in the world, built in Los Angeles. So I took that job and worked there for six years.

I took it without having yet completed my doctoral degree. I went up to Los Angeles and bought myself the de rigeur suit of the day with wide lapels and stripes. I went downtown and interviewed with this kind of smiley old guy who'd been the manager of the World's Fair in San Francisco. He looked at me. I was so god damn stiff and scientific that he was kind of afraid of me. On the other hand, I had good recommendations and so he hired me. His two first orders were to go down to the cave, a sea cave on the cliff below the oceanarium and get rid of all the rattlesnakes that were in there. Well, there weren't any rattlesnakes in there, but that's all right. And the other one was to take care of his goldfish.

Unlike most people I didn't give up my Ph.D. thesis. I set up equipment in the basement of the oceanarium and continued the work on my thesis and finally finished it in 1959.

Jarrell: So you were really doing two things at once?

Norris: Oh, man.

Jarrell: Well, I mean two main roads here; you were working. And what was the nature of your job?

Norris: I was the curator; I was in charge of the exhibits.

---

*Kenneth S. Norris, "The Functions of Temperature in the Ecology of the Percoid Fish, *Girella nigricans* (Ayres)," (Ph.D. diss., University of California at Los Angeles, 1959).

Jarrell: Did you have any previous experience with things like this?

Norris: No, I didn't know a damn thing.

Jarrell: But that didn't matter?

Norris: No, it didn't matter because I was a young Turk all full of enthusiasm and Boyd Walker knew that I would work my buns off and that I was smart.

[phone rings] "Oh good, Fred, thank you."

Fred [Carlson] is my salvation. He's a magnificent instrument maker.

Jarrell: What does he build?

Norris: He builds violins and guitars and special instruments. He's amazing. He's the best craftsperson I ever met.

Jarrell: Where did the funding come from for Marineland? It was not a non-profit institution, was it? It was a commercial enterprise?

Norris: Yes. It came from a group headed by one of the heads of the Texaco Oil Company. They just up and built it and it was successful.

Jarrell: Where did they get the idea?

Norris: Well, from the first one in Florida at Sarasota, out in the middle of a palmetto swamp.

Jarrell: Did you visit Sarasota?

Norris: Yes. It had been built for making movies. That's why it was called Marine Studios.

Jarrell: It was a backdrop for making movies?

Norris: That was the original plan. But the first day they opened they had 14,000 people down this lousy dirt road to get in. They knew they were in the tourist business. That was the first one and we were the second. I had to figure out how to catch dolphins and fish and God knows what else. What I did was to listen to a couple of people who said, "Ken, you can't do this yourself in a skiff. You're going to have to have some real help. Go get yourself the best fisherman you can find." So we did and hired him. We bought his boat, a cute little thirty-seven-foot gill net boat and spent the next six years at sea much of the time when I could get out.

I found myself in total terra incognita. Nobody knew anything about the marine mammals that went by our door. I was well-trained in taking good notes of my observations of these mammals. For example, I published papers from that which documented the passage of 60,000 Dall porpoises a year, when they were thought to be rare, and known only from two or three strandings on the beaches. It was like that throughout the whole fauna. Nobody knew anything about them. So I was in hog heaven. I went out with those guys as much as I could. We captured the first pilot whale together.

My head fisherman was Frank Brocato, who was terrific; he was one of the brightest people I've ever worked with. He knew how to build anything. He was always doing what he called "snootin' around." He'd go out and look his boat over every morning before we'd go to sea. Heaven only knows how many times he saved the boat from sinking in one way or another, you know, from fuel leaks or whatever else it might be. In other words I'd found myself a jewel, a Sicilian fisherman with a temperament to match. Boy was he pyrotechnic! But I loved him and together we learned about the marine mammals of Southern California in all kinds of dimensions. Because I wasn't a taxonomist I didn't just classify them and count them. I wanted to know how they swam and when they gave birth and everything about them. So I published a series of important papers based on these experiences and observations at sea.

Then I set up a laboratory to finish my doctoral degree and built this beautiful machine called an ichthyothermataxatron: icthyo is fish, therm is temperature, taxi is movement, and tron is marvelous, wonderful, mysterious machine. And then I did my thesis work in that.

Jarrell: You know, to backtrack, what I find so interesting is that when you went to Marineland, you left UCLA and it took you a long time to finish your dissertation and get your doctorate. But even though you were working in a non-academic setting, you published all of these papers.

Norris: I did it anyway. I started a publications series out of the oceanarium and we distributed the best of our papers. We were getting to be known as a research institution before I left, from that.

Jarrell: So you never stopped.

Norris: No, I never stopped.

Jarrell: I can imagine that many of your counterparts in other oceanaria later on might have gone and designed a Marineland and not had any interest at all in doing the kind of research and publications that you continued to do?

Norris: Yes, that's certainly true. I think most wouldn't have. But it had to do with this excitement about what I was doing. I was so swept up in these discoveries and the joy of the work. God I loved the work!

Jarrell: During that period in the 1960s were you in contact with other scientists involved with marine mammals or the work that you were doing at Marineland? Did you have correspondence or get to know or consult with other scientists?

Norris: I found myself in a cadre of about forty people, not just nationwide but worldwide, who were concerned with these animals. We met and formed a group and met in Washington, D.C. We published volumes on our work.

I edited one of the first volumes, *Whales, Dolphins and Porpoises*, which was published by UC Press.*

They came from all over the place, from the British Antarctic Survey, from museums, etc. So I was still in the middle of the scientific swim. After all, I was producing some of the most original material that was coming out because I was actually watching the animals in the wild. So it was an exciting time. Sheer physical excitement carried me though there too. Also the bits of integrity that I had picked up from my professors were crucial. I was a good reporter.

Jarrell: Did you have young scientists, graduate students, at Marineland?

Norris: We had a string of them. Welcomed them in the door. They enlivened the place endlessly. And my friend who was also my assistant, John Prescott, who later on became the curator at the New England Aquarium, was a very much respected figure at Marineland.

Joining the Scientific Priesthood

Norris: By God, in 1959 I went up and got my Ph.D. degree and listened to the chancellor tell us how few of us there really were who got those degrees, and what we would mean to the country. I listened to him and was impressed by that, that I really had entered some kind of priesthood, if you want to call it that. Because it was kind of a priesthood then.

Yes, that always struck home with me, that speech. I didn't think it was just formulaic. It was also true. I found it to be. The minute I got my degree I was elevated. A lot of people expected a lot of things out of me that they hadn't expected five minutes before. I entered kind of joyfully into the priesthood. It was indeed a priesthood at the time.

Jarrell: It was that old model, wasn't it?

---

*Berkeley, 1966.

Norris: Yes. It was before people began to find the warts on science; before they began to find ways to avoid science.

Jarrell: What do you mean by that?

Norris: What I mean is that science had always been a sticking point. Here are these ponderous guys in their white lab coats who'd come up and nail you with facts. Your testimony before congress which was going along just fine until the scientists showed up, would crash. Well, the maneuverers, the politicians, who had run things forever, began to find ways around that. They de-mystified science. That's what has been happening in recent years. It's pretty easy to push a scientist off in the corner. But one thing, we always demand proof. Proof is hard to get. They never did enough of it to satisfy themselves. As a result you just talk about that and then pretty soon you've got them. Science has been fighting that battle ever since.

Appointment at UC Los Angeles

Norris: I finally decided that I really was an academic and that I wanted to go back to it. So I went back to UCLA about 1961, I think. I walked in the door and asked my biologist friend [J.] Homer Ferguson if they needed a biologist. He said, "Well what do you teach?" I asked what they needed. He asked if I could teach general biology. Sure. So they hired me. That was the personnel process, for Chrissakes. So I went to work at UCLA. As the story goes, Ray Cowles, my professor, was going to retire and I think it's true that he asked that I replace him. So later on there was a kind of almost tearful transition when I was settling in at UCLA where I said to him his junk wasn't as good as my junk and I'd have to replace it and the desk.

Boy, it was amazing. But then of course they knew me. So I went downstairs and replaced Cowles and became a desert biologist again.

Jarrell: Oh I didn't know you sashayed back and forth between the desert and the sea.

Norris: I did. We were entering the decade of the Sixties. [And the next part of my story demonstrates] why bad judgment's my most important product.

Jarrell: How so?

Oceanic Institute, Hawaii

Norris: Well, we'll see if I can tell you. I had started the job at UCLA and I was doing great. I was just tearing up the turf. I really was. A guy drives into my driveway and in the back of his pickup truck were two giraffes in boxes, with their necks sticking out. This was the director of the Honolulu zoo, Paul Breese. Paul said he would really like me to come over to Hawaii and look at a project over there. He was talking about building an oceanarium there. I said, "Gee Paul. Sounds good." And off I went. I became involved in the construction of Sea Life Park. I was actually their sort of animal man and designer.

I told them about marine animals. They didn't know anything about marine animals. But I knew all about them from my experience at the oceanarium [Marineland of the Pacific] where I worked. So I ended up splitting my time between UCLA and Hawaii. Believe it or not I became the director of the scientific institute that we built alongside the oceanarium at the same time as I was a professor at UCLA, which [was] insane. On the other hand, I was introduced to the central Pacific fauna of marine mammals that was totally unknown. Nobody knew anything about them. I'll just tell you a story. We had a French-Hawaiian collector, Georges Gilbert. He called me up one day and said, "We've got a polka dot animal; the polka dots are pink. Tell me what it is." I said, "I don't know what it is. I better fly over and take a look." And so I did.

The dolphin swimming around in the tank was the second or third record for the rough-toothed dolphin for the Pacific ocean. That sort of thing kept happening. That animal, by the way, turned out to be a wizard. It was a creature that never came closer than about eight miles offshore. It would open gates with its mouth, things like that. It manipulated things. We trained it, my colleague, Karen Pryor and I. She was the wife of the founder of the place and an amazing person. She was Philip Wylie's daughter. And smart. Oh boy. So Karen and I became colleagues in experimentation. We worked with the rough-toothed dolphin. She taught one to innovate. This was supposed to be a characteristic of humans but it's a characteristic of dolphins too, at least rough-toothed dolphins. She taught an animal to do new things; she taught it the concept of new, and it picked it up and over its head was the little light bulb going on when it got it. Then in one day it poured out twenty-three new behaviors that nobody had ever seen before. Think about that. That begins to tell you something about what lies in the heads of those dolphins. So it was a terribly exciting time.

Jarrell: Now you said that at this time our scientific knowledge of marine mammals was virtually nil.

Norris: Well, that's not fair.

Jarrell: You said there had been a lot of work in terms of identification and taxonomy in the nineteenth century, but that it was a very neglected field?

Norris: Well, the Pacific was neglected; nobody knew what the hell was in the Pacific. I landed in the middle of hog heaven for somebody who was interested in that.

Jarrell: Paul Breese, who asked you to come to Hawaii, what was his background?

Norris: Paul Breese was the director of the Honolulu zoo, and a total character. His wife worked for a while at Long Marine Lab, Mary Lou Breese.

Jarrell: So there was a zoo and they had you come for awhile to oversee the development of the—

Norris: Of the oceanarium research institute. Then I became the director of the research institute at the same time as I was a professor at UCLA.

Jarrell: How did that sit with UCLA?

Norris: Well, finally UCLA told me to go jump.

Jarrell: Into the ocean? (laughter)

Norris: Well, they gently said, "Hey Ken, this is crazy. You really have to come back and do your job here," which made every bit of good sense. I knew it was right. But I looked at Los Angeles; I was driving clear across L.A. every day to go to work. God, I hated being on the freeways behind the semi-trailers and stuff. So instead of going back to UCLA I came to [UC] Santa Cruz. I inquired up here and there was a job for someone to establish their marine station, what became Long Marine Lab. So I came here instead and brought my family into this lovely forest instead of driving across Los Angeles every day.

Jarrell: So you wound down at UCLA, decided you did not want to continue teaching there. What happened to your work in Hawaii? Did you continue with that?

Norris: I left the oceanarium.

The Norris Family

Jarrell: How did you meet your wife, Phylly?

Norris: Well, I was twenty-nine and I could feel it coming upon me. I started looking for a mate. That's a messy process. I think an awful lot of people don't know anything about the person they marry. I knew something, but I didn't know very much. Anyway I used to go to whale-watch up on top of Ritter Hall at Scripps, which was a thing that my professor did. He was counting the gray whales that went by.

In a little alcove in the hallway sat this beautiful, black-haired woman. The most important thing was that she was the queen of the campus because she had the rattiest lab coat available, all covered with acid holes. That was high-toned at Scripps. Actually that's unimportant, but nonetheless that was part of it. So I finally asked her if she wanted to go up and whale-watch with me. So we went up the ladders and out onto the roof and into this little kiosk where we counted the whales. And six weeks later we were married.

Jarrell: My goodness!

Norris: Wow! I took her home and introduced her to the family and she was very reserved and very nice and they all liked her. She is the daughter of a Pulitzer Prize winning White House reporter who went to Washington, D.C., in a Model T Ford in 1923 during the Harding administration.

Old Papa [Richard Lee] Strout, he used to write a column; he got a job at the Christian Science Monitor, even though he wasn't a Christian Scientist. Anyway, he told the story about [President] Harding coming over to the press building. He walked from the White House, mind you, and knocked on the door. They opened the door and there was the president. The president was lonely; he wanted to play cards. So they took him upstairs and played cards with him. I think that tells you something about the times. Anyway, Papa Strout was very much like Phylly. He had it all together. Oh boy, did he have it together. And so does she. Phylly never missed a beat. I couldn't have picked a more wonderful person, or one who filled in all the gaps in my own psyche, than her. She's the one who does all the investments; she pays all the bills; she just generally runs everything from her position while I'm allowed to go off and be dreamy. So that's the way it's been. It's been an absolutely wonderful marriage forever. Still is.

Jarrell: And the two of you have raised four children.

Norris: Yes, Richard Norris. He is a biological oceanographer and staff member at Woods Hole Oceanographic Institution. He was the co-leader of a recent expedition which proved the impact of the asteroid on earth that killed the dinosaurs.

Jarrell: Down by the Yucatan Peninsula?

Norris: Right. He led the drilling expedition which took the cores on the other side over in the Florida area. He actually works in paleontology, mostly with little foraminifera and radiolarians, and things like that. He's made a world-wide reputation for himself. I'm so proud of him. He's just a pretty amazing young man. He has two children. He married one of my students.

Jarrell: From Santa Cruz?

Norris: Yes, Teresa Burns, now a Norris as well. Then next is Susan [Norris] who lives here [on the property]. She's a violin maker. If I ever met a carbon copy of myself, it's her. There's all the art there; there's all the love for the environment, the deep love for the environment. Finding yourself alongside a stream or amongst the wildflowers or whatever. There're all those things. She's a marvelous teacher as well. She takes people on herb classes here.

Jarrell: Here on the farm, on the property?

Norris: All over, all over the hills. She knows every trail. She's an instrument maker as well. She makes lovely freeform violins which she calls suzalynes* and other instruments. She just finished a xylophone.

Now my next daughter is Nancy [Littlestone]. She's married to a mathematician at a think-tank at Princeton. Nancy is absolutely one of a kind. You totally never know what she's going to do next. It's always full of imagination and joy. She just had a little girl and watching little Eleanor grow up is something to see. I just treasure her more than I can say.

Then our last child is Barbara [Gaskell]. Barbara graduated in geology. She married an astronomer from UC Santa Cruz and they've settled in Lincoln, Nebraska, where he teaches at the University of Nebraska. He's one of the

---

*Phyllis Norris described Susan Norris's suzalyne as a five-stringed violin-like instrument with sympathetic strings and the combined range of a violin and viola, inspired by historical Norwegian stringed instruments.

world's authorities on quasars, the most distant objects in the universe. He's a very, very smart guy.

They're both church members. This has been a wonderful experience for me. I haven't been a church member. I went to church when I was a little kid, but never seriously. Barbara has taken me in, unlike most people where there's almost always a distance between people of faith and people who are on the outside. But Barbara will have none of it. She'll talk to me about anything. And we do. She's totally wonderful. As a result I've been able to creep up to the boundary between faith and my Darwinian position as an evolutionary scientist, and find out how far I could go. What I found was that I couldn't make the leap. I couldn't get over the top of that.

Jarrell: The leap. What would the leap be to?

Norris: The leap to faith. I couldn't accept a lot of the world metaphysically. I was too much of a scientist to do that. So that's where I am now. And my daughter still loves me. She's just totally wonderful. She'll talk about everything with me. She was on the phone every night while I was in the hospital. She's raised two kids while her husband's on soft money at the university there and it's just been scratching by. But she's raised her family in the most wonderful way. They haven't missed anything, the kids, you know —so that's my family.

Robert M. Norris

Now, I didn't tell you about my brother, Robert. He's three years older than I am. Let me tell you a little about him. He's a very well-known California geologist; he wrote the major book on the geology of California.* My father was an engineer. And Robert really was an engineer, too. My father could make the most beautiful drawings. He had a little box all full of sharpened pencils, and really down to his core he knew how things worked and could do engineering things. Well, my brother can, too; he can fix anything. Old cars. He loves old cars. He put up with this improvident brother of his who

*Robert M. Norris, *Geology of California* (New York: Wiley, 1976).

would end up sleeping on the front porch of the apartment we shared in La Jolla because I would forget my keys.

He has the sweetest, most wonderful temperament. He put up with his brassy little brother in the most wonderful way. When we were in college he used to take me on these trips in his old cars and we went all over much of the west in a 1926 Dodge laundry wagon that we cut the back end out of and covered like a Conestoga wagon.

He's a wonderful teacher; he's won awards as one of the best teachers at UC Santa Barbara. He teaches in a totally different way than I do. I've also won a teaching award but he's done his because he went right by an outline of everything he was going to say written on the blackboard. Tick tick tick tick: the students never lost track of anything. When he would talk to them it was like going before a compassionate judge; they didn't fool him for a minute about anything. On the other hand, humanity is where my brother is. So basically I love him.

Appointment at the University of California, Santa Cruz

Jarrell: Ken, you said when you'd come back from Hawaii to UCLA, the whole congested environment was not conducive and you wanted to make a change. You thought of UC Santa Cruz. What did you know about Santa Cruz?

Norris: Well, let's straighten out one thing.

Jarrell: Okay.

Norris: I loved my colleagues at UCLA, and I loved that department. I was in a very good place there. But I was separated by Los Angeles from my home on the south side of the Palos Verdes hills. I just had to make a choice. UCLA is a wonderful place; it's full of resources, all kinds of things, concerts going on there. I would have loved to continue being part of it, but I couldn't. So I thought I better move and so I did.

I checked to see what was available at Santa Cruz, whose campus I thought was the most beautiful of all. I found out that there was a position at UCSC for somebody to put together their [marine] program. They had some money and they were designated as one of the marine campuses. I didn't know there were certain campuses that had been assigned to have a marine science emphasis and Santa Cruz was one of those. They had some money and they needed somebody to direct it. Dean [E.] McHenry was good enough to assign me to it. So I switched.

Jarrell: What was the background of those initial discussions? You made it known to Dean McHenry that you wanted to come up here? How did that work?

Norris: I don't really remember, exactly. Obviously he looked into me and found out that I had been directing a marine institute and that I had a very good record as a marine scientist. So up I came.

Jarrell: Was your initial appointment in biology?

Norris: In biology, Yes.The confusion here is whether or not there was a marine program that I was in. I'm not quite sure about that.

Jarrell: UC Santa Cruz environmental studies wasn't yet established.

Norris: That came later. That was Matt[hew] Sands, the physicist who went around and asked if there was anybody who was interested in environmental studies. I said that I was. So off I went to a partial appointment in E.S. I was one of the original guys there.

Jarrell: Did it have the status of a board [department] at the time? Or was it a little constellation of faculty interested in environmental studies, at first?

Norris: Well, I think it was a board, but I'm not sure. That kind of administrative stuff never stayed with me.*

*Environmental Studies was established as a board/department in 1970.

Jarrell: The Institute for Marine Sciences and the establishing of Long Marine Laboratory: how did you involve yourself in these?

Founding the Joseph M. Long Marine Laboratory

Norris: Well, the job that they'd asked me to do was to bring marine science into the cluster of people in environmental studies, which at the time was heavily social science-oriented. I said sure, that I'd like to try. So I was given this little pot of money for planning the marine program. I found the staff busily spending that money on their research programs. I took it away from them. I don't think they were particularly happy with me, but I did it anyway and began to use it in planning for the marine station. I went to Dean McHenry, as you can imagine, and said, "Hey, what do we do next? Here's what I think we need. Can you help? Do you agree with me?" What I told him was that I'd seen too many marine stations set up where they were so far away from the campus that people could go off into them and be troglodytes, but that you couldn't engage the campus with it. Over and over again the main campus had grown to ignore such stations. For example, that happened at Hopkins Marine Station.

Jarrell: I was going to ask you about that, about Stanford and Hopkins.

Norris: Yes. Hopkins is so far away that it loses contact with the Stanford campus. The contact that's needed is subtle; it's seeing each other over a cup of coffee; it's talking to people about your family, making friends, sharing one thing and another. The idea of being isolated and alone is something that appeals to a lot of scientists. Many of them would be just as happy to be out in a situation like that. But it inevitably leads to rot.

Jarrell: What kind of rot?

Norris: Rot of the organization you're trying to build, particularly because the students can't get there. So I drew a circle on a map of Santa Cruz [which I showed the Chancellor] and I said this is how far a student can go in between classes on campus and at a marine station, and this is where we've got to place our marine station [in the Younger Lagoon area].

Jarrell: What an interesting way to look at it.

Norris: Yes. That's exactly what I did, and so my circle didn't go very far. I did calculate that we could have bus transportation between the marine station and the campus so there was a little bit of extra space but it limited us to the west side of Santa Cruz, to the pier, places like that. I said to Dean McHenry, "Do you know anybody who's got any land here?" He piped up and said, "Yes, I do."

Jarrell: Did he mention Donald Younger?

Norris: Yes. What he said was that he thought we could bargain with him. I thought, wow, more power to him. So we started dealing with Donald Younger. He had an agenda. I guess that Dean McHenry knew this, so that was another thing in our favor. The agenda was that Younger owned a lot of land on the west side of campus over on Meder Creek and was looking for access to it so that he could develop it.

Jarrell: Oh, so this negotiation was in the nature of a quid pro quo?

Norris: Yes. Then I got to meet Donald Younger. Oh boy, was he a tough old bird. He was a lawyer and knew exactly what he wanted and was prepared to drive up a bargain on it. So we set about obtaining Younger Lagoon. I looked at that lagoon and saw that it should be a reserve; this place had to be saved; there are hardly any coastal lagoons of that sort left in America. There are special flora there. Then Bill [William T.] Doyle popped up. I had a party working with me, of whom Bill Doyle was very important. So we went ahead.

In the middle of it all there was a great tiff between Younger and the chancellor. Our first chancellor was a tough guy. A lot of people didn't know that. But I fell under his lash once, and it was enough to scare the hell out of me. He knew exactly what he wanted to do and how he wanted to do it. He once said that if he couldn't run the whole campus out of his hands he didn't want to do it. I think that was true. Anyway, I very much followed in his steps about obtaining the land. I once asked Donald Younger if we could get a setback from the cliff edge, since he'd agreed to give us the lagoon. He said something to the effect that, "young man, if you push me one more inch it's all gone." So I shut up and we ended up with boundary lines right at the top of Younger Lagoon and not an inch more, which is really dumb on a lot of counts.

Jarrell: What was the logic of Younger's refusal?

Norris: The logic was that he didn't want to be pushed by the likes of me. He wasn't going to be pushed.

Jarrell: You wanted more than he was willing to give?

Norris: Yes, I wanted three feet so that people would stay away from the edge of the cliff and that we could protect it better and so on. But anyway, I bit my tongue and shut up. So we have a reserve down there which comes right to the absolute brink of that lagoon. But that's the way Younger wanted it. So that's the way it is.

Jarrell: Were you involved with Dean McHenry in these negotiations?

Norris: To a degree I was. Yes, he was certainly the one who was running it all. I was about to tell you that in the middle of all this Younger got angry with McHenry. Oh boy, could Younger get angry. Oh, woof! I mean he was pyrotechnic; he turned McHenry's picture to the wall in his office down there, over this tiff. I never did really know what the tiff was about. All I know is that by shutting up I was able to get us that site down there, where the marine station ultimately was established. So those were the early days in the development of the marine lab at Younger Lagoon.

I was able to get Joe [Joseph M.] Long, head of Long's drugstores, once again a contact through McHenry, to fund the first two buildings and to help us to get our salt water system in and some other things. Tough old Joe Long liked me. We always had a good time together. I think it was because in me he saw a fellow entrepreneur, perhaps. But also a person of imagination. He loved the thrust of the ideas that I had; he loved to talk to me. We'd go up to his house and he ran this imperious soirée up there.

Jarrell: Up in Orinda, was it?

Norris: Yes. Anyway, I think he was happy to see me come in the door. I always excited him with some stories or whatever else it was. Tough old Joe Long had a capacity for making business decisions beyond anybody I have ever met. He just didn't go wrong. Whatever he picked up seemed to make money. God knows, that's not me. But in this curious way we struck sparks with each other. I found him to be a fascinating human, certainly not one I could emulate, but nonetheless an amazing person. He had a clear vision of where he was going, clearer than anybody I think I've ever met. He just didn't make a mistake. He equipped himself with the best minds he could get. For example, he decided to drill for oil in the overthrust belt all along in the mountains up by Denver. He was a druggist, for godsakes. But he just didn't miss. Anyway, he was a pretty amazing old duck. He ran his household like a battleship. I used to feel for his wife a lot. I liked her. She collected children; she had all these waifs there that they were caring for. I liked her. I was more like her than like him. Anyway, those are some of the first things.

Jarrell: In designing what Long Marine Laboratory would become, where did your conception come from? You mentioned the salt water system, okay. What went into conceiving this marine lab, its emphases? What did you want to specialize in? And also just the physical plant?

Norris: I don't think any marine station is worth a damn unless it's got a good salt water system.

Jarrell: Why?

Norris: Because you're supposed to be studying the sea. You better have some sea to study. There better be good stuff. You want flowing water where scientists can do real experiments. For the invertebrate people, that means they have to have unfiltered water which has in it the reproductive products of other little organisms that the invertebrates feed on. So you have to be very careful and have a good supply of that.

Jarrell: So you are trying to replicate a natural system?

Norris: You are trying to provide for an experimenter who's going to work with a natural system. Yes. The natural systems come in different flavors. Keeping dolphins is a whole different sack of cookies than keeping invertebrates. Yet in my mind the invertebrate work is every bit as important as the dolphin work.

I terribly much wanted a system of plurality down there. I wanted all sorts of representatives from campus to use it. I went to different departments and gave speeches about the opportunity. I went to the chemistry board, for example, and told them about the opportunity at the lab and for them to take a place in it. I was met with cold and gimlet stares, mostly. Oh boy.

Jarrell: Why do you think? Was it so unconventional what you were inviting these faculty to participate in?

Norris: I suppose it was. At least I didn't get very far. In that case I didn't get anywhere. I got suspicion. Maybe when you try to give something away in the University it's that way.

Jarrell: So you wanted to open it up?

Norris: Yes. I wanted terribly much to have a number of disciplines involved down there. My view about the kind of disciplines involved went all the way to art. I thought to myself, gee, we've got some beautiful opportunities down here. I'd love to have some artists sitting around working on it. Wouldn't that be wonderful? I wanted the physical scientists; I wanted the geologists. I got almost none of them; almost all I got was biologists.

Jarrell: How do you account for that?

Norris: It's kind of the history of familiarity with marine stations amongst biologists. They know that they're expected and liked there. I think it's different with chemists. It's very hard to move a staff member in a university from his or her path because they're trying very hard to make a career and they have to plan ahead, and as a result I finally realized that I wasn't going to reach these people through their own programs. I was going to have to do it through their students; it was going to have to be a place where students came and the more diverse the better.

Jarrell: Subvert the reigning paradigm? If you couldn't get the faculty members from other disciplines because of their career paths and specializations, then recruit the students?

Norris: I finally came to that realization. I didn't like that a bit because I sure wanted this diversity. But I realized that faculty are forced by the system to stick to certain paths in their careers.

Jarrell: You were saying you wanted the invertebrate people to be involved at the Long Marine Lab; you wanted it to be to be a very wide-ranging marine lab.

Norris: I did get the invertebrate zoologists down there. We got John [S.] Pearse. Good old John Pearse and his colleagues. They came right along. And Todd [Andrew T.] Newberry, also.

Jarrell: You said you wanted access for the students so that they could work there as part of their campus experience.

Norris: Yes, exactly.

Jarrell: So it wouldn't be an isolated little lab off there somewhere. You said if you couldn't get the interdisciplinary stuff going that you were going to work with the students.

Norris: Well, we did get interdisciplinary stuff to a degree and then Bill Doyle, who followed me in the directorship, did that, too. He was wonderful about outreach; he was Mr. Outreach. He reached into the community and involved them in what we were doing there. Bill Doyle brought in the community. He was the one who made sure that we had good citizen involvement with tours and things like that. Then the students built a little aquarium, and so on. That was a wonderful contribution.

Jarrell: It really has become a community resource in that way because they have the docents, the teaching programs, the students—the little school kids.

Norris: Yes. That's very much his responsibility.

Jarrell: Is there anything else you'd like to say about Long Marine Lab?

Norris: Well, let's see. I want to say this: I hate trailers; I think trailers are at best temporary places to keep people out of the rain. I would have fought as hard as I could to get permanent buildings down there. I think that's now happening. But it's taken a long time.

Jarrell: I thought that Joe Long funded the first two buildings there. Has funding subsequently been a difficult problem?

Norris: Well, funding is as difficult as you make it. I've found that if you have a good story, something that grabs people, you can sell it. That's been my experience. So you can take the easy way out, and keep the rain off of people or you can fight harder for something more permanent. My impression is it has everything to do with personal salesmanship. Do you have a vision? If you've got the vision people really will buy into it.

Natural History Field Quarter

Jarrell: Tell me about the history of the Natural History Field Quarter, its importance for you, and your approach to teaching.

Norris: Well, let's see, when I was at UCLA we would do our field trips. There was lots of opportunity then in the mountains and the deserts. But we had to get to it. So we would caravan. One dreadful night which I will never forget or forgive, one of my students got lost from the caravan. He had all the sleeping bags.

Jarrell: Oh!

Norris: God it was cold! We were down at the Algodones Dunes, the big Yuma dunes in the southeast corner of the state, out in the desert. All we had were some jugs of red wine and ourselves and we slept huddled together in the back of those trucks. I have never quite forgiven the jerk who ran off and didn't pay any attention to where we told him to go. I'm not one to bear grudges, but he's got my grudge after all these years. You'd think I'd forgive him. But anyway, that experience made my mind up that I had to do something different. This caravaning business tied us to the campus. You had to go a long way just to get to where you were going and it ate up most of the time you had.

Jarrell: Just getting there, instead of being out in the field?

Norris: Yes. So I conjured up this notion at UCSC of us getting vans and loading them with our food and so forth and off we went. We could go anywhere. That turned out to be a wonderful way to go. We could stop on the way and look at the plants we found or the geology or whatever else it was, and then we could move on. Far, far beyond that, our little moving organism across the state became an organism into itself and it was terribly different than teaching in a laboratory or a lecture hall on campus, where you're propped up in front of the students and the students are taking down your every golden word. In this case, you're living your life with them in a very real way. We divided up who would cook, who would wash dishes and all that sort of stuff. We ate each other's dreadful food, which I still consider dreadful for the most part. We wove ourselves into each other's lives. We contrived to teach three classes in the field, me and my buddy, whoever that might have been. There were three or four different people over the years who taught with me. Steve [R.] Gliessman was the longest running, and the last one. Botanist Ray [T.] Collett taught with me. The Keeler-Wolfs taught with me; they were students who knew the vegetation of California like the backs of their hands.

Then there was Larry [Lawrence D. Ford]. He was our general factotum student. I taught the natural history of California, the geology. I had almost graduated in geology, as I guess I told you. I knew a lot about geology. So I taught them about that. I myself was never tied to a single discipline at all, Randall.

Jarrell: You were much more freewheeling?

Norris: Yes. I liked the plants as I well as I did some of the little bugs and stuff. I liked the geology a lot. I wanted to know about the weather. I really did want to know about how the world worked. That came very early on in my career from my discussions with my old professor Ray Cowles. He was a wonderful generalist, too, and influenced me that way. But I think I came built that way, anyway. I really did want to know; I really did want to gulp the world whole. It was perfectly natural for me to go to Scripps to get a degree in the ocean after I'd worked in the desert. I still feel that pull as strong as ever. Then I got the central core of evolutionary theory when I was at UCLA. I fell in with a group of people who were working with the greats in the field. We went into the field with Theodosius Dobzhansky and Ernst Mayr and others and watched how they worked, and were part of their work. What we saw above all were people who wanted to get it right. That was exactly what they wanted. They would do anything to get a correct answer. I was really struck by that. I've been that way myself.

Jarrell: So all of these experiences informed the way you conceived of the Natural History Field Quarter. How many students were in this class in which you would be gallivanting all over the state?

Norris: Well, we got ourselves a great, big bus. Old Blue. We had a loudspeaker hung on the roof of the bus and a microphone we could talk into and which the students used for giving oral reports while we were on the road. We had 23 students, usually 23.

Jarrell: That's a big bunch!

Norris: Yes. We had all of our food and gear strapped in the back. We had a resource person along. I would invite one per trip. These people came from different genres. For example, I looked at the student body I was carrying and saw that there were a lot of people who were going to end up as outdoor educators. So I brought along the best outdoor educator I could find to help teach them. Or I brought a poet. I've always thought that poetry was a dimension of the wild world that needed to be thought about. We had Cosmic Joe. Cosmic Joe [Jordan] knew more than the Lord about the atmosphere and things like—he just knows the damnedest bunch of stuff. He works at NASA-Ames [Research Center] on auroras and things like that. So we brought him and his galfriend Mary Moreno in quite a lot and they were wonderful.

Jarrell: How long would you be gone for, typically, in Old Blue?

Norris: It was a series of four to six trips, each for a week, a week and a half. I'm not sure we were out two weeks. We may have been.

Jarrell: How did you decide where to go?

Norris: We found places that would take us. Reserves that would let us camp out and cook our dreadful meals.

Jarrell: Were they really uniformly dreadful? (laughter)

Norris: Well, I'm sort of an obligate carnivore and obligate carnivores hardly have a place in the present-day fare. So that it wasn't too infrequent to find Steve [R. [Gliessman] and me showing up at the local breakfast parlor for a bunch of fried eggs and bacon.

Jarrell: A little survival food?

Norris: Yes, I even carried a salami in my sleeping bag.

Jarrell: In your sleeping bag! (laughter)

Norris: Yes, I did.

Jarrell: Get pretty raunchy. (laughter)

Norris: Well, it was in plastic. But I did munch on it.

Jarrell: You showed me your bound books of students' field notes in your office. So what was expected of the students? What were you trying to get them to experience?

Norris: We worked the hell out of them. They didn't mess around. They kept that daily journal, for which there was a very careful format. Steve and I went through every journal; we read every journal after every trip, which was a lot of journals. We made comments in the margins. Then a lot of the students would give oral reports. Amazingly to me, sometimes these were the first oral reports they'd ever given in college. My Lord! They'd stand up there and give their reports and then they would be discussed and so on. They talked about everything, just damn near everything.

Jarrell: Did a student have to have fulfilled prerequisites in order to be in the class? Did they have to have basic biology? Or were there students from different disciplines who'd never done anything like this?

Norris: I militantly wanted us to select broadly. That's changed now. They've gotten to the point that there's pretty much a pure diet of environmental studies students, which I decry. I selected poets. I had a wonderful poet, a really good poet. He was afraid because he was in the middle of all these damn scientists and was inhibited by them. But finally we got him relaxed, and he gave the most marvelous reports over that speaker system on the bus. He emerged as one of the real strengths on the whole trip. I thought he was extra special. That happened over and over and over again. The releasing of people.

Jarrell: Do you mean their opening up?

Norris: Yes. And then some of these students got married. Their lives were all woven together. They were all woven together with my life, too. You know, it was far, far beyond the experience in a regular class. It was life.

Jarrell: Larry [Ford] told me that you taught the Natural History Field Quarter class continuously over a period of twenty years.

Norris: The first class I taught at Santa Cruz was in 1973. That's when I began to form an idea and perhaps more, to understand, what it was I was dealing with. I was dealing with the lives of 23 young people, all bright, all special in their own ways, who were busy trying to find their place in the world. I was part of it. I wasn't just on the sidelines. I was a part of that search and it marked me for life. It wasn't anything, anything, like getting up in front of a class and then teaching it and then sitting down. It was a slice of life. Very many of my best friends came out of it.

Jarrell: Would you talk about some of these students? It doesn't seem as if you were trying to create scientists but were giving these young people an opportunity to experience the world in a new way.

Norris: In fact. Absolutely.

Jarrell: It seems there was something larger that you were after? Because you said you would have a poet, an artist, non-scientists. Those barriers are so artificial.

Norris: I had a dancer who danced these beautiful movements in the trees. She had a bear dance, in which she made bear claws out of pine cones and snorted and then danced the dance. That sort of thing. What an experience.

Jarrell: You asked me to remind you to talk about the down side, or the problems, that you experienced. Let's start there.

Norris: Okay. It's pretty simple. There are two approaches that one needs in a moving environment like that. You're taking a whole cadre of students out at the most fragile time of their lives, and you can't help but be part of their lives. As a matter of fact that's what you become. There are different approaches to how you teach a student. For one thing they need some discipline; they need to be kept in line some of the time to do the work that needs to be done and not to go off in extravagant behavior. They need some control. On the other hand my style of teaching was to reach into who each student was and to find out what their hopes and fears were. That's a very fragile thing to do.

Jarrell: Very delicate.

Norris: Yes. In some ways it's the opposite of the discipline needed in order to run a venture like that. So it was totally necessary, I found, to have two of us, one of whom would say, enough's enough, and the other who would relate to the student's hopes and fears. Those roles really don't come in the same person. But that meant that I had to have a good partner who would help me do what I was trying to do. At the same time the reverse is true. So my trips were much the best when we had those two sides to them. Our position, that of my partner and me, was that of "uncledom." We were caring uncles. But we couldn't ever be part of what was going on. If we decided that we were going to be students—well, we could have done that but we would have lost everything. We had to be above the fray; we had to be the givers of direction. My part was as the giver of hope and guidance. My partner was more the one who said, let's get the bus loaded. But he also had his position with the students in the same way that I did.

Jarrell: Who were your partners?

Norris: I've had several partners all the way along. Steve Gliessman, the agriculturalist, was my last partner, and was with me the longest. Steve was on his own trip; he had his own concerns and was trying to find his place in the world, if you will. There was a cadre of students that collected around him as a result of that. Then I had my cadre around me. But there was a complex interaction in this rolling community in which we were very much in each other's lives. But there had to be a balance since one person really couldn't do it very well. So that's what I mean.

Jarrell: You were talking about hijinks or extravagant behavior on the field trips. You'd have to lay down the law, tend to business?

Norris: Yes. There were times like that. I wasn't very good at laying down the law because I was trying to have them tell me about their hopes and fears, their problems. That kind of runs against laying down the law, in a way. So that by having two of us who were doing different pieces of it, it worked wonderfully. But without the two—I did it alone a couple of times—it was very hard and was not nearly as successful, I think.

Jarrell: What were some of the classes that you taught besides the Natural History Field Quarter?

Norris: I was involved in the core course in environmental studies. I taught regular, doctrinaire lectures there. Except I have always had trouble behaving myself.

Jarrell: In what way?

Norris: What I mean by that is that my lectures tended to be iconoclastic ones, in which my blundering and messy mind wouldn't let me just shovel the stuff out the way it often is. I think I may be a lot better teacher. But I was different. Does all that come clear, Randall?

Jarrell: Yes, it does. In your approach to students, the way you have just addressed it in terms of the trips, traveling with the students, you said you liked to get very intimate and to really get to know the students.

Norris: Intimate's the wrong word. I was very careful about my limits. I knew my place and it was as this caring uncle. I wanted the young women, especially, to trust me so that they had never a worry from me. I was very careful about that.

Jarrell: I think I used the word intimate just to say that you were interested in students' personal aspirations. Some professors are not particularly interested in the inner lives of students, in their hopes, fears, dreams, shortcomings, weaknesses.

Norris: I was terribly interested in that. I found that we were in the company of peers. That they were, yes, new-formed, and yes, they were struggling their way through, into, life. But yes, they were also every bit our match when you came right down to it. We were amongst peers. What we brought was history; we could bring the dimension of time.

Jarrell: And experience.

Norris: That's what I mean.

Jarrell: Yes.

Norris: Bringing that dimension of experience is a priceless thing. For so many students who became part of my life, like Dawn, for example, I ended up marrying [her and her fiancé], but I think it was seven couples [I married] out of the class in some of the most wonderful ceremonies you ever saw.

Jarrell: You would officiate?

Norris: Yes. Two of my students came to me and said, "Ken, would you marry us?" I said, "I can't marry you." They said, "Oh, yes you can. We'll fix that." So they went out and bought me a certificate and we married them up on the hill over here. The groom had a lizard in his hair; he had this great mop of blond hair and a lizard darting in and out, sticking its head out of his hair. A grandmother came up to me and said, "Oh, how I wish when I was married I could have been married like this." I thought that was kind of fine. The ceremonies were very serious ones in which I tried to tell them what I thought lay ahead for them, and that sort of thing.

Jarrell: I'd say that's rather extraordinary, that particular role.

Norris: Yes, it didn't come easy at first. Then a couple of times it was difficult. But mostly it was a joy. Like a couple I married up on top of the mountains by Boulder Creek. They said that the marsh up there where they were going to have the ceremony would go away by the time of the wedding. Well, it didn't go away. There were ducks swimming in the place when we went up there.

Jarrell: You were supposed to be standing there?

Norris: Yes. They had built giant stilt puppets. They were marvelous great things with long, swirling banners. They came out of the forest and did a dance of the east wind and the west wind. The head puppet sank in the marsh. We could see her go. She had a little radio up in her puppet and—oh there she goes. Anyway, they fished her out. They stood her up again and the ceremony went on. But then the bride had forgotten to file the papers, the marriage license, and the county is not relaxed about that. After a certain number of days the whole thing is null and void. So I said we'd better go down and do it all over again. I asked them to take me to dinner at the

Ristorante Avanti. So we went down there and got the waitress to act as the flower girl. God, she loved it! So we remarried them. Anyway, that's been an experience. They've been some of the most touching times in my life, those ceremonies. You know? It's hard to say it, but our lives are all woven together.

Jarrell: It seems unusually so.

Norris: Oh yes, absolutely. I've never experienced anything like it.

The Tuna/Dolphin Fishing Controversy and the Passage of the Marine Mammal Protection Act

Jarrell: I'd like you to tell me about marine mammal politics and your involvement in the passage of this legislation in 1972.

Norris: Well, I have a friend who is a lawyer and also a biologist. He got me involved in helping to write the Marine Mammal Protection Act of 1972. We got an office in the Smithsonian and went back there and spent a lot of our time talking to the senators' aides, one of whom was writing the first draft of the Marine Mammal Protection Act. We spent a lot of time with him.

I arrived in Washington, D.C., absolutely zonked. I'm a basket case with jet lag. I'd be sleeping on the floor in this little office that we had and then we'd go off and talk to various people. We ended up having quite a lot to do with the shaping of the Marine Mammal Protection Act.

Jarrell: What was the impetus that led to this legislation?

Norris: Well, there was an enormous kill of dolphins going on in the tropical Pacific. 325,000 a year. I had been approached by a wise old fisherman who was a great, close friend of Donald Douglas, of the Douglas Aircraft Company. They knew that this kill couldn't continue going on. They came to me to see if I could help them. This is while I was still at the oceanarium in Palos Verdes.

I had some suggestions for them but I couldn't really solve the thing sitting around a table. So from that came a series of dedicated cruises, dedicated to the science of trying to find out why the kill happened. I led one of those trips out into the Eastern Pacific. That was quite an experience.

Jarrell: What were you looking for?

Norris: I was trying to find out what killed the dolphins.

Jarrell: You said there were 325,000 dolphins a year being killed. Who came up with that number and how?

Norris: They counted the dolphins as their dead bodies sluiced out of the nets of the tuna fishermen. We went out there to try to figure out what killed them because it wasn't at all obvious. Most of them were killed in what's called the back-down operation, where the net is strung out into a long finger and the animals roll around on the bottom of the net, and they drown; then their bodies go over the end and the sharks pick them up and that's that. The question was how to get them out of the net. We studied this. They'd circle their nets and they did what they call back-down. They'd back away from it, and draw the net out into a long finger and then into this the dolphins would come. Then they would try to get them over the lip and free.

Jarrell: Why would the dolphins go towards the net? Would they just be scooped up in the net?

Norris: Yes. We figured out how that worked and devised a way to prevent their being caught in the nets. They were stopped by bubble barriers; they wouldn't go through a bubble curtain. This has to do with their echolocation. They'd send an echo train out and they would get these bubbles which look like a wall to them when they echolocate.

Jarrell: And then they'd stay away from the nets?

Norris: Yes, the fishermen could use this to corral them. We learned a lot of things like that. One of the fishermen, a guy named Jim [M.] Coe worked at the National Marine Fisheries Service. He went and dived down in that channel which was scary, because there were sharks there. He came up and said, "Ken, those dolphins on the bottom of the net aren't dead. Their eyes are rolling around." So I went into the net, into that back-down channel and sure enough, he was right. The animals weren't dead; they were just lying on the bottom. So there was a chance of getting them out of the net and we worked on that. That particular maneuver has now reduced the kill from 325,000 animals a year to just a scant two or three thousand animals that die. So we made an enormous difference. It was done because we had a couple of naturalists loose, who really looked at the animals to find out what was going on and learned things they didn't know before. So that's that story.

Jarrell: They drowned. They were asphyxiated. Was that the reason?

Norris: Yes. They got their beaks caught in the nets. Then they would sluice around down there until they actually did drown.

Jarrell: What was your contribution to this legislation?

Norris: Well, I was their dolphin guy. Nobody else knew anything else about dolphins. They'd just kill them. So I was able to contribute a lot of information about how the animals lived. I was able to contribute this business of their being stopped by bubble barriers, and in the setting up of schools which taught the skippers [tuna fishermen] how to get the animals out of the net and some regulations. But mostly through teaching. The best of the skippers hardly lost an animal after that. The worst of them were disasters and would kill everything in the net. So they began to license who could fish and who couldn't. But what you never knew was what happened over the horizon.

Jarrell: Because how could they enforce the law way out in the ocean?

Norris: Yes, trying to enforce such things in an area five times the size of the United States, an absolutely huge area of ocean, was difficult. So there was a terribly careful political game that was going on between the ones who were trying to solve the problem and the fishermen.

Jarrell: Was it pretty antagonistic at first?

Norris: Yes. Often it was totally antagonistic. But then the very best of the skippers just hardly killed a dolphin. So that the way was showed for solving these problems in different countries in all the Central American countries, in Vanuatu out in the New Hebrides. Anyway, it's a very complicated thing. People still sneak in loads of tuna that are caught just any which way.

Jarrell: Illegally according to the legislation?

Norris: Yes. Some of the watchdog conservation groups have been able to run those things down, using genetic markers generally. The fish can be marked by where they come from, so they can be identified; when a load of fish comes in from the wrong place, it has certain other markers which they can look at. In other words, it's a cat-and-mouse game between the forces of good and evil as clearly as you can imagine.

Jarrell: What particular kinds of dolphins were being killed in this way? Were there certain dolphins that were more susceptible?

Norris: Yes, the spotted dolphin took the brunt of it. These are all animals that feed on what's called the scattering layer out in the ocean, which is a layer of fishes, shrimps, and squids that hang down in the dark water during the day, where they're protected by darkness. Then they move to the surface at night and feed themselves, but they're also fed upon. That's a major, major, movement of life; it's the major movement of life on earth. It's also a major source of the energetics of the ecosystems on which the tuna live. Most people don't even know there is such a thing. Anyway, it's quite a story.

Jarrell: Would you say that the tuna fishing in the old way affected the population of the spotted dolphins significantly?

Norris: Yes, I wanted to say, the spotted dolphin is the one that bears the major brunt. And the spinner dolphin—

Jarrell: That you've written so much about.

Norris: Yes. Which associates with the spotted dolphin, is next. They both get hit pretty hard.

Jarrell: Do you think that subsequent to the 1972 legislation that was almost thirty years ago, that the problem has mainly been solved in that part of the ocean? Or is this going on in other parts of the world?

Norris: I would say that there was a major reduction in the problem as a result of our work. But then it turned into this cat-and-mouse game, between, literally the forces of good and evil. That goes on today. There always seem to be forces of good and evil out there. This is certainly a case where that's true.

Society for Marine Mammalogy

Jarrell: Could you talk about the Society for Marine Mammalogy, its origins and how you were involved in that group?

Norris: Well, we had a meeting in 1971 in San Diego of the marine mammalogists gathered there. We had had two or three meetings in the Washington, D.C., area and then this one in San Diego. There developed a stress in these meetings between the conservation-oriented people and the scientists. The conflict was centered around the fact that the conservation-oriented people didn't pay any or enough attention to factual material. We scientists felt very uncomfortable being represented by them.

Jarrell: Okay, and the conservationists were non-scientists who were interested in safeguarding—

Norris: They were trying to save the dolphin, and with very good cause. There were wonderful people amongst them. Yet the scientists felt very uncomfortable having them as mouthpieces because they weren't hewing to the truth as we knew it, with the rigor that a scientist would. So we had this really very painful breaking away from the conservationists in which they felt affronted by the fact that we couldn't accept them in their form amongst us. You can see the dynamic there.

Jarrell: What was the conservationist group's organization?

Norris: The best of their organizations was the American Cetacean Society, which was formed in a room underneath the oceanarium where I worked. So I knew all the people and furthermore I liked them. We were all trying to do the same thing. We were using different tools. But the scientists simply couldn't be professional under those circumstances, so we moved toward setting up our own society.

Jarrell: Was it the politics that made everything so difficult?

Norris: It was simply that they knew full well that they were working hard for the same thing we were, and we knew that, too. We couldn't bring up a cadre of young scientists under the terms of the conservationists who very often didn't give a damn about science. Our requirements were much more rigid than theirs. So we had to break away, and it was very painful. But we did it.

Jarrell: Did the activists have some kind of difficulty with the nature of the science you were doing with the dolphins?

Norris: We had difficulty with the fact that they didn't pay any attention to the science.

Jarrell: They'd ignore it?

Norris: Yes.

Jarrell: Why?

Norris: Well, because they were conservationists and science wasn't their thing. Science has got a lot more rigor to it. We wanted to bring our young people up with the canons of science intact. We were also under a lot of fire from others in the scientific community because they viewed our science as not being rigorous. That came from being all mixed up with the conservation group. Can you see what I'm saying?

Jarrell: Yes.

Norris: We knew we had to correct it. We knew we had to teach our young scholars what real science was. And the conservationists were out of all good motives, in the way. And so we did it.

Jarrell: So the genesis of the Society for Marine Mammalogy was a way to legitimize, to express your concerns, but also to do it in a scientific way?

Norris: Yes. It was in a hotel room in San Diego. There was a funny cast of characters there. But we started the society and I was elected the first president up there to try and escort all this through. My biggest problem was the Internal Revenue Service. God, they were awful!

Jarrell: Why?

Norris: They simply refused to recognize that we were a legitimate scientific venture.

Jarrell: They thought you were a political activist group of some kind?

Norris: I think they were just being a pain in the tuchus. I think they were just being awful. And it's sort of like some of the things you've been hearing lately about the IRS. We just couldn't get past them. At least I couldn't.

Jarrell: And you wanted to set up as a non-profit, educational—

Norris: Yes. Like any other scientific society.

Jarrell: You couldn't get the nonprofit status?

Norris: I couldn't myself get past the IRS. The next presidents succeeded. But not me. The society started out local in California, then it went national and international. They have offices overseas. It's the major marine mammal society in the world now. We have a fine journal, Marine Mammal Science. We have very good meetings, very well controlled. So there really is a target for a young person coming out. Teaching the young is the most important thing a society like that can do. Teaching them the canons of their craft. Our society does a very good job of that now.

Environmental Field Program

Norris: The Environmental Field Program was set up by me in my office in the environmental studies board to put students in teams on issue areas throughout wild California. The Environmental Field Program sent these teams of students out. We built a collapsible house out of plywood that we could bolt together; we put it on a flatbed truck and drove it wherever we wanted to and set it up. It had a little bunk room, a dark room, and a place where you could cook. Like that.

Jarrell: Whose idea was this?

Norris: Me. I thought it up. We built it here in the backyard. It was about forty feet long and had little rooms in it. It was tight going for people who stayed in it. We would identify an issue area and we'd take this thing out and set it up and then attack the issue. For example, one of the sites was in the Kingston Range in the desert south of Death Valley. We thought it ought to be a wilderness area. They're big, high mountains, over seven thousand feet. We put our team out there to study this, and they ended up doing an elegant report.* They discovered twenty-six new Indian sites while they worked out

*R. Doug Stone and Valerie A. Sumida eds., *The Kingston Range of California: A Resource Survey: Natural and Cultural Values of the Kingston Range, Eastern Mojave Desert, California.* (University of California, Santa Cruz: Environmental Field Program Publication, 1983).

there. They mapped the geology. They did all kinds of stuff like that. By golly, we got the thing in as a wilderness area. That was a successful one.

Jarrell: Who oversaw this inventory or survey of the whole area?

Norris: Larry [Ford] was my straw boss. He took charge of making sure that they got it all done. The first thing the students did was to draw a base map, and then everything went on the base map. One young woman discovered, I won't get the number right, probably twelve old Indian trade trails around the mountains. She discovered them by finding beads and old coins and things like that. You can imagine what an impact a thing like that had on a student who was doing it. It was a marvelous program.

Jarrell: How was this funded?

Norris: I raised the money from foundations.

Jarrell: How would you identify these issue areas?

Norris: Well, I knew where there were issue areas. Mostly.

Jarrell: How large a group of students would go out and do these inventories and make the maps and—

Norris: I hope I'm going to get this near right. But I would say twelve. Something like that.

Jarrell: These would be advanced students?

Norris: Yes. Most of them had gone through the field quarter. I knew who they were and I knew what they could do. If we needed a geologist I'd go pick a student whom I knew and we'd build these teams. It was pretty neat stuff.

Jarrell: What was the publications side to this?

Norris: Each area was written up and a report published in a very carefully edited volume. I have them all in my office here at home. We had an Environmental Field Program team who did the whole resource survey for the Granite Mountains before it became a major part of the UC Natural Reserve System, a University reserve.* They're seventy miles west of Needles and about ninety miles east of Barstow. We published it just like the other ones. It's a beautiful publication which has become a mainstay out there. We published resource surveys on Big Creek in the same kind of general format.† But I separate that out because we didn't move the house down there. We weren't attacking a specific research problem.

Jarrell: How many of these issue areas did you identify? How many survey teams went out over the years?

Norris: Under the direct banner of EFP I think we sent out five. They took a long time. We had to raise the resources for them but that turned out not to be too hard. People were excited by the idea and I had a friend in a foundation back in Boston who helped us out.

Jarrell: That's also a very intriguing part of your modus operandi.

Norris: Yes, it's so typical, isn't it?

Jarrell: I've heard some quite amazing stories from several people about your capacity for fundraising, for raising money for things you think need to be done. Not just for your personal research, but for projects such as the one you've just mentioned in the Environmental Field Program.

---

*Bruce A. Stein and Sheridan F. Warrick, eds., *Granite Mountains Resource Survey: Natural and Cultural Values of the Granite Mountains, Eastern Mojave Desert, California* (University of California Santa Cruz: Environmental Field Program Publication, 1979).

†Two reports were published by the Environmental Field Program on the Landels-Hill Big Creek Reserve. Clarisse Bickford and Paul Rich, eds., *Vegetation and Flora of the Landels-Hill Big Creek Reserve, Monterey County, California* (University of California Santa Cruz: Environmental Field Program Publication, 1980) and Ava Ferguson, ed., *Intertidal Plants and Animals of the Landels-Hill Big Creek Reserve, Monterey County* (University of California, Santa Cruz: Environmental Field Program Publication, 1984). See Appendix IV for a listing of all EFP publications.

Norris: There's a secret to it, Randall. It's not very hard; if you have an idea that can excite people they'll buy in. If you have a sort of a drab idea you can fight like hell and not get any support.

Jarrell: I was told that some of your colleagues were quite jealous. I think you had a pretty singular ability to come up with wonderful visions.

Norris: It was solely because of visions. I mean if you've got something that excites people, and they can see that there's a vision there, you can get support. It wasn't magic. I worked at it. You know, I have a sort of an eye for how to get things done. I know how to get things done and I get things done.

Research Interests

Jarrell: I'd like you to tell me about your research over the years, your fields and how they've evolved. I think I mentioned to you that Paul Rich told me, "You know, Ken seems to kind of regroup and embark on a new path or a new development every seven years." I have a list of your publications starting with your master's thesis on the iguana.

Norris: There's a thread that goes through it all, Randall. I couldn't be dissuaded from my path. I was very hard-nosed about that. What I mean is that I had a vision at the very start about where I was going and nobody really could dissuade me from it. I was kind of difficult sometimes, I think, for some of the administrators. They'd try to put me in a box and I wouldn't fit. You know? But I knew where I was going and I'm damn near there, Randall.

Jarrell: You are?

Norris: Yes, this book. It's called *Beyond Mountain Time.**

---

*At the time of the original publication of this oral history biography, *Beyond Mountain Time* was being completed posthumously by co-editors Shannon Brownlee and David Hart. This work was later picked up by Larry Ford and Eric Engles and is still in process under the direction of Susan Gee Rumsey of the UC Natural Reserve System.

Jarrell: To pick up that thread which Paul Rich mentioned, that you seem to change directions or shift gears, about every seven years.

Norris: That's about right, too.

Jarrell: You can start with the iguana or where you want. I'll ask you questions as you proceed.

Norris: When I was in high school I got all wrapped up in chemistry. We had a teacher who took us all over California in a truck. I was fascinated by the history of chemistry, but it turned out, not the actual practice of chemistry, which I found out wasn't my cup of tea. It was smelly and it was conducted in a basement and—oh, while I was excited about the Curies boiling down a ton of pitch plant to get a tiny bit of radium out of it that they didn't know quite how to handle, what excited me most was the history of it, really. So I never did any chemistry. But I fled upstairs at UCLA to the light and geology and I entered geology. I was a really good student in geology. I was just tearing up the turf in the place. It was kind of my cup of tea. It's basically a naturalist's discipline. You go out and try to figure out things out on the earth someplace. I actually did some work in geology.

Sand Dunes

Norris: I published a long paper on the Algodones Dunes, the sand dunes of southeastern Imperial County, with my brother [Robert M. Norris]. My brother was the main instigator of the work and I was his helper. But that still engages me because it's that dune amongst all the sand dunes in the west, that doesn't sing. Right now I'm engaged in the study of why sand dunes sing. That's the great puzzle of that dune. Because it's forty miles long and not a single bit of it will produce the loud sounds that are typical of many dunes when you start them sliding.

Jarrell: When you say sing, you're not talking about the wind at all?

Norris: It's a slide.

Jarrell: Like an avalanche?

Norris: It's an avalanche. That's exactly right. It puts out a sound which is something down around forty hertz. We've made the first recordings of it. We've got the first decent data, really, me and a physicist friend of mine who lives across the bay.* He and I have had a good time all over the west looking at sand dunes and collecting the sands. I'm just about ready to write a paper about that with him. So anyway, I was in geology and my brother was working on sand dunes as well. He did a paper on barchan dunes,† which are these little crescentic dunes that march along. They're all over the world. We have them on our deserts.

We took this one sand dune and mapped it with a plain table survey. We mapped along the back of it, on the crest, and the foreslope. We followed that dune across the desert and it moved four feet a month. I said to myself, four feet a month—well, I'd found some canon shells in the sand. We knew that the dune was being used as a target by the navy aviators down there. So I thought to myself it must have been used as a target during World War II. So I calculated the number of years between when we were there and World War II. I walked backwards that many years at four feet a month and I came to a great circle of canon shells which had been fired in the dune which of course wouldn't blow, which I thought was kind of tricky.

Jarrell: Wouldn't blow?

Norris: Yes. The wind couldn't move a canon shell.

Jarrell: Oh, I see.

---

*Norris is referring to his friend, physicist Evan C. Evans with whom he investigated the phenomenon of singing sand dunes. Evans mentioned a recent paper (P. Sholtz, M. Bretz, and F. Nori, "Sound-producing sand avalanches," *Contemporary Physics* 38 no. 5 (Sept.-Oct. 1997): 329-42), which addresses the current understanding of this problem, but does not offer an explanation.

†Barchan dunes of Imperial Valley, California," *Journal of Geology*, 74 (1966): 292-306.

Norris: So they just settled out. Anyway, that was my work with sand. Except that during my master's thesis work in biology I worked on a sand-dwelling lizard. We went all over the desert. I went 14,000 miles looking for sand dunes, and collecting the animals that lived on them. I wrote a great long master's thesis, which explained the history of these animals and how they got where they are, how they managed to go up washes and over divides and this kind of thing. That paper was published in the American Museum Bulletin series and is still an important paper for that species.*

Jarrell: How did you get from iguanas to marine mammals?

Norris: Well, I started to look around for a thesis. I did this great huge tome, it's 300 plus pages, on *Uma.* I went to almost every sand dune in Western North America in the process. I got to know the desert very well. I survived in spite of the fact that I'm a dreadful mechanic and cars fall apart in my hands.

New Mexico

Norris: We went all over the place. There were three of us up in this lab who did a job in New Mexico in 1948. Charlie Lowe who's now a professor at Arizona, and Dick Zweifel who's the retired curator of reptiles and amphibians at the American museum, and I had gotten this job with the Atomic Energy Commission. This was a couple of years after the first atomic bomb had gone off. We were sort of geeks who walked the desert. We walked up the center of where the bomb fallout had gone.

Jarrell: At Alamogordo?

Norris: At Sierra Oscuro where they blew it up out in the middle of the desert. Our hope was that we could collect reptiles down there. We walked up the center of the cloud and we'd walk out a lateral, until the background dropped to two times normal and then we'd turn around and go back and then go back up the center of the bomb cloud again. When it blew up it was fairly close to dawn and was caught in a thunderstorm series which blew it

*Kenneth S. Norris, "The Evolution of the Iguanid genus *Uma*," (Master's Thesis, UC Los Angeles, 1951).

across New Mexico, across the tip of Texas, and into Kansas, leaving its trace of fallout all along the way. We were tracking it to find out where it went. But we also did what we went down there for: we collected reptiles all over New Mexico. We climbed all of the highest peaks in New Mexico looking for the cloud chamber effect, which was expected to have caused fallout on those mountains but most of them didn't get any dusting at all.

Jarrell: Was the area radioactive?

Norris: Yes!

Jarrell: Were you wearing protective clothing?

Norris: We had film badges which told us how much radiation we'd taken. If it got too high and if there was too much radiation exposure, they sent us home. Tom [Thomas A.] Lehrer's songs floated like a wraith over New Mexico, "all through the sagebrush and the cactus. I'll watch them fellows practice. Droppin' bombs through the cool desert breeze." Anyway, he later became a staff member at UCSC. His songs drifted through the establishment down there. I never met Tom Lehrer either there or here. Anyway, it was quite an experience. I got to do a lot of herpetology of New Mexico.

Jarrell: What was the charge that you were given by the Atomic Energy Commission? What did they want you collecting all these reptiles for?

Norris: They didn't want us to collect the reptiles.

Jarrell: What did they want you to do?

Norris: They wanted us to collect plant samples, which were then ground up and tested for radiation.

Jarrell: Because at that time the toxicity of radiation really wasn't completely understood?

Norris: The notions varied widely. The Russians were reported to have five times the radiation tolerance that we were allowed to be exposed to. Anyway, I just throw that in because it was a piece of my history which was very much alive and important to me.

Desert Iguana, *Dipsosaurus dorsalis*

Norris: I came back from New Mexico and started looking around for a thesis project since I finished this one with *Uma*, *Uma scoparia*, the fringe-toed sand lizard. I ended up deciding on the desert iguana and set up this plot. I drove out of Palm Springs to the east, painted a line of green paint around a telephone pole. I can't tell you why. Walked a thousand feet north into the trackless dunes and set up a plot to study the desert iguana. Then I began to do it. I learned a lot about that little animal, that sweet little creature. Then one day I looked up and half of my plot had been plowed under for a motel. And they built it. It was a terrible place for a motel because it was right in the sand stream. It did in fact finally get defeated by the sand that came in the doors.

Jarrell: What is the sand stream?

Norris: Well, the winds blow down the Coachella Valley and they carry sand with them. It's stronger in some places than in others. They happened to have picked a place right in the middle of the strongest sand stream and it was the end of the motel. But I published a paper on the desert iguana.* I also published some papers along the way from New Mexico, one on the mating behavior of the box turtle, a clandestine little paper that the Atomic Energy Commission looked at and decided they'd have to run through their hierarchy to see whether it could be published or not. Well, they finally did release it and it was published with a little disclaimer at the bottom telling about how it had been done under AEC authority. We thought that was very funny.

Jarrell: You mean it might have been classified?

---

*"The Ecology of the Desert Iguana *Dipsosaurus dorsalis,*" *Ecology* 34, no. 2 (1953): 265-287.

Norris: Yes, it was all but classified. We thought that was the height of hilarity. The bureaucrats were above us in fleets and droves; oh my God, there were a lot of bureaucrats. Anyway, so I'm standing out there on the desert, my study plowed under, trying to figure out what in heaven's name to do. I had at that time been sharing a seminar under Dr. Boyd Walker, who was the ichthyologist at UCLA, and a wonderful guy. I went on some of the trips they had taken to Mexico. He was going to do a revision of the fishes of the Gulf of California, which was an enormous job. I teamed up with him to do this. I was his library guy who went in and got all the history and all that kind of stuff. I worked very hard at that. We never published a paper but we produced a mimeograph that became a standard for knowledge of the fishes of the Gulf of California. I collected all up and down the Gulf, clear into Sinaloa and Nayarit, Mexico, over on the mainland. Some of the most exciting fieldwork I've ever had. Goodness, it was fun! And adventurous, too. All full of adventure.

But anyway, that's all prelude to saying that it really wasn't much of a jump for me to go into the study of fishes from desert reptiles. I'd impressed Walker with the same thing, I think, that impressed other people, that I was always up for what was going on. I gave absolutely everything to it. I was a dependable quantity with a lot of horsepower. That won me entré from one place to another. People would say, they didn't know what I was trying to do next, that they could never pin me down. But one thing you could depend on was that I was going to give it both barrels whatever I did. So they let me do it.

Carl L. Hubbs

Norris: So Boyd Walker, finding me at the end of my tether with that study on the desert iguana, said he could send me to Scripps at La Jolla, under the great Dr. Carl [L.] Hubbs, America's greatest ichthyologist, at that time. So I went. I signed up and ended up at Scripps under Hubbs.

One of my professors at UCLA said when you go to work under the great man, remember that some great men have feet of clay. What I found out about Hubbs was that he was a magnificent worker who worked on a relatively slim skeleton of ideas. I was an idea person. Ideas are pouring out of my pores all the time. I didn't find that with him. I found a person of enormous solidity. Whatever he said was going to be true. He won many a battle in the conservation world simply by snowing people with facts to the point that they were gasping for breath trying to find out how to get out. Literally he won many a battle that way. I found him honorable, except around women. He was a terror there and his wife was constantly trying to keep the ship upright, which she managed to do. She actually ran the place. She was one of these people behind the scenes who ran everything. I grew fond of her. She was tough as nails but she was a fine person.

Echolocation in Dolphins

Jarrell: [The tape is inaudible here.] You were talking about your being a card-carrying dolphin up in the sky.

Norris: I was the card-carrying dolphin up in the sky. There were two or three of us who had led the way about the understanding of dolphins. We found out that significant work had already been done in a very spare and pretty experiment at Woods Hole.

Jarrell: By whom?

Norris: By [William E.] Schevill. Bill had been the librarian at the Museum of Comparative Zoology at Harvard.* He loved books; his mind kind of operated like a librarian's. He was a person of great caution and he had admonitory advice for all of us. God knows, I needed it. I was the idea guy in the whole thing. He didn't really know how to deal with idea guys, and yet he became one of my closest friends. I think that was because I was honest; he knew that he could trust me when I told him something, and that bridged across this really great gap in our temperaments. I learned the world from Bill.

He did the first experiment which showed that a dolphin had echolocation, that it used its sound to find its way around. The experiment was simple and yet it was hidden. It was one of these things that got published in a

*W.E. Schevill and Barbara Lawrence, "Food-finding by a captive porpoise (*Tursiops truncatus*)" *Brevoria, Mus. Comp. Zool.*, Harvard 53 (1956): 1-15.

miscellanea of the Museum of Comparative Zoology but nobody noticed it. When they did come across it, it was written in such careful language that nobody understood what it meant.

About six years later I, too, began to suspect that dolphins had echolocation. I did an experiment that demonstrated it for the world. What we did was to design blindfolds for a dolphin. This was John [H.] Prescott and I. He later became the very capable director of the New England Aquarium.

Jarrell: When you were doing your original experiments you didn't yet know about Schevill's work?

Norris: No, I didn't.

Jarrell: You were working independently, trying to figure out how to make these blindfolds to confirm your notion that dolphins had echolocation?

Norris: Yes. It was at Marineland of the Pacific. We couldn't figure out how to make a good suction cup that would fit over the eye. Finally, either John or I, I can't tell you who, got the bright idea to use a mold. The mold was a brassiere with falsies, junior teen falsies. We were all very excited about our choice of molds. They worked. John [Prescott] came in my office and said, "Ken, you gotta see what they're doing!" I said, "What who's doing?" He took me out there and a dolphin was swimming around the tank with the falsies on its eyes as if there was nothing wrong with it at all.

Jarrell: In spite of the blindfolds?

Norris: With the blindfolds on. We did the first test, well, other than the Schevills' test. I should include Barbara Lawrence in this, Bill's wife, who's a consummate anatomist and a wonderful person. A real Yankee, though, if I ever met one. I learned to love them both. Anyway, we did all sorts of things with that blindfolded animal. We ran it through mazes and listened to its sounds; we had it locate targets real close to a wall, which is hard to do. Then we changed the maze. The maze was made out of metal poles. Our tests were incontrovertible. Then we published, but before we published I found out about the Schevills and I very carefully cited them in the paper. That cemented our friendship for life, I think, that I was honorable enough to recognize that they really had done the first experiment about four or five years earlier.

Jarrell: How could you have done anything different?

Norris: Well, some people would have. But not me.

Jarrell: So then you later met him and his wife and—

Norris: Oh, we became very close friends. Yes, I always thought I was a little bit of an odd bird every time I'd show up at his house. Phylly became good friends with them, too.

Jarrell: What year did you publish the paper confirming echolocation?

Norris: 1961.* The Schevills' two papers were published in the mid-fifties. Anyway, that was the way that went. It ended up with a lifelong friendship.

Jarrell: Was that was the beginning of your research in this area?

Norris: Yes, certainly. It led to whatever else I produced in the field of echolocation. We produced quite a bit. We had two tanks at UCLA.

Jarrell: On what kind of dolphin did you do the original work on echolocation?

Norris: A bottlenose dolphin named Kathy. She was a peppery lady who told us off frequently. Then we had sweet, dear old Alice at UCLA. We taught Alice, too. We taught her to tell us the difference between the sizes of ball bearings, which were hung in a tank in front of her. She could tell within a

*K.S. Norris, J.H. Precott, P.V. Asa-Dorian, and P. Perkins, "An Experimental Demonstration of Echolocation in the Porpoise, *Tursips truncatus* (Montagu)," *Biological Bulletin* 120, (1961): 163-176.

matter of a couple of percent the difference in size by hitting them with about a second's worth of echolocation. She'd go brrrp and then that was the answer. We found out many other things from her, dear, sweet old gal that she was, frightened about the world. Then one morning a call came and someone said, "do you want your dolphin on the ground?" I said, "Well, no." "Well, she's on the ground. Your tank collapsed." So what do we do with a dolphin in West Los Angeles? Well, I remembered there was a test tank in the bottom of the physics building for testing acoustic stuff. I called and on an emergency basis got permission to put Alice in the test tank. We went through the Christmas party with a wet dolphin and put her in the tank down there. Anyway, there you are.

Jarrell: Once you got to UCLA, did you have any colleagues with whom you worked on dolphins?

Norris: I continued my work with Alice. I worked with a young psychologist, Ronald [W.] Turner as the main person. One of my grad students turned out to be well trained in acoustics, Bill Evans. So the three of us worked together. Turner was a class master at Skinnerian psychology; he was able to bring all the power of that paradigm to work on the training of Alice. He was really good.

Jarrell: Then during that time that you were at UCLA you became involved in Hawaii.

Norris: We enter my incomprehensible decade.

Jarrell: Yes, the 1960s, about which you told me, "I still haven't figured them out myself."

Norris: Oh God. I had no control over my enthusiasm for doing things. So I was kind of released into doing a whole lot of things all at once. I ended up helping build an oceanarium in Hawaii and spent half my time there.

Jarrell: I'm interested in the thread of your research. Were you research-driven, dolphin-driven?

Norris: Well, I found myself in the central Pacific about which people knew even less than they knew about the California coast. It was true terra incognita. We didn't know what animal we were going to see next. We didn't know what their classifications would be. I mentioned earlier that our collector caught a rough-toothed dolphin, the third ever, during this period. Stuff like that went on and on.

Jarrell: What is the difference between a dolphin and a porpoise?

Norris: Well, that's kind of a nomenclatural tangle. The British used to like to eat what they called the puffing pig, which would swim up the Thames and other rivers. The Queen liked it particularly well.

Jarrell: And that's fresh water?

Norris: It was a marine animal that would go into fresh water. It had no beak. It had a very low dorsal fin, and a few other features. It was a very small animal. So the British classified any animal that looked like that as a porpoise since that's what they called it. That name became associated with that particular, distinct group of cetaceans. They don't live as long as others do and those characteristics are more or less there.

Jarrell: For the porpoises?

Norris: Yes. But if you go from one porpoise to the other you'll find that they disappear like that. They're supposed to have tricuspid teeth, but there's one that has a whole mouth full of tiny, little needle-like teeth. Well, so you have to shift the definition there. Is that good enough?

Jarrell: Yes, that's just fine. You know we're almost at the end of the tape now. When we pick up next time I'd like you to talk to me about Gregory Bateson and your work with him.

Norris: Sure. There was a lot of research in Hawaii.

Jarrell: Thank you very much, Ken.

Norris: Oh, Randall you're a delight.

Jarrell: Well, thank you. You are, too.

Norris: I really look forward to your coming.

Jarrell: Well, I love coming here. And I love the way I'm greeted by all your animals.

Editor's Note: This turned out to be my last interview with Norris; shortly after this meeting he was hospitalized for several months and died on August 16, 1998. Because we were unable to discuss so many important facets of his work and career, the following interviews with his colleagues and former students touch on many subjects I had originally planned to discuss with him.

Part II.

The Scientific Legacy of Kenneth S. Norris

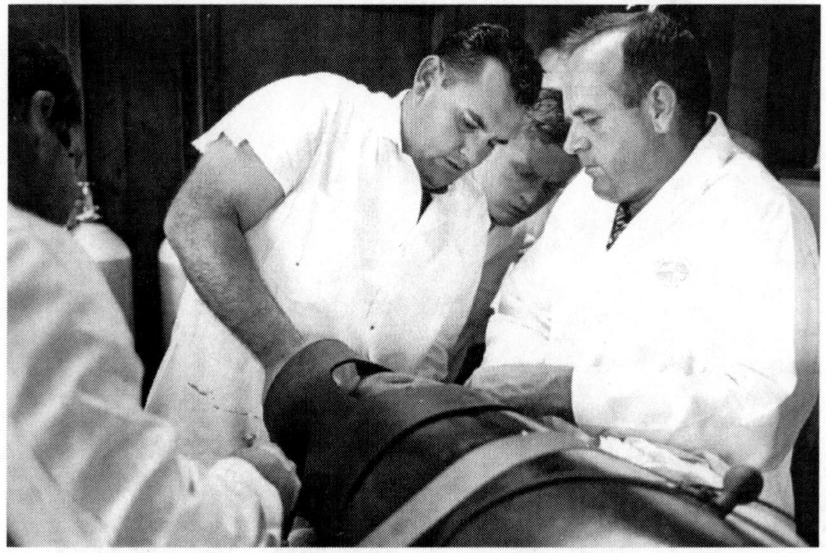

Sam Ridgway and Ken Norris attempting to remove a foreign body from "Keiki," a male dolphin Oceanic Institute, Hawaii, July 1965. Photo courtesy of Sam Ridgway.

Evan Evans and Ken Norris at Kelso Sand Dunes explaining sand dune dynamics in the Mojave Desert, April 1993.

William N. McFarland

Raymond B. Cowles

McFarland: I started at UCLA as an undergraduate. I was a chemistry major. That's what I loved. I didn't realize then, I didn't think in terms of what I'd seen when I was a kid swimming out in the ocean. And like Ken, as a youngster I went out in the deserts when I was young and chased lizards. Even around where I lived. I lived in the Culver City, Baldwin Hills area. Hardly any houses there.

It was during 1951 that I ran into Ken Norris. He was working on his master's with Ray Cowles. I should say something about Ray Cowles. Ken, when he was a boy, as Bob Norris said today at the memorial, did a lot of lizard chasing. He talked about Ken setting up this field area out in the desert and learning about everything in it. I think that naturalist desire was in him. In fact in my remarks at the memorial, I suggested that somehow a naturalist gene snuck into his genotype. But there was more to it than that. Something turned that gene on. It wasn't quite stated that way, but I should have said that.

I think one of the things that turned him on was his past experiences and interactions with Ray Cowles. I knew Ray Cowles quite well, too, and he was a fascinating guy. He was, like Ken, a naturalist, but he was what I would call a new naturalist. Ken, in my words wasn't just a naturalist; he was everything. He was a functional naturalist; he wasn't just interested in describing the animals he saw in a system, but in how they all interact. This is what Ray Cowles did. In conjunction with some of his students, he approached problems like

Ken did later, but not as full strength as Ken did, because we build on each other through time.

Ray was just a fascinating guy. Let me give you an example. In the Natural History Field Quarter, what Ken did with students, he had done with Ray Cowles. I know because I took Ray Cowles's course and I did the same thing. We'd go out to the Mojave Desert for two days. We'd be running around collecting snakes, lizards—any reptile you could get your hands on, all day. At the end of the day we'd come in and everybody'd cook dinner. There'd be twelve students and Ray. The sun would go down and you'd say oh boy, now we can have a nice fire and drink a beer. Just about then Ray would come up and say, "Okay, Mack and George," or whoever else it might be, "come with me, you two guys." He'd pick up a Coleman lantern, and a bed sheet and walk out two or three hundred feet away from the camp. He'd lay the sheet out on the ground, put the lantern in the middle of the sheet and say, "I want you to sit here for the next two hours and collect and learn to identify every insect that falls on that sheet." Of course at night a lot of insects are out flying.

This is what Ken was doing as well. Ray forced us to observe what was happening. Ray Cowles knew every bush in the desert, every animal that lived out there that had ever been described. He knew a lot about their interactions. Ray was the son of missionary parents in Kenya. He was always a very dignified-looking professor. You know, tie and coat. Of course in those days most people wore them all the time. But he rode a Triumph motorcycle and he'd come into school on his Triumph. That really set me up. This guy's great!

Jarrell: Ken talked about Cowles's deep pockets. He would be collecting things all the time. He'd take something out and it would be wondrous, like Blake's grain of sand. He would talk about a Joshua tree seed pod or something and he would just open one's mind.

McFarland: Ken was the same way. Ray may even have gotten it from Padre [Loye] Miller, who was a very senior emeritus professor from UCLA, who was also a naturalist. When we were graduate students Ken must have encountered him. Because every Wednesday he would come to coffee. He'd sit and wait for the professors to leave because he wanted to talk to the students. We all got to know this so three or four of us would go late to coffee on Wednesdays. Art[hur O.] Flechsig whom Ken knew at Scripps was also in this group. After everybody was gone Padre would say, "Well, gentlemen," and he'd pull something out of his pocket and put it on the table: "What can you tell me about this?" Everybody would look and then this would lead to an hour-long discourse on the natural history and everything he knew surrounding that object. It was just fascinating. This was the old school approach. It wasn't a modern ecological approach with all the interactions and physiology. It was just sort of a natural history of the object. Something about interactions. But not a probing study of interactions. Anyway, Padre must have affected Ken. We talked about Padre Miller. In fact he wrote a not very good book with a fascinating title, *Lifelong Boyhood.* That's what a lot of field biologists are, really. It's a lifelong boyhood for men.* I'm sure it's probably the same thing for women. I know that Ken and I talked about Padre. I'm sure we must have been at UCLA together. I just don't recall sitting with him in that group because once he finished his master's he went right down to Scripps.

Jarrell: You finished up and got a bachelor's in zoology. Then you were at UCLA for your master's and doctorate and knew Ken during all this period?

McFarland: I met Ken from the first semester he entered graduate school at UCLA. We'd talk but we weren't real, real close at that time. We'd be in a seminar together and got to know each other. But we weren't going out and drinking beer together then. We talked a lot at coffee and things like that. But he was doing reptiles and I was doing fish.

I had two professors at UCLA. Boyd Walker, who was the ichthyologist and Fred Crescitelli, who was the comparative physiologist. I started out with Boyd for my master's. I finished my master's with just Boyd. But at the end — I was going to go to work for the California Fish and Game Department. I came from a background like Ken's. I don't think my parents ever finished

*Loye Holmes Miller, *Lifelong Boyhood: Recollections of a Naturalist Afield* (Berkeley: University of California Press, 1950).

high school. Quite frankly, when I entered college I hardly knew what a Ph.D. was.

Jarrell: Being an academic was like—

McFarland: The furthest thing from my mind. In fact, I went for a master's because I had been diving and I said, well, California has a fish and game department and I like that sort of thing, maybe I should learn about fish for a master's and then I could work for fish and game. But apparently I did well enough with Boyd that he was impressed with me. I took my master's by written exam. I didn't write a thesis. He told me not to. In fact he didn't like his students going for a master's thesis. So he suggested that on the general exam I take the Ph.D. qualifying exam and if I passed that it satisfied the master's criterion, except for a specialty. You'd have to take a separate little exam. So I took that exam and I studied with Art Flechsig. He also went to Scripps to work with Hubbs to get his Ph.D. and never did.

Ken Norris's Ph.D. Dissertation

So I worked for my Ph.D. That gets back to Ken now, okay? I finished my master's about the time that he did. I started on my Ph.D. Ken went to Scripps Institution of Oceanography to work with Carl Hubbs. I'm not really quite certain why Ken went to Scripps. It may have been [because] he knew Boyd Walker very well. Anyway, Ken worked with Carl but his thesis topic— Dick Rosenblum and I were just speaking about it at dinner—was suggested to him by Boyd, I think, at UCLA. Because Boyd had got his degree at Scripps under Carl Hubbs. He told Ken that he should work with Carl Hubbs. He was down there for maybe two years. That's when he met Phylly. A lot of things happened to him at Scripps.

You know Ken and his personality. He was always dancing, horsing around, doing things. He did a couple of things, as we understand it, that sort of ticked off Mrs. Carl Hubbs. She was in the laboratory all the time; she was Carl's secretary, his assistant. If Laura, for example, took a dislike to one of the graduate students she would keep pushing Carl about the slight negative things about this student and kind of turn Carl off on the student. She sort of did that a little with Ken. But it never got full force so that he dropped him and so forth. It would have been a crime if he had.

Ken's Ph.D. thesis is just beautiful. His master's thesis is great, but it's not nearly as great as his Ph.D. thesis. But it leads to his continuing natural history approach and putting on top of it his incredible imagination. He was really unusual to be around.

Jarrell: Tell me about his dissertation and why it was so singular.

McFarland: Well, his dissertation was to try to relate the role of temperature and how it might influence the ontogenetic, the life history development, of fishes. It shows specifically the California opaleye. There was a reason for that which was that they are herbivores as adults but as very, very young fish, like most fish, they're planktivores, they eat plankton. In Southern California waters and down in Baja, they invade the tidepools when they're very, very young. They're still silvery, almost larvae-like. They grow there for awhile feeding initially on plankton and then start to pick things off the bottom. Then as their teeth develop, they have very special teeth, they become scrapers and they scrape algae off the rocks. What Ken did first of all was to study the natural history of the fish. The reason I think Carl Hubbs may have had some influence there, I'm vague on this, but Carl was fascinated by past sea temperatures up and down the California coast. He was studying El Niño differences but he didn't know it at the time, and Ken was his assistant.

As a result of that they also got into the work of Uri of Chicago, who was a chemist working with the oxygen sixteen, eighteen ratios which recorded the way oxygen sixteen and eighteen incorporated in the calcium, for example, of a mollusk, a shell, is dependent on the temperature, the chemical reaction rate. In other words it will select one isotope more than the other, depending on temperature. Uri used a mass spectrometer to get these ratios, and so you could predict or even suggest what the temperature was if you knew the age of the shell. Now a lot of this was due to Indian middens and they could age them, they could use carbon 14 as well to age them, and so forth.

Jarrell: Depending on the concentration you could tell temperature?

McFarland: You could tell what the temperature was at that time. So they tried to reconstruct these past histories of sea temperatures. I saw that they fluctuated. But this, I think, got Ken very interested in the role of temperature in fishes. Of course Ray Cowles was one of the first people who ever started sticking thermometers up the anuses of lizards and snakes and seeing what the body temperature was. Somebody mentioned this today at the memorial. The students were always sticking thermometers up— you know. At any rate, that must have led to it.

But his thesis is beautiful. I was involved in helping a little bit. I assisted him in the field a lot. He assisted me in the field, too, when I'd go out and collect for my thesis and so forth. Because we both did our research in the laboratory at Marineland of the Pacific. I was working on my doctorate in late 1954, when they were building Marineland of the Pacific.

Anyway, Ken, for his Ph.D. thesis, won the Mercer award for its sheer excellence, the best paper of the year the Ecological Society of America published in any of its journals. That was stunning for a graduate student to win that then, you know. It was synthetic. In his paper, he took the physical attributes of the environment, particularly temperature, how it changed through time up and down the coast, and related the life history distributions of this fish through time and season. He talked about different foraging habits as a function of size and then tried to explain why the fish distribute differently. Why do the young go into the tidepools? That's where he was able to measure tidepool temperatures and find that the young fish sought higher temperatures in the tidepools. It stands to reason. The babies do. Why? They grow faster. They digest their food faster, and so forth. All of that's in that thesis. At the time it was unusual for an ecologist or a naturalist to do. He not only did all this field study but then he came back and built this marvelous ichthyothermataxatron which was a fifteen-foot-long tank with a bunch of compartments and glass doors, with little narrow compartments all the way up and down. First of all, what he would do— I helped him with this. He had cold water going in a pipe in one direction and hot water in the other direction. By varying where the hot and cold was he could create a temperature gradient down this tank. And each of these —from cold to hot and so forth. Well, what he would do is start out with the same temperature in all compartments, and then introduce fish, three or four fish.

He would randomize it. They might flock together, as fish tend to be social. Then he would record over time where they spent most of their time. Were there end preferences or middle preferences? What he tended to get was basically random distribution with a constant temperature. Then he'd introduce a temperature gradient. What he found was the fish tended to hover around certain temperatures. They might occasionally go down to the cold end, let's say, if they were little ones. But then they'd come back. They'd spend most of their time, statistically, in the warmer waters. Now even though somebody said Ken never found a statistic he ever cared for—that's baloney. But he didn't like statistics. That came partly, I think, from also knowing my major professor, Fred Cresetelli, who said, if you need a statistic, it ain't worth doing. (laughter) In other words you get a yes or no answer.

But what was so important about that study was the synthesis of a very broad natural history approach, distributions, everything, coupled with experiment, to actually prove what he was saying, within the realm of scientifically proved possibilities. That was fascinating. I was there all the time. In fact we'd bounce things off each other, you know. I'd be his alter ego and critique and he did the same with my research. "So, why are you doing that Mac? That's stupid." You know? So that was great.

Jarrell: You were Ken's first hire at Marineland. Is that right?

McFarland: I think I was, Yes. He hired me because I had almost been a chemistry major and he was worried about the tanks; he needed somebody to study the chemistry in the oceanarium's tanks. So he hired me for that but also to be an assistant biologist, or whatever I wanted to do. I was delighted, because I had to have some sort of income.

Jarrell: So you were working there and concurrently doing your thesis research?

McFarland: Right. I went there, I guess, in late summer '54. He came up to UCLA and was looking for an assistant and sought me out. He talked to me and told me about the position. He said why don't you come down and take a look. So I did and took the job. It's really worked out to be a wonderful relationship. Because I wasn't so much his assistant as I was his colleague.

Ken and I and his secretary were the only ones in the laboratory. Then there was David Brown, who was in charge of the mammals, the display and stuff. Ken was curator of all of the animals at Marineland. So he was in charge of the design, not the design of the basic tanks, but the displays themselves. Marineland was designed before either of us went to work there. It was under construction when we both started. When I went down there, Frank [Brocato] was already there.

Jarrell: The fisherman. Ken said he was such a terribly strong influence.

McFarland: His influence on Ken and me was incredible. I think it was our first real experience with a non-academic person who knew so much about the sea. I mean it was just incredible what that man knew. He had a wonderful personality. He was Sicilian and like Ken and me—we all had a certain irreverence about things. Frank was raised as a Catholic and he used to tell Catholic jokes.

I stayed there through '58 and I left when I finished my dissertation. I had gotten a job with the University of Texas marine lab. Ken stayed on for a couple more years.

Jarrell: Yes, he stayed on at Marineland until 1960.

McFarland: '60. So it was two more years after I left. But several things happened there. Let me first of all talk about Ken's research in general. I don't have his c.v. I can't tell you every paper he published as a graduate student.

But he published two major ones. One was his master's thesis, the lizard paper I mentioned. The other was his Ph.D. thesis which was not published until 1963.

Uma notata

The lizard paper was on *Uma notata*, if you want the scientific name. If you look at the thesis there are three or four different species in the southwest deserts. He specialized in *Uma notata* because it occurred in sand dunes in the southwestern Mojave there. But he also compared it to the *Umas* in other sand dune areas. The fringe-toed lizard he was studying, and they're insects that are also adapted, have all these adaptations on their feet, the fringes, so they can run on sand. Their feet allow them to burrow. They literally burrow under the sand in the middle of the day when it's so hot they couldn't be out on top. Bob Norris also mentioned his study on the iguana. Well, *Uma's* an iguana, too. But they were talking about the lizard *Dipsosaurus. Dipsosaurus* in the middle of the day, instead of burrowing, often climbs up on top of the creosote bush and takes advantage of the slight cool.

At any rate, Ken's primary orientation was the evolution of adaptations in the same genus in different sand dunes. For example, he studied *notata* as his prime species. But there's another species, *Uma inornata*, which occurs in Arizona. I can't remember exactly where. I'd have to go back and look at his master's thesis. But he studied its evolution. He'd been with Ray Cowles, remember. He'd gotten interested in the environmental interactions of these adaptations. Even though his focus was the adaptation in different species, and its convergence in this particular case—what he really got interested in was the sand dune as a dynamic moving system, and what happens in that process. In fact, he and Bob Norris were going to go study this together again. Because Bob's a geologist and moving sand is geological, so to speak.

The last time I saw Ken was last New Year's Eve day. I spent the afternoon with him, and he talked about going back to his sand dune research. So that even though he became one of the world's leading cetologists, his real love was deserts, I think, going back to his boyhood.

Marineland of the Pacific

I want to talk a little more about his research at Marineland and as a graduate student because that's really what people are going to know Ken for. At least, in most of his scientific papers. Certainly he was more than that.

Jarrell: He was a naturalist, a herpetologist, an ichthyologist, a marine mammalogist, and totally into cetaceans. Where did he get this interest in cetaceans?

McFarland: Well, certainly Ken wiyell really be known for this through his scientific papers. It just came out of his inherent curiosity. There he was at Marineland of the Pacific in charge of obtaining porpoises, whales, and dolphins in the tanks. Because that was the main drawing card. We had a lot of problems trying to get the first animals from the St. Augustine Oceanarium in Florida, while we were there. I remember it distinctly. Ken went back to Florida and flew with a bottlenose dolphin clear across the country with F. G. Wood, who was the curator at St. Augustine.

Jarrell: How did he transport it?

McFarland: In canvas stretchers where they could pour water over them. Frank Brocato, Bruce ("Boots") Coladrino, who was the assistant fisherman, and I, drove the truck to meet the airplane. Boy, this was real excitement, and he brought back two dolphins. Ken had to do this. This was applied; this was necessary for our job. We were a functioning oceanarium. It was to make money, you know. I think we ended up with four dolphins. There was another trip that brought two more in. F. G. Wood, who became a very close friend of Ken's, and me too, to a degree. Woody, we called him always. Sam Ridgway mentioned at the memorial that he was a product of F.G. Wood. They had the same jobs, Ken on the West Coast and Woody on the East Coast. We decided we had to get other kinds of porpoises. Why don't we try pelagic porpoises?

Jarrell: Would you define pelagic for me?

McFarland: Pelagic is an organism that lives at sea. Well, it doesn't have to be the upper waters, but usually, I think of it as the upper waters. It means, really, even something in the deep sea is pelagic. Tunas are pelagic. There are some that come in pretty close to shore. But they never associate with the bottom, in that sense. That's pelagic organisms. Whereas, you know, bottlenose dolphins live in lagoons. I've actually seen them underwater. They use their nose, their echolocation can sense things in the sand. Then they use their snouts and burrow and grab the fish. And they're extremely good at it. I've watched them many, many times. It's very interesting.

We've got the San Pedro Channel. We got more porpoises or dolphins than we knew what to do with, you know. Frank Brocato, Ken, and I went on these trips. What they did, initially, is they had to harpoon an animal.

Jarrell: Wait, I'm not quite following you.

McFarland: We had to somehow get the dolphin, the common dolphin, which is strictly a pelagic animal, on board our ship, the catching vessel, so we could get it back to Marineland. Well, how do you collect it? I mean we didn't have nets we could wrap them with. Since they would run the bow of the vessel, Frank said we had to harpoon them. So he took a long pole and a big hook without a barb on it, tied a line to it, and this was taped to the end of the pole. There was a line tied right here that went up, a long line with a float on it. A 10-foot long pole. This was taped so it would break away. So he would harpoon the animal and then yank on the line which would turn the hook around. So that the harpoon would go in the animal's body and come back out. So there'd be two holes in the animal. It was just in the dermis. It might have been a little into the muscle, and we tried to hit them in the back, usually. Frank Brocato was an expert at this sort of thing.

Ken always said try to think like the animal. I tend to think like the animal, too, partly from my relationship with Ken. Frank always thought like the animal. He'd even imitate porpoises. "This is how they go, Mac." It was a riot. But anyway, they'd come back in and we'd put them in a big round tank about twenty feet in diameter.

Jarrell: So you'd have the line in them. What kind of a line was it? How heavy?

McFarland: It usually was parachute shrouding, nylon, braided line. Very strong.

Jarrell: So how would you wheel this dolphin in?

McFarland: Well, the line would be there. We'd throw a life preserver or some type of float tied to the end, and let the animal swim around. It would be bleeding a little. Then as soon as we could, we'd pick it up, and start to horse the animal in. Sometimes it would start fighting so you'd let it go again, and then pull it back, until it got very tired. Then you'd pull it up alongside. Often what happened, was that Boots or I would jump in the water alongside the animal, and we'd get a stretcher underneath it. Then Ken with the boom, and Frank, would pull the animal up, and put it on the deck. We'd bring the animals in. It was always exciting because there was a dock right at Marineland and everybody would come to see when we'd come in with a porpoise. I was on many of these trips, but not all. The upshot of that was we had sick animals. We had to really worry about abscesses.

Jarrell: Did you use antibiotics?

McFarland: Oh yes, we did. In fact, one of my jobs when we had an animal, was to jump in our four-foot deep tank, and cradle it. Dave Brown and I did this. Ken did some of it, too. But I was the assistant and Dave was the curator of mammals, so to speak. We would put cotton swabs into the wound, with antibiotics and so forth. I don't think we should say much about it. We probably lost more than half the animals.

Jarrell: I was just going to ask you that, yes.

McFarland: The first one we got through was the first Elsie, a *Lagenorhynchus*, Pacific white-sided dolphin. But at any rate, that was a serious thing. Because we were losing too many porpoises. Several things happened. We'd even get them in the tanks, healed up, and the pelagic porpoises performed beautifully once you trained them. They were just fabulous animals. But we'd keep losing them, even after they were healed. So one day, the fifth Elsie died. I came in that morning and Ken said, "Elsie died, Mac. I want you to do an autopsy on her." The animal was in the room in a stainless steel tank. I started cutting and dissecting it and looking everywhere, heart, brain—I couldn't see anything. I finally got into the lungs and, oh my God, its lungs were just totally congested. I didn't have gloves on. How stupid we were about certain things in those days. I ran into Ken and said, "Ken come here. You've got to look at this.

I think the animal's got lung congestion." He came in and he's just like me. He says, "God, yes!" So we were at least smart enough to take some of the stuff and put it in petri dishes and send it out and have a bacterial investigation on it. It was a really bad human pneumonia. I came down with it. Three days later I was sick as a dog and so was Ken. He went to the doctor and they did a swab; he had the same bacterial infection. He had a mild case of pneumonia. I got double pneumonia. I could have died, actually, except for penicillin, thank God.

Jarrell: It never occurred to you to wear gloves, to take precautions?

McFarland: Oh, it sure did after that. But then the question was what was causing it?

Jarrell: You said you were losing about half of the dolphins and that it wasn't just due to the wounds from the harpoons?

McFarland: It mostly was from the wounds. It was a really traumatic way to collect a dolphin. But we didn't have any other way. We couldn't think of any other way to do it. The only way they got the bottlenose dolphins in Florida was they'd get them up a lagoon and put a net across it. But we couldn't do that out in the open ocean. How do you do it? The only thing we could do was harpoon an animal. The other part was this loss in the tanks.

So we started thinking about that. I'm not certain whether it was Ken or one of the attendants, the gatekeepers, who would go out and watch the crowds. Before the show the porpoises would swim around the tank and we saw people spitting in the water. Of course if somebody's got even a mild cold, this bacteria, these animals are just totally susceptible to it. So we were able to lick that, once we figured it out, because then in all their food they got streptomycin constantly. We never had any more problems that way. Once in a while a porpoise would die. But we still had the problem of harpooning them. In *The Porpoise Watcher* Ken described what happened. I always feel kind of bad about this, but not really, because we finally devised a way to catch porpoises at sea without harpooning them. The person who came up with the idea was myself and one of the divers, Ted Davis. We were drinking coffee together one day. Ted and I were pretty good friends. He'd been an old tuna fisherman before that. We got to talking and trying to figure out a way of doing this. I don't know whether he or I suggested—well, why don't we lasso them?

So Ted went to work and I walked out to the welding shop. I happen to be a pretty good machinist. I asked for ten feet of quarter-inch rod and one electrical conduit tubing, steel tubing. I bent this quarter-inch rod into a long "U" and then I welded the end to the rod so it was a pole with a big "U" on the end of it. Then I took some of the parachute shrouding we had and I made a lasso with the line going up to the end of the pole and then it would be coiled so this "U" held a loop. I tied it, taped it very lightly at the end.

Then we had a round tank where we had porpoises, dolphins, actually swimming around, being trained for the show. So I just went out and I was very careful about it. The animals would come around. They were used to being fed. So I initially just held this thing up over the tank. The animal would go underneath it. Then when it would come up. It took me a couple of times to learn how to do it, the animal would swim through the "U." I didn't do anything. The animal swam through the loop. It wasn't really frightened by it. Then one time when it got in, I yanked, like this. The lasso closed around its tail and ripped loose from this thing. Here was this dolphin swimming around the tank with this lasso on it. It was really important because we didn't have to harpoon porpoises anymore.

About four days later Frank went out to sea to catch a porpoise. He used this lasso and came back two days later with two or three *Lagenorhynchus* on the deck without a mark on them. No harpooning, no nothing. He radioed in that he had three animals with no marks on them whatsoever. Later on Frank took the "U" and the line and wove a large, very big net, silk stocking, so to speak, over the end.

Jarrell: For whatever reason this reminds me of a lacrosse stick?

McFarland: Yes, very much like that. Then he would tie that up with a piece of string. So the net was up. When the porpoise went through the lasso it was very translucent, kind of white, very hard to see. The porpoise would go through the lasso, hit the net, and trap itself in the net. The lasso wasn't just around the tail.

Another person I'd like to mention is John Prescott. He later became the curator at Marineland. He was a graduate student at UCLA and had been a student in my ichthyology class. I knew John and you know how these things work. I suggested to Ken, why don't you interview him and see if you like him. John had had a lot of commercial fishing experience as well. So it worked out very well.

Echolocation in Dolphins

McFarland: What Ken discovered from watching and doing experiments with the porpoises in the tanks, was that they scanned, and that as they approached an object, the scanning would become more rapid. He thought that what they were doing was listening with each side to the echoes and sort of nulling it out, so to speak, to hone in on it at the end. The frequency went up as they got closer to an object. It's a very high frequency. So he built all of that. That was to me, brilliant. It really was. It doesn't sound like much now. But just from out of nowhere—and it turned out to be just so controversial people wouldn't believe him until Ted Bullock showed that that was indeed what was happening.

Three months before I left Marineland John Prescott was brought in so he could learn all the chemistry and stuff he had to do. While I was still there he got interested in dolphins and the tank in the back. We were all wondering how we could work experimentally with these animals, if we could in some way blind them temporarily. You can't wrap something around the head. John went out and got some falsies; he went out every day and he'd get the dolphin up and he'd start by bringing the falsies near the eyes. He worked about a week and we knew what he was doing. Ken was in typing most of the time. One day John came running in and said, "Ken! Mac! Come out! I got a blind dolphin out here." We went out and sure enough here was the dolphin swimming around with falsies near the eyes. He worked about a week and we knew what he was doing. Ken was in typing most of the time. One day John came running in and said, "Ken! Mac! Come out! I've got a blind dolphin out here." We went out and sure enough here was the dolphin swimming around with falsies over its eyes. That led the two of them to do all of these experiments on echolocation using ball bearings. We worked on the *Phocoena sinus*, mentioned by Sam Ridgway at the memorial, this little porpoise from the northern Gulf of California. *Phocoena phocoena* is the harbor porpoise you'll see around San Francisco and up in Puget Sound and in those areas. It also occurs over in the North Atlantic. What we said in this paper, because there're a lot of other kinds of relic marine organisms in the northern Gulf of California, was that they got isolated there during the Pleistocene as the ice ages came and went. Now since the glaciers were there the pole proceeded further south so the harbor porpoise could go around lower California and enter the Gulf.

They like cooler temperatures. If you've got glaciers coming down, in the Pleistocene, it's going to be cold further south. So the water was cold down that way. In other words, the tropics receded, so to speak, to the south. The harbor porpoise came around everywhere. There's fine habitat for them. But then as the glaciers went away the warming came back and trapped this population in the northern Gulf of California. They couldn't go around and so became a relic population. They are a miniature harbor porpoise; they're much smaller than the ones in San Francisco.

Coral Reef Fishes

Anyway, as I got to work with Ken on that, he also worked with me on problems I was working on on the side. We published a couple of papers together on applied problems. Because Ken was a basic scientist, and so am I. I love basic science but I am quite willing to work on an applied problem. Particularly if I can use basic approaches to it. We had the problem of bringing tropical reef fishes into Marineland. We'd get a big four-box shipment from Hawaii, let's say. We had displays of coral reef fishes. But we'd open the tank up and they'd be all dead. Not always. Or half of them would be dead and the other half didn't look very good. What could we do? I set up some experiments in sealed tanks. We took local fish, because we had lots of them, and asked how long could they live in a sealed tank under different conditions. We measured things like oxygen in the water, and it would go down because they'd be breathing it. We measured pH, the acidity of the water, because they'd be releasing acids and ammonia into the water and carbon dioxide particularly and we found out reducing oxygen was serious. But what was really serious was the build-up of carbon dioxide. As pH drops it affects the hemoglobin's ability to take up oxygen. So it exacerbates the fact that the oxygen is going down. We said, what do we do? Let's put buffers in the water to serve as a seal, too. It worked like a charm.

Jarrell: What kind of buffers?

McFarland: We used trizma buffers which worked very well and were easy to use. They're not toxic to the fish. I think there was one fish, actually it was the opaleye that Ken and I both worked on for our Ph.D. dissertations in which it didn't kill them or anything, but their respiration rate slowed way down. But other than that, no effect. So we solved an applied problem. Then we could bring in tropical fishes and never lose one. That worked very well. We did a lot of things like that.

What else can I say about Marineland? There was so much more.

Wild and Crazy Antics

One thing I haven't talked about is our antics. We were crazy. You have no idea. I said sort of jokingly, that if I said anything about what we did as graduate students Phylly would claim I would get arrested. And she and my first wife—

Jarrell: You were pretty wild and crazy?

McFarland: Oh we did some pretty wild things. Ken was wild. So was I. Let me tell you a couple. Just a little bit of flavor.

As Shannon [Brownlee] and several people said at the memorial, there was the other side of Ken, this fun in life, to do something against the grain. In the '50s when we were at Marineland it was a time in Southern California when there were a lot of funny religious groups all over the place. Everywhere you'd see these "Jesus Saves" signs. There'd be very formal ones and home-made ones, and we used to keep talking about it. Ken said, we had to do something about this. We said why don't we have our own religion. Let's form a little group. We'll meet Sunday mornings in the Norris garage and we'll call ourselves the Society for the Preservation of Evil, I think that's what we called it. I was elected the Archdeacon of Evil and Ken was Bishop of Sin, or something like that. (laughter)

There were two other fellows. One of the artists and one of the gatekeepers joined us. We'd meet every Sunday and drink beer and compose music. Because music was a part of Ken's life even though he really was not a musician in the strict sense of the word. I should have asked Phylly about it today, darn it! Because I talked to Ken about it on New Year's Eve. We composed a symphony. We had what we called the All Ghoul Orchestra. We wrote a symphony in four movements and the instruments were unbelievable: the octopus tank bollen, which we'd bang, and Ken was extremely good on funnel and "taigon" tubing. He'd take a big funnel and attach tubing to it and sort of make a trombone-like thing out of it. Anyway, we'd do crazy things like that. But, the upshot of this, since we'd decided to preserve evil, we had to get rid of the "Jesus Saves" signs. So we would sometimes together or when we were alone, start stealing "Jesus Saves" signs and bring them home. You had to always show up on Sunday with at least one sign. It would go on the wall. This went on and on. The word got around, what we were doing, so that graduate students at UCLA started collecting signs all over Los Angeles County for us. In about two months there wasn't a wall in his garage that didn't have a "Jesus Saves" sign on it. They were just everywhere, okay. Both Phylly, and particularly, my wife, said that we were going to get arrested. I think Phylly's final response was to let the boys have their fun.

I left and took a job as staff physiologist at the University of Texas marine lab, in the late summer, '58. Ken stayed on for two years. I stayed for four years in Texas. I kept coming back to Los Angeles. In fact I came back and did a research project with John Prescott, who was the assistant there, on production in California kelp beds, which was another story, that has nothing to do with Ken, other than that we used the lab. But I kept coming back and we kept talking and the friendship, the bond, was there.

Designing Oceanariums with Ken Norris

In 1960 Ken called me and said he was leaving Marineland. He said, "I've been in touch with a fellow named Tap [T.A.] Pryor in Hawaii who contacted me," while he was still curator, "and they're going to build an oceanarium in Hawaii." Ken wanted some consulting help and asked if I could join him since he needed somebody to do all the chemistry. So in '61 we flew out to Hawaii together, and consulted, and ultimately designed the oceanarium. We had a lot of experience by that time. We were paid, in those days, in 1961, quite well. We decided to form a consulting firm, got a lawyer and incorporated Aquatic Consultants. We consulted then on the Philadelphia oceanarium which went defunct. Ken and I designed it for them, the concept. But we disagreed about its location in Philadelphia next to a baseball stadium. There was no water anywhere around for a mile or two. We suggested that they put the oceanarium in Atlantic City or on the edge of the Skullygil River or something like that, near the museum, where they'd get a lot of crowds. They built it and it lasted about two years and went under.

In the interim we were approached by the promoters for Sea World in San Diego. We designed Sea World together. I kept flying out from Texas all the time and Ken would send me stuff and back and forth. The whole initial concept of the first Sea World, which has expanded since then, was ours. They said, for consulting what they'd like to do was pay our expenses and everything, but they didn't want to pay us. They wanted us to take promotional stock. So we took promotional stock. Both Ken and I did extremely well because it went up. After Texas I went to Cornell and I thought I'd last a year at an Ivy League college and I ended up spending 28 years there. Through all that time I kept seeing Ken off and on. The beauty of it was that our bond was so close that even if we hadn't seen each other in three years, the minute we'd sit down we'd pick up the conversation right where we left off practically.

On New Year's Eve day [1998] we got to spend a couple of hours just talking. My wife and my daughter and one of my sons and his wife visited. Ken knew my son who's a very good guitarist and musician. Ken used to love to hear him sing; because he not only sang nicely but made up anti-religious songs which Ken loved. He loved the one especially about the Seventh Day Adventists coming around on Saturday morning when you're trying to sleep.

We then we disbanded our corporation. About five years later Ken consulted on the Hong Kong oceanarium. In the '60s while Ken was working on the social behavior of spinner porpoises, off Oahu, I was into vision in fishes, and I had all the equipment at Cornell. Very little work had been done on cetacean vision; there had been one paper published a long time ago on a humpback by H. J. A. Dartnell, a physical chemist in England who worked on vision, whom I happened to know quite well. Nobody had done anything. I wrote Ken and told him about this research. I went out and started with him. I got spinner porpoises and then later whenever a porpoise would die somewhere, if they'd tell me, I'd go. So it took me about two years, but I ultimately published the paper on cetacean visual pigments. Then I couldn't go back to it because it's so hard to get to them now. If you want to sit around and wait for an animal to die in an oceanarium fine, but—

I had done studies on the metabolism of fish schools a long time ago. In fact, I started that when I was at Marineland. The way I did it was the same way that Ken did. I keep saying, think like an animal, which he taught me. One time we were on the *Geronimo* collecting fish for the oceanarium. We pulled into Catalina harbor for the night and it was like 4:30 in the afternoon. There wasn't anything to do but it wasn't time to do dinner yet. I climbed up in the crow's nest and was sitting there looking around and noticed these schools of anchovies swimming along. They were eventually going out of Catalina harbor, but they didn't go in a straight line. They kept zigging all over the place. I thought, what the hell are they doing? Why not just go out? Your net progress is out but it's done in this very random walk sort of way. I got to thinking. I was high up enough so I could look down on them. I could see that when they moved the school just kind of turned on themselves. Why were they doing that? The first thing I thought was that they could be feeding. By changing direction the fish at the back of the school would later be in the front. I saw that they were very dense. I wondered if they were not reducing the oxygen in the water or adding carbon dioxide, the very same kind of applied problem that Ken and I had worked on in the lab for transporting fish. I wondered if by changing direction the leaders become the tail end and through time they averaged out their impact on the water.

I told Ken about it that night and he said, "Go for it! That really sounds great." We were going out of Cab harbor the next day to catch albacore tuna for the oceanarium. As we were going out I looked over to the left, off the bridge, and said, "Frank, what's that?" There's a big sandy beach out there, with surf. You could see this black streak in the water. The waves were breaking—just behind the waves. The wave would break and they'd kind of go in and out. The black streak was five or six hundred feet long. So Frank turned the boat and we went over there. It was solid anchovies. They were so dense you could have walked on them. The only thing I could figure was they had a natural aerator; they weren't moving. A wave would crash and bring fresh oxygenated water back there. Well, that led later to experiments.

What I'm trying to say was that Ken and I were constantly observing and asking questions. He was concentrating mostly on cetaceans, toward the end. But that's the way we operated. We constantly bounced ideas off each other. It was marvelous. When I spoke at the memorial the last two sentences I wrote were: "For me what began as the camaraderie of graduate students, flourished as a lifetime friendship," which it really did. I said, "We shared the creative joy of simply doing science, asking questions and," and I didn't put it this way, but it's what I think Ken would have wanted me to say, "trying our damndest to be that animal." That was really it for me. Ken was so many things. But to me, he was one of two or three most imaginative scientists I've ever met in my life. He was just fascinating.

Jarrell: I was going to ask you about his imaginative capacity.

McFarland: Oh, it was incredible. Well, it must have been. Dr. Van Denburgh sightings—these things didn't come out of nowhere. Ken's was an imagination incredibly creative in so many different ways. Not just as a scientist, but his sense of fun in life. He was just a great joy to be around. I mean, why would we sit on Sunday morning in a room and admire "Jesus Saves" signs? He ran counter to the stream of conventional thinking; in fact, he contributed more by doing it than by going in the same direction everybody else was going. Listen to those students today at the memorial who had been in that natural history course. Those people loved Ken because they got something they would never have gotten anywhere else. Never, ever. To me that was an enormous tribute to Ken. To see that many people who just took a course from him stand up in an ovation at his memorial. Now I know some of them became very close.

Jarrell: Over four hundred students took the Natural History Field Quarter.

McFarland: I've had a lot of friends in life but I have had two very, very close friends. Ken was one of them. I considered him a brother. The other was a young man who was my postdoc, whom I consider my younger brother. Fortunately he's still with me.

Then there was the other wonderful side of Ken Norris, and that's Phylly Norris. She's just an incredible lady. I mean, anybody who could put up with

Ken's antics had to be marvelous! (laughter) It was a full partnership. I think she said, oh let the boys have their fun.

It's been enjoyable talking about these things. Phylly put it so nicely at the end of the memorial when she said, "He needed—he loved you." That was so true. I said something about that as well. "Ken loved life and was fascinated with the people who surrounded him. He had a strong influence on his colleagues and got strength from each of them as well." But it's what she said, that he needed us; he absolutely needed us. Phylly was so right. Yes, I think it was perfect coming from Phylly. In fact my colleagues at dinner tonight both commented and said, "What a beautiful memorial service that was." Well, thank you.

Jarrell: It's been a pleasure and I thank you for meeting with me at this very unorthodox hour.

McFarland: Oh, it doesn't matter. This is what Ken and I would do. It's only 10:30 p.m.

William F. Perrin

Meeting Ken Norris

Jarrell: To start, Bill, where did you do your undergraduate work?

Perrin: I spent a year at UC Berkeley in the mid-50s and I finished up after a stint in the air force, at San Diego State University, in 1966.

Jarrell: Where did you do your graduate work?

Perrin: I started a master's program at San Diego State. Then after I talked to Ken, he invited me to come up to UCLA and do a Ph.D. on the same research. That was in 1967.

Jarrell: What were your research interests? Why did you want to go to graduate school?

Perrin: Well, originally I started out with the idea of becoming a secondary school teacher. I took some courses in that direction. But I didn't care much for it. I decided to continue with biology. I had hoped to perhaps teach junior college, something on that level. I really wasn't expecting to get into a Ph.D. program. My master's advisor at San Diego State said I should talk to Ken because he was interested in dolphins, too. I caught Ken sitting in his pickup truck behind the aquarium at Scripps, just leaving for L.A. He said, "Sit down. Tell me about yourself, what you're doing." I sat in the truck and we talked for about half an hour or so. Then he said, "Well, why don't you come to UCLA and do a Ph.D. instead?" I was utterly flabbergasted. I had no idea that I was being interviewed as a possible student. So of course I went and that's how I got to UCLA.

The Tuna/Dolphin Fishing Controversy

I'd gone out in 1966 on a tuna boat to collect information on tuna purse seine performance for some developmental work that was going on, for the [National Marine] Fisheries Service. I saw the dolphins being slaughtered by the hundreds, over a thousand, on the trip that I was on. So I thought I'd look into it. When I got back to San Diego I found that there was nothing to read and that the situation was completely under wraps.

Jarrell: Under wraps?

Perrin: Well, nobody was talking about it.

Jarrell: It hadn't been defined as an issue yet?

Perrin: No. There had been some talk about it within the agency and so on, but it wasn't publicly known. I decided to work on that. I started the master's program at San Diego State. My idea was to work on the relative vulnerability of the different species of dolphins to the fishing operation. That's the kind of problem I was outlining when I talked to Ken. He was very interested in that because he had heard about the problem and was happy to have a student who was working on it.

Jarrell: Who were the people you worked with who were saying, there's this slaughter going on that's part of catching the tuna. Who identified it and said this is crazy?

Perrin: Well, it wasn't identified at that point.

Jarrell: So how did you—

Perrin: Well, I went out and saw it. I went out for a different reason. It was a purse seine development project. I was hired as a technician.

Jarrell: Who sponsored this project?

Perrin: The National Marine Fisheries Service. I was hired to go out and look at net performance.

Jarrell: What does that mean, net performance?

Perrin: Well, how fast the purse seine sinks, how fast it can be retrieved, the technological aspects of the fishery.

Jarrell: So it was a study of how to be more efficient in terms of fishing?

Perrin: Yes, right.

Jarrell: There wasn't any intrinsic interest in the dolphins?

Perrin: No. There had been a previous research project by a young biologist from Kent State University who had gone out and collected some specimens and was working on the natural history of the dolphins. But he had left and didn't carry through on it. When I came along there was nothing happening.

Jarrell: Someone I spoke with prior to this interview described your work, your doctoral thesis, as the seminal work in the whole tuna/dolphin issue.

Perrin: Well, I was a young graduate student, and fairly naive. In 1969 my professor, the co-chairman of my committee, was Carl Hubbs.

Jarrell: Oh, I didn't know you worked with Carl Hubbs, too.

Perrin: Yes. He suggested that I give a talk at a meeting in Palo Alto at the Stanford Research Institute. The meeting was run by an old friend of his,

Thomas [C.] Poulter. It was a conference on diving mammals. I took some film that I had taken in 1968 of the tuna/dolphin problem, put it together, and gave a talk on it. I made an estimate of the mortality, about a quarter of million a year. I suggested that it might not be sustainable. When I finished the talk, during the question period somebody stood up and said, "We realize you may lose your job because of this. We're very glad that you broke the issue." My response was kind of, say what? I got back to San Diego and sure enough, they tried to fire me.

Jarrell: Why?

Perrin: Because I'd let the cat out of the bag.

Jarrell: What was it that you said that put you in such jeopardy professionally?

Perrin: I presented data and film showing that thousands of dolphins were dying in the tuna fishery. That was the first public awareness or notice that this was going on.

Jarrell: Who was your opposition?

Perrin: My opposition?

Jarrell: Yes, you were in jeopardy and you said that you would lose your job.

Perrin: Well, the Fisheries Service didn't want this information known.

Jarrell: So somebody already knew about it before you identified it?

Perrin: Well, certainly the California Department of Fish and Game knew about it, the National Marine Fisheries Service knew about it. But they didn't want people talking about it. It turned out that any talk that was given was supposed to be cleared with the higher authorities, with the regional director and so forth. I hadn't done this because I was a new employee; I didn't know about these requirements. I naively just went and gave a talk.

Jarrell: You just presented your data.

Perrin: The Fisheries Service didn't like that at all. The regional director then ordered me fired. But my laboratory director, Alan [R.] Longhurst, went to bat for me. He said that he had okayed the talk.

Jarrell: He took the heat.

Perrin: He took the heat and I kept my job. In 1969, because of public pressure, and the word being out, we got some money from Washington, [D.C.] to start a research program to try to solve the problem.

Jarrell: So after this talk at SRI, the cat was definitely out of the bag.

Perrin: Yes, I have to emphasize that I did this very naively.

Jarrell: Right. You weren't some political gung-ho activist.

Perrin: No.

Jarrell: You were just saying, here are the data.

Perrin: Right.

Jarrell: This is what's going on.

Perrin: Yes.

Jarrell: Okay, could you talk about your graduate research?

Perrin: Well, I started the program at UCLA in 1967 and spent a couple of quarters in residence. That was required. Then, in early 1968 I moved back to San Diego and was hired full time by the fisheries service. The man who hired me told me I could work on my research, provided I did this other work in a different area. I was a full-time employee.

Jarrell: Right, kind of like Ken when he worked at Marineland and he was working on his doctorate concurrently.

Perrin: Yes. That's when Carl Hubbs became the co-chairman of my committee because he was at Scripps. Ken at that time was in Hawaii, actually. He was still, I guess, a third-time at UCLA. I didn't see Ken very often during those years. A handful of times. I pretty much knew what I wanted to do on my research. So there was no day-to-day supervision or guidance.

Jarrell: Ken talked to me about this in his oral history, but to what extent was your dissertation—

Perrin: My dissertation didn't come out until 1972.

Jarrell: 1972 was the year the Marine Mammal Protection Act was passed.

Perrin: Yes. My dissertation was really more on the animals themselves, on their distribution and morphology, taxonomy. It was not on the conservation problem.

Jarrell: To what extent were you involved in the conservation activities and the ultimate crafting of the legislation which led up to the act?

Perrin: Well, Ken was very much involved in the drafting for the act, with [G.] Carleton Ray and some others. They sent me a copy of the act, the draft, to look at. There was no provision in there for consideration of the tuna/dolphin problem. The public pressure for legislation, the act, came about because of the killing of baby seals in Canada. That was really the impetus. In the very early drafts there was no recognition of the tuna/dolphin problem. I suggested that there should be something built-in that would regulate that situation, number one. And number two, that would allow some kind of transition between what was going on right then and hopefully some time in the future a changed situation in which the dolphin-kill would be reduced a lot. Because as the act was written, legally, the tuna fishermen would have to start obeying it when the act was passed because it didn't allow for large incidental takes like that. This obviously was not going to happen because it was a very important industry, a very important fishery. What would likely have happened was that it would be a big, head-on collision between the act and the economic interests. I thought the act would probably lose. So I suggested that there be some provision for recognizing the kill and reducing it in a rational way.

Jarrell: Not just overnight, but—

Perrin: Well, it couldn't be done overnight. It wasn't going to happen; it was not in the cards.

Jarrell: And that's a multi-million dollar industry.

Perrin: Yes. That was not going to happen. So that's how I was involved; I helped draft some language to make that possible.

Jarrell: How did you interact and work with Ken over the years? You finished your thesis in 1972 and then where did you go?

Perrin: I stayed where I was, at the Fisheries Service. I had a research program to try to reduce the mortality. That lasted until 1981. During that period we contracted Ken to do work on dolphin behavior, primarily in Hawaii, to try to understand the behavior of the dolphins, what made them die in the nets, how to get them out, and so forth.

The first thing we did, actually before Ken was involved, was an experiment at the Oceanic Institute. We built a crowding chamber out of netting and put dolphins in there, and crowded them to see how they would react to the pressure. This was at a period when Ken was director of the Oceanic Institute. Later we let the fairly large contracts to Ken and his research group, who worked for several years on spinner dolphins in Hawaiian waters. During this whole period, of course, Ken was relating to people in Washington, D.C., and working there to try to make sure that adequate attention was given to the problem. He was an advisor to the Marine Mammal Commission during that period.

He saved my career at one point. I went to a congressional hearing in Washington. An administration person gave testimony that I thought was not entirely accurate. I reacted with a letter to the head of the agency [The National Marine Fisheries Service], saying I thought this was not entirely truthful testimony and I wanted to disassociate myself from it, etc. Unfortunately somewhere along the line somebody got ahold of the letter and posted it in a corridor where all the people in the agency could read it. It was embarrassing to the head of the agency, to say the least. Again I did it out of political naiveté, as much as anything else. They wanted to get rid of me again. The way I did it was not the best way. You don't want to embarrass your chief. But I did. Not intentionally, but I did it and Ken stepped in and talked to them and talked to me and saved my job for me.

I was in La Jolla and he was in Hawaii for that period. Then he moved to Santa Cruz. By the time he went to Santa Cruz I was out of the system as a student. So we related to each other pretty much as colleagues during that period, from the time he came to Santa Cruz, until now, until recently. I just thought he was a great guy and saw him from time to time and we talked. He asked me for advice; I asked him for advice. He was one of my favorite people in the world.

Jarrell: When did you become a faculty member at UCSD?

Perrin: In 1983.

Jarrell: What was the backdrop for that? You left the federal government?

Perrin: Oh no, I didn't leave. Our laboratory is on the Scripps campus; we have a very close relationship with Scripps. Several of our staff members are adjunct professors there. I was doing research in which we got students to work with us and wanted to be able to advise students. The University agreed and made me an adjunct professor. I'm not employed by UC. I'm still employed by the fisheries service. I'm an adjunct professor at Scripps. And so I've had some students.

Norris as a Founder of Cetacean Research

Jarrell: I'd like you to give your assessment of Ken's contributions to cetacean research over these years. What's your overview of his work, the kinds of questions he asked, the consciousness-raising he did in the political realm? How important was Ken as a scientist in this field?

Perrin: Well, he virtually created the field in the United States. There were some people here and there working on things. But he chaired the first conference ever on cetaceans. That was in 1963, in Washington, D.C., a bit before my time. About the only book around at the time I started my student career was the proceedings of that meeting. That was the only book on cetaceans available in the United States, by a U.S. author.

Ken went on from there to define conservation issues and to create research programs, first at UCLA, and then in Hawaii, and then at UC Santa Cruz. That produced many of the people who are now heading up cetacean research programs around the country. He really is the Abraham Lincoln of our field. He was always this person we heard so much about during the memorial, the kind, generous sponsor of students and so on. But he was also a very rigorous scientist. A lot of what we heard about was just his way of presenting himself and conducting himself, when he talked about not worrying about data and so forth.

Jarrell: That's not true?

Perrin: That was completely untrue. That was a just a style because he never, ever, said anything was so without having the data to back it up. He never said that "a" was bigger than "b" without measuring it. He did some very, some truly excellent, purely scientific work in his earlier career with reptiles and fishes and later with dolphins. He measured speed; he demonstrated echolocation. This cuddly exterior of his was wrapped around a truly rigorous scientist.

Jarrell: You said earlier that basically cetacean research was minimal at best, maybe a few people in the world, in terms of his predecessors; there was not a clearly defined field with a critical mass of research prior to Ken in the U.S.?

Perrin: There wasn't in the United States. There were some people in the U.K. Most of the whale research in the United States before Ken came on the scene was associated with whaling. There were people who were working on data from the U.S. whale fishery at Richmond, for example; or out of Seattle on the biology of the great whales; or out of Australia, South Africa, the United Kingdom—various places around the world where there were whale fisheries. Norway, Japan. But there wasn't a field of cetology, in terms of looking at the animals in their environment and as parts of their ecosystems.

Jarrell: Was there any umbrella organization such as the Society of Marine Mammalogy, prior to—

Perrin: No. Ken was the co-founder of the society, of course.

Jarrell: So those researchers were kind of working in isolation?

Perrin: Well no, they knew about each other. There was the International Whaling Commission, of course. That was the main organization that brought researchers together. There were annual meetings of the scientific committee of the whaling commission. But there really was no field of cetology. There wasn't much going on about behavior, on ecology, on ethology, which is behavior, in a different light. The kinds of things that were being studied for all other groups of animals weren't being done for cetaceans. One reason was because they are so hard to study out there in the open ocean. Ken really brought all this together and created a new field in the United States. He was a very good communicator and a good socializer, and generally just a force of nature in his field.

Society for Marine Mammalogy

Jarrell: Can you tell me about the genesis of the Society for Marine Mammalogy?

Perrin: Well, there had been a series of annual meetings convened by Tom Poulter at SRI, mainly having to do with diving physiology, primarily in pinnipeds, seals and sea lions. Somewhere along the line there Tom Poulter was getting pretty old and everybody wanted the meetings to continue. They became a more general marine mammal meeting. Ken helped that to happen. Subsequently there was a lot of feeling that since we had these annual meetings or bi-annual meetings, we ought to have a society made up of the same people, to sponsor the meetings and at some point to launch a journal. Ken was the main organizer in that effort. So the marine mammal conferences go back to those days. They were originally the meetings that Tom Poulter held at Stanford Research Institute and they evolved into the present series of meetings. When those expanded to include cetaceans and other areas of biology, and diving physiology, the time was ripe for a national society, and then an international society. Ken recognized that need, and because of his great influence and abilities, he brought it off.

Jarrell: What year was it founded?

Perrin: The first meeting after Tom Poulter's meeting was I believe in 1975. That was here in Santa Cruz.

Jarrell: And that's where Ken was the co-founder and first president of the society.

Perrin: Well, it wasn't a society yet. That was the first.

Jarrell: Oh, this was the precursor?

Perrin: Yes, this was the transition between the earlier meetings which were primarily on diving physiology and so forth of pinnipeds, to a broader marine mammal meeting. The next meeting was in San Diego in 1977. The third meeting, I believe, was in San Francisco in 1979. But the third meeting was the one, if my memory is correct, at which the society was actually formed.

Jarrell: Then the journal was launched.

Perrin: In 1985.

Jarrell: I know you are the current editor of *Marine Mammal Science.* I got your e-mail about the plans for the *Fieschrift* issue.

Perrin: We were talking about doing something like this before Ken died. We didn't expect him to leave us this soon. It's a shame that we didn't get our act together and get it done while he was still around. But we're carrying through and the last issue of next year will be dedicated to Ken. It will have a memorial tribute edited by Sam Ridgway, with contributions by lots of people dedicated to Ken. That's a long time in the future but it takes a while. So far we have half a dozen papers or more coming. It's not very much but I guess it's more for us now, of course.

Jarrell: If you'd like to add anything about your thoughts on Ken or whatever, I would be happy if you have any more to say.

Perrin: I think it's all been said. The memorial yesterday was really good. I would agree with everything that was said.

Jarrell: Okay. Thank you very much.

Photo by Norden H. (Dan) Cheatham

Part III.

The Founding of the University of California's Natural Reserve System

UC's Natural Reserve System was founded in 1965 in response to the increasing loss of the state's natural habitats due to population growth and land development. Ken Norris came up with the idea of developing a system of reserves, "living laboratories," representing diverse habitats for research and educational use. Today the NRS manages over thirty reserves, encompassing more than 120,000 acres throughout the state. Although other universities in the country have one or two sites available for field work, the NRS is unique in the United States for both the number and ecological scope of its reserves.

Photo by Donald J. Usner, Landels-Hills Big Creek Reserve

Roger J. Samuelsen

The University of California's Natural Reserve System

Jarrell: To start, Roger, when did you first meet Ken Norris, and what were your initial impressions?

Samuelsen: Well, it was early in 1967. I had just joined the University and Ken came to Berkeley and visited me in my office in University Hall. I was just immediately taken by his charm and warmth, his charisma. He started to talk about his dream of the Natural Reserve System, which was then called the Natural Land and Water Reserve System, and of the need to move expeditiously, before it was too late, on some very key acquisitions. As I recall we spent most of our time talking about Año Nuevo Island and the need for a use-agreement with the [California] State Department of Parks and Recreation. That led to a visit to Sacramento some weeks later that Ken and I took to meet with officials there and start negotiations on what ultimately turned out to be a long-term use-agreement for Año Nuevo Island as part of the system.

Jarrell: What was your position at the University at that time?

Samuelsen: I was coordinator of special projects under Earl Bolton. Clark Kerr was then president and Earl had persuaded me to leave the practice of law and join the University as coordinator of special projects on January 1, 1967.

Jarrell: How did you end up working for the University?

Samuelsen: I was active on the UC Berkeley campus as an undergraduate; I ended up becoming president of the student body in my senior year, during 1957-58. Clark Kerr was then chancellor of the Berkeley campus and during my senior year he was named president of the University and became president, I believe, on July 1, 1958. So he and I had developed a relationship during that time. I was in the army for two years and upon my return I knew I was going to go to law school but there were nine months before I was to start. I approached President Kerr and asked if there might be some work there that would be helpful to him and suitable to whatever background I had. He introduced me to Dean McHenry who was then the University's dean of academic planning. I worked for Dean McHenry during those nine months, starting in early 1961. During that time I had no idea that Dean McHenry was destined to become the founding chancellor of UC Santa Cruz. He would send me over to the library to look up various and sundry documents having to do with the collegiate system in England. I prepared papers on various collegiate systems, which of course eventually he utilized in the founding of the campus.

He gave me other assignments as well. During that time the office next to mine was occupied by Earl Bolton, who was then special assistant to Clark Kerr. Earl was very instrumental in the founding of the Santa Cruz and Irvine campuses. His basic job was to negotiate the transactions establishing those campuses. Earl and I became very close during that period. He had a legal background and kept talking to me about going to law school and then perhaps someday returning to the University. I pretty much followed the course that he had taken. I went to Boalt Hall and worked for Earl during summer vacations. So it was almost destined that someday I would come back to the University. But Earl was the first to say I should practice law for two or three years just to get my feet wet, to find out what it was really like. We stayed in close touch. He offered me several opportunities. The opportunity to join the University, as I say, in 1967, was afforded largely to help Earl and Clark Kerr negotiate still additional campuses for the University which would have been, at the time the tenth, eleventh and twelfth campuses. At that time the thought was that those would be in place by the mid-seventies, because the population was growing and there still seemed to be quite a need for new campuses.

What none of us anticipated was that three weeks after I joined the University, Clark Kerr was fired by the UC Board of Regents. There I was, not sure where my career was going to lead, but it was clear that new campuses were going out the window. Ronald Reagan had just been elected governor. There wasn't that much support for the University, let alone its expansion. It was about that time that I met Ken and all of a sudden a void in my portfolio was filled by Ken Norris and his dream of building a natural reserve system into what it's become today.

Jarrell: In terms of the history you've just outlined, and the firing of President Kerr, it seems an inauspicious time to have started such an ambitious and pioneering program, which I know had been in the works since 1963. By that time Charles Hitch had become UC president, and you were working under Vice President Bolton, overseeing the coordination of the Natural Land and Water Reserve System. At the time all that existed was a University-wide advisory committee, of which Ken Norris was chairman, and faculty members from different campuses: Hartzik, Leopold, Davis, Majors, Stebbins, Mooney, Mayhew, Hubbs and Cushing. Originally seven sites had been designated. This became a major part of your job.

Samuelsen: Yes. But at the time, Ken Norris, while he was chairman of the committee, was really serving almost as the first director of the Natural Reserve System, which was then known as the Natural Land and Water Reserve System. To Ken's considerable credit, he was devoting what he later told me to be about half of his time in trying to piece together the early stages of the system. As he and I developed more and more rapport, of course, I was able to pick up more of the responsibilities. Then when he had to step down as chairman of the University-wide committee.

Jarrell: When was that?

Samuelsen: June of 1968. He was replaced by Mildred Mathias, herself an extremely competent individual. I started to pick up even more responsibility. It just grew and grew until finally so much of my work was involved in the development of this program that in 1974 I was named director of the

Natural Reserve System. So I was the first director, from a technical standpoint, but in so many ways Ken was the director during all of those formative years, from the time the system was established in 1965, until he stepped down in 1968.

Jarrell: I want to read you a quote here from an article that Ken wrote in *Bioscience* in 1968. He said, "I toured the state from top to bottom, inspected nearly ninety sites, hiked shorelines, mountains, grasslands and deserts and emerged from it not only with a firm grasp of what is needed, but also with a reaffirmation of the magnificence of our opportunity and the importance of rapid action. Time is short. Habitat destruction is appalling and everywhere evident. Although some habitats are gone, we are generally in time."

So he had, with his own fieldwork, and then with the committee, identified habitats all over the state of California, from top to bottom. I know it was a three-tiered system, where you had the coordinator, you, under UC's vice president for agriculture and natural resources; and then the systemwide advisory committee; and then, as sites were designated, individual campuses oversaw those sites. What was Ken's involvement in the NRS over the years?

Norris as Visionary and Activist

Samuelsen: Well, Ken really put the blueprint together for the whole program. He, first of all, was the visionary; he was one of these amazing people who not only had a vision or a dream but also had an action plan to carry it out. It is very rare that a person can be both a visionary and action-oriented. So he had the vision; he was the one who put together a report that influenced the UC Board of Regents to establish the program in January, 1965. And then, as you suggest, he literally took an entire semester in the spring of 1966 and toured the state. He took the time off from his teaching responsibilities and I've read reports of how he borrowed a jeep and a dictating machine and was off and running. He visited eighty to ninety sites, prepared a lengthy report that evaluated not only the natural features of those sites, but also what might be possible in terms of acquiring them either by purchase, gift, or lease or use-agreement, whatever the mechanism might be. He followed that with an acquisition plan which literally listed, by priority, the various sites he had visited and suggested the order in which they might be acquired. The list included a combination of sites that might be lost if they weren't acquired right away, or opportunities for the future. Now admittedly, he did all of this under the auspices of the University-wide committee, but he was the chair and clearly, as I look at the record, he was the one who drafted the reports and made sure they were finalized; made sure they were presented to the pertinent people in the structure of the University, and just kept pushing, pushing, pushing. I can't imagine anybody else being able to do that.

Jarrell: Whom did he push?

Samuelsen: I think he was pushing everyone from Clark Kerr to Earl Bolton to when I came on board, Samuelsen. I mean he had an ability to push with a big smile and an "aw shucks" attitude that was awfully hard to turn down.

Jarrell: To resist.

Samuelsen: There would be times that he would go before the board of regents, or before a donor. His charm and eloquence were such that you could just not turn him away. You said a few minutes ago that after Kerr was fired that it was not an auspicious time to launch a program of this magnitude, and you are absolutely right. These were rather austere times.

Jarrell: And the University was not getting all of the support that it had been used to getting?

Funding for the Natural Reserve System

Samuelsen: Absolutely. That was largely true throughout much of the first part of the evolution of the Natural Reserve System. In fact it was just within the last several weeks that the University made a commitment for the first time of a permanent base of funding for the operation and maintenance of the program, $500,000 is now available from permanent state funds for the program. That was a long time in coming. I wish Ken were here to know about that. Because one of his concerns was that the program kept growing, because it had to grow if it was going to grow at all, or the system would never have materialized. These sites would have been lost. But it was operated in many ways on a shoestring. In the latter part of his life Ken made a point to try and work through this and stayed very influential until the very end. It was largely on that basis that the Packard Foundation made its grant of four million dollars just before Ken died. Even the $500,000 I just mentioned, which is from University sources, I think in part was stimulated by the Packard grant, and that was part of Ken's strategy. Ken, in a variety of ways, kept pushing for more support, so that this dream would not fold under its own weight.

Jarrell: I read an article from *Bioscience*, 1988, written by Ken Norris and Lawrence Ford entitled, "The University of California Natural Reserve System: Progress and Prospects." They wrote: "The present budget in 1988 for staff and operations is about one-third of the level necessary to elevate the NRS to be comparable with other University of California activities." So you're saying that the NRS was operating on a shoestring, in terms of maintenance, of facilities, that funds were always in short supply?

Samuelsen: Yes. But the NRS kept going for a variety of reasons. First, there were very dedicated people like Ken at a faculty level; very dedicated people at the reserve manager level; and people living, caretaking, on the sites. It continued because people found very interesting ways of making do with less than standard types of housing and equipment and the like. But there was an underlying feeling that the NRS was terribly important, and that in due course people would come to appreciate it more and more. I think we are starting to see that as time goes on.

Ken believed that we couldn't just acquire lands and mothball them; that it wasn't our purpose to simply hold the reserves under the auspices of the University of California. These were sites that had to be developed and maintained and used as outdoor laboratories. In order to do that it took money. You had to have basic housing; basic equipment; basic campgrounds. You had to keep the trails and roads open. We had no business being in the natural reserve business unless these sites were being utilized. So Ken pushed all along for basic support to allow that to happen.

Jarrell: So you had to be active stewards?

Samuelsen: That's right.

Jarrell: This was just not some kind of a holding operation to preserve habitats, but to be actively utilizing them for research and teaching. In order to do that you needed money to establish the sites for students and faculty.

Roger Samuelsen as NRS Coordinator

What was your job as NRS coordinator? Eventually you were the director. But you were dealing with individual campuses, with new site acquisitions. You had a myriad of activities. Please describe, in detail, what your job was.

Samuelsen: Well, much of my time was devoted to acquiring new sites and making sure that they received the appropriate evaluation from one of our faculty members before we started negotiations. Then we had to work out agreements not only with the landowners but also with the campus that would eventually administer each site, that would pass muster, and would eventually coalesce and be presented to the board of regents for approval.

Jarrell: Was it difficult getting support from other campuses, because there wasn't a Ken Norris on every campus?

Samuelsen: Yes and no. I think it was not difficult to get support from the faculty on several campuses because Ken had counterparts, very strong and able faculty members, who shared his vision and like Ken, they needed these sites for their own teaching and research use. What was more difficult was persuading the administration to take on the responsibility because there were financial ramifications and again, because we were working on a shoestring, we had to piece together funding strategies that would work.

Jarrell: So you might have a campus where you had a very passionate geologist or geographer or botanist who was totally in support of working at some particular site that would be under the aegis of that campus. But then you'd have to have the chancellor on that campus commit funds to maintaining that site?

Samuelsen: That's right. We did have some systemwide funding available, largely through gifts that we were able to raise over a period of time and we could utilize those for matching purposes. What we didn't have though, were state funds. That's what I alluded to previously about the $500,000. We were having to draw upon these private funds in order to make this all come together.

Jarrell: Could you tell me the story of a particular site from the time, let's say, that Ken identified it in his initial inventory, and then of course it had to go through the whole process of having the faculty advisory committee verify and say yes, we want to get this site. I've read that twenty percent of all the NRS sites are actually owned outright by the University. What would be the story of one particular site that you'd like to tell me, from beginning to end?

Samuelsen: Well, let me talk first kind of generically and then I think I'd like to use the Granite Mountains as a specific siting question because it involved Ken and his brother Bob [Norris] from the very beginning.

In general, sites would come to our attention more often than not through a faculty member, who had perhaps used a site over the years or had heard about a site through a fellow faculty member or a student or just because they were active in their field. We would then ask a given campus to look at the site through its own Natural Reserve Committee, made up of faculty, to see if they felt it passed muster. We had a list of criteria that a site needed in order to qualify to become part of the Natural Reserve System. If the campus committee recommended that we proceed then we would call into play the University-wide committee, made up of a chairman and a representative of each of the nine campuses, plus myself as an ex officio member. So that would be a group of about twelve. We would always insist that any proposed site be reviewed by at least three separate campuses. We wanted to make sure that it passed a systemwide or statewide test and wasn't just something that any given campus or even a given faculty member wanted for his or her own private research.

Once the University-wide committee endorsed the acquisition, then I would start getting involved even more actively in terms of meeting with the landowner, ascertaining what it would take to acquire the site, and start the negotiation process. At times I would involve members of the general counsel's office, because of the legal ramifications. Other times I would involve the real estate office, because in the end before we went to the board of regents any site had to have the signoff of those two offices before we could present it to the president and then to the board of regents. Quite often I would need to cultivate a landowner. This was where we needed Ken Norris, even after he stepped down as chair. Although he went to Chile and then to Hawaii for several years, as you know, he came back and became active on the UC Santa Cruz campus with the Natural Reserve System. So from time to time I would bring Ken Norris or Mildred Mathias or some other faculty member with me to cultivate a given landowner. This was true throughout my career. At key times I would just sense that it would be important, notwithstanding their very busy schedules, to ask Ken or Mildred if they would join me. It might be in some remote part of the state but they would always say yes. They never turned me down. Sometimes it would be beyond that. We would want to make a presentation to a foundation or to the board of regents. I would more often than not have one or both of them along just because they were who they were, and they were so persuasive. And Ken continued on, even after he retired, being available for that type of endeavor.

1967 Ford Foundation Matching Grant

Jarrell: I wanted to ask you, when you were talking about foundations, that in 1967 the regents made an allocation of $500,000 over a three-year period. That was I guess the first expenditure for the Natural Land and Water Reserve System. The Ford Foundation also gave a matching grant of $500,000 in 1967. Do you know how the Ford Foundation got involved?

Samuelsen: Because of one person—Ken Norris. Ken Norris paid a visit to the Ford Foundation in New York, met a program officer by the name of Gordon Harrison and told him about this brand-new program and persuaded him to become interested in the Natural Land and Water Reserve system program. One of my first recollections of my own association with Ken was a meeting with Gordon Harrison at Ken's office at UCLA. I flew down and this was all part of Ken starting to get me involved and excited about this brand new program, and frankly, I just sat there and listened. The two of them were just going back and forth, obviously energizing one another, and out of that came the proposal that we took to the board of regents, as you said, in September, 1967. It was a one-for-one matching provision; that is, we persuaded the regents to put up one dollar up to $500,000 for every one dollar that the Ford Foundation pledged.

Jarrell: That was a lot of money in those days.

Samuelsen: That was a lot of money and that was Ken Norris. As a matter of fact there followed further negotiations with the Ford Foundation. I had one letter from Ken, dated around February, 1968, or thereabouts, where he told me that he planned to step down as chair of the committee. But one of the reasons he didn't want to go public with that information quite yet was that he realized he was central to the final negotiations with the Ford Foundation. Keep in mind that we had the authority in September but it took these additional months to work out all the final details. Not until the Ford Foundation said absolutely yes on the grant and then a few other things that Ken wanted to do, did he announce publicly that he was stepping down in June, 1968. So Ken was absolutely central to that; it would not have happened without Ken, just as the Packard Foundation grant just this last year would not have happened without Ken Norris. Probably the two biggest grants in the history of the Natural Reserve System could be attributed to Ken's persuasiveness as a fundraiser, among all the other wonderful attributes that he had.

That Ford Foundation arrangement was crucial in another respect, because several years later we decided we needed to raise even more money in order to acquire sites for the Natural Reserve System and again this depended on private funding. State money wasn't available. In that instance we still had about $175,000 left from the original Ford Foundation grant. So we went to them again and persuaded them to increase that figure to $250,000, which again was big money at the time, and to allow us to use it on a three-for-one matching basis as the centerpiece of a major fundraising campaign. Over the next few years we raised quite a bit of money, largely utilizing the good name of the Ford Foundation as a means of persuading not only foundations but corporations to join forces and give us the wherewithal to acquire sites that we might not otherwise have been able to acquire.

Acquiring the Sweeney Granite Mountains Desert Research Center

I suppose I should go back to go to the Granite Mountains, because you asked me to pinpoint one site where Ken was very much involved. This is a lengthy story and I could go on and on, but it really started in the early 1960s, before there was a Natural Land and Water Reserve System, when Ken and his brother persuaded the Southern Pacific Land Company to give them a ninety-day renewable license, for something like one acre out in the middle of nowhere, in what is known as the Granite Mountains.

Jarrell: Is that where they built the Bunny Club?

Samuelsen: Yes. The wonderful Bunny Club was built by these two brothers and their families and henchmen and the stories about that—I wasn't there but I've heard the stories about begging, borrowing and stealing a little bit here and a little bit there. So that turned out to be a place, not only where the Norris brothers would visit, but where many, many students and researchers could be housed when they conducted their research in the desert. It wasn't until some years later that we were able to negotiate with the Southern Pacific Land Company the outright acquisition of three sections of land, on one of which the Bunny Club was located. We would have used money that we raised through the Ford Foundation challenge grant that I just described in order to acquire that. I don't think it was until the late 1960s, or thereabouts. So for all of that time until we acquired the sites, Ken and Bob were really allowing students and faculty to use the sites, but it took us that long to formalize the arrangement. Ken was right in the middle of those negotiations. He and I met numerous times in San Francisco with the Southern Pacific Land Company in order to persuade them to give us a price and they were reluctant to sell the property for whatever reason.

Jarrell: I would think they might be pretty difficult to deal with; they might not appreciate the uses to which this land was going to be put?

Samuelsen: I think that was part of it. I think also they were trying to decide what to do with the checkerboard holding of land they had throughout the desert and they were hoping to consolidate through exchanges with the Bureau of Land Management or other parties so that they could have a huge block of land to develop and make money from. Asking them to separate three sections of land for the purpose of this rather exotic program called the Natural Land and Water Reserve system was somewhat difficult, but we finally did persuade them. Ken almost single-handedly negotiated with the Bureau of Land Management to give us a long-term use-agreement on many, many other sections of land, to greatly expand the holdings in the Granite Mountains. Again it was his persuasiveness, not only in a very direct way, but also his willingness to serve on an advisory committee for the Bureau of Land Management and therefore to cultivate the support and interest of these people in what he was trying to accomplish, that softened them up enough so that I could come in at the right time and actually seal a legal document that would pass muster with them as well as with our board of regents. So that did materialize.

But Ken wasn't through. There were several other private holdings in that area owned by a gentleman by the name of Art Parker. Ken continued to cultivate Mr. Parker about the possibility of selling these two holdings, one called Granite Cove and the other called Dorner's Camp. It wasn't always easy. There were times when the two of them would kind of get after each other because Mr. Parker was concerned that Ken's vision would jeopardize his cattle operation out there and that Ken was trying to force him to move his cattle away from very strategic raising-land and the like. But Ken finally compromised and suggested that there were times of the year when the cattle could run on the University's property without jeopardizing the natural values that were being protected. It was an example of Ken's willingness throughout his lifetime to compromise in order to maintain the larger vision which he had in mind. There were some, I recall, who were critical of Ken, who felt that he should be more strident in his approach, particularly certain conservation elements and the like who thought he was selling out too soon and so forth.

Jarrell: Ken indicated in the *Bioscience* article that he believed in compromise for that larger vision, and not just that it had to be his way or no way. So he got criticism for this.

Samuelsen: Yes. Well, I think much of his success in founding the Natural Reserve System, in founding other wonderful enterprises during his lifetime, was because he recognized the need to compromise. But the Granite Mountains is a real testament to Ken and as you may know, several years ago, a portion of the Granite Mountains, what I describe as Dorner's Camp, which is a facility plus the surrounding campground, was dedicated in Ken's name as a permanent part of the Natural Reserve System. I'm so glad that that occurred, because people came from all over the country for the dedication. I was privileged to speak at the program. The chancellor of the UC Riverside campus also spoke.

Jarrell: When was this?

Samuelsen: I think it was in 1995 or 1996. At the time, of course, we had no idea that we wouldn't have Ken that much longer. As I look back at it now I'm just so pleased that a number of us had a chance to say publicly how much we loved and admired what Ken had accomplished. Ken insisted that it not be just all serious speeches, that there be music and laughter and fun. We all stayed there overnight and there was a big gathering that evening, and it was just typical of Ken Norris. It gave a lot of us who had been privileged to know and work with him over the years a chance to get to know one another and to swap tales, talk about the Bunny Club and so on.

Jarrell: Now is that the Sweeney Granite Mountains Desert Research Center?

Samuelsen: That's right. So that's the name of the whole of the Granite Mountains.

Jarrell: And then this one component—

The Bunny Club

Samuelsen: Is named for Ken. That's right. It is a wonderful tribute to him. One other story, while I think of it, I want to tell about the Bunny Club. I took early retirement in 1991, having served for many years as director of the Natural Reserve System. One of the promises I made to Ken and Bob Norris was that before I retired I would take to the board of regents some formal documentation for the Bunny Club, because in reality after the University acquired the land, their right to be on the land and maintain this funny little, exotic Bunny Club was a handshake agreement among the three of us, myself, and Bob and Ken Norris. But nothing was in writing. They were concerned that once I retired some successor might say, wait a minute—

Jarrell: What's this all about?

Samuelsen: What's this all about? You need to leave. So we negotiated a license and I think the license itself is about thirteen or fourteen pages long. Then I prepared an item for the board of regents, the last item I prepared, I think, during the course of my career. I had prepared maybe 125 to 150 items for the board of regents related to aspects of the Natural Reserve System. But I did not refer to it as the Bunny Club. I just referred to it as the cabin.

Jarrell: (laughter)

Samuelsen: I used appropriate language about how the Norris brothers had utilized this for a period of time, that there had been an oral agreement that they could stay on, and so basically the right that we negotiated was that they or the survivor of the two of them has the right to use it during their lifetime and then after the survivor passes away, the University then is obligated to grant a twenty-year license to some member of their respective family for that period of time, so it assures Ken's and Bob's family of at least twenty years after, in this case Bob, passes away. But part of the deal too is that they will allow, which is consistent with what they've always done, researchers and students to utilize the cabin at no expense for up to half of the year. Now a given visit can't be longer than seven days, as I recall, but it means that in essence these two brothers and their families have use of it half the year, the other half, at no expense to the University or each other, you know, there are variety of other technical aspects, but with kind of tongue in cheek I took that to the board of regents and they approved it. (laughter)

Jarrell: You just had to omit the name Bunny Club?

Samuelsen: We had to omit Bunny Club. Fortunately no one asked me for a picture of the premises. (laughter)

The Future of the UC Natural Reserve System

Jarrell: Right now, according to the website of the NRS, there are thirty-four sites, eighteen in the south and sixteen in the north. You told me that in the planning of UC Merced, with which you're involved now, several more NRS sites are being contemplated.

Samuelsen: Yes.

Jarrell: It's interesting, because in the *Bioscience* article, Ken wrote, "The northern part of the state, the giant inland valleys of the San Joaquin and Sacramento Rivers and the west slope of the Sierra will remain sparsely represented in the NRS. Inevitably many important habitat types will not be included in the NRS." I read that and when I spoke with you on the phone the other day you said, "Oh yes, they are already planning a couple of sites." So I guess they've been identified?

Samuelsen: No, we're in the process of identifying them. I say we. We have a faculty member at UC Santa Barbara who is taking the lead in identifying one or more sites. We hope to make it part of the fabric of UC Merced from the very get-go which of course will be different than has been experienced on existing sites, because the Natural Reserve System was established after the campuses were developed. It's very, very exciting, because it not only can be brought into the fabric of the academic programs right from the beginning, but hopefully will become part of the strategy we are pursuing in order to meet the standards of the Endangered Species Act and the Clean Water Act with regard to wetland protection and mitigation, and endangered species preservation and mitigation. So I see a cornerstone of UC Merced becoming closely associated with natural history, with the use of the entire Sierra Nevada as an outdoor laboratory. We have ongoing discussions with Yosemite National Park, Sequoia National Park, and Kings Canyon National Park. So the involvement in some way of the Natural Reserve System is very consistent with the central thrust of the campus as it's evolving today. I was able to share this with Ken before he died and he was very, very excited, because again it's the fulfillment of his vision. He realized, as you just suggested in quoting that article, that there was a void up and down the San Joaquin Valley and particularly in the Sierra foothills regarding the Natural Reserve System.

Jarrell: Up to about 1988, I believe, that seventy percent of the major California habitat sites were represented in already existing NRS sites, leaving thirty percent not yet represented. Originally there was a committee that identified all of the different habitat systems in the state and an inventory done. So as you said, it wasn't just that some faculty member at a campus wanted a site; it had to fit into this larger conception of representing the habitat sites of the most diverse ecological habitat state in the union. So you are adding on these other areas that have not yet been represented. What's the future of the NRS?

Samuelsen: I think, first of all, it's going to become more valued and more appreciated with every passing day. People are going to look back and just say, wow, see what Ken Norris did, how far-sighted he was, what a visionary he was. Because it really was a now-or-never proposition. That's why it was terribly important to push forward.

Jarrell: Ken's conception of the NRS was way before the first Earth Day, before the establishment of the EPA.

Samuelsen: That's right. I think with the allocation of the $500,000 it suggests that the Natural Reserve System is going to become more and more part of the mainstream of the University. For so many years I think there were those who felt it was kind of outside of the main purpose of the University of California. I'm not speaking now of the Ken Norris-type people but about people who didn't appreciate the importance of protecting our natural environment, just for all the unknowns that are out there to make sure that there's still, as Ken would always say, a bulwark of sites that were available for natural scientists still to come. My hope is, led by UC Merced and other campuses, that these reserves will be at the cornerstone of principal academic endeavors and will be the basis on which to attract outstanding faculty and students from around the world because of the opportunity these sites provide. I think that there will be, as Ken often advocated, more and more of an appreciation that to really make these strong functioning units you need to have basic facilities, basic resources at the site, so that as with any other scientific endeavor, people will have a place where they can hang their hat, a place where they can put their instrumentation, where they can get out of rain and snow and whatever. I think we're going to see far more sophisticated equipment brought onto the sites than perhaps Ken ever envisioned at the beginning. It's the wave of the future and that interplay between sophisticated equipment and the natural habitats that are there is going to spawn all sorts of research productivity that's beyond our wildest imagination. I think the future for the NRS is extremely bright. It's going to be a strength that goes along with many of our laboratories and attributes that we often value when we think about what makes UC such a quality institution of higher learning.

Ken Norris's Legacy

Jarrell: How would you describe Ken's legacy?

Samuelsen: There are so many aspects. I think beyond the obvious—the Natural Reserve System, the coastal [Long] Marine Lab, or the Natural History Field Quarter, was the way he inspired so many hundreds, if not thousands, of students and faculty and people like myself to carry on his work. He obviously had a tremendous impact on my life, personally and professionally; so much of what I'm doing now at UC Merced really goes back to the times that I spent with him, and some of the lessons he taught me. I'm only one. There are so many who were influenced by him. He was way ahead of his time so that if I can continue in my work right now at UC Merced and help develop a few more reserves in the system and tie this into the fabric of the campus in whatever way, then I'm carrying out his legacy. So it's continuing to be a very important component, I think, of our endeavors.

Jarrell: You're of the older generation. As you work on the new Merced campus, are there people you encounter in the new generation who are like-minded in this regard?

Samuelsen: Definitely. If anything they are even more enlightened than my generation. Ken was in many ways ahead of himself, as were Mildred Matthias and other people of that ilk. But yes, I think there are many, many people who are here to build upon the foundation people like Ken Norris have laid, and to help us be more environmentally conscious and sensitive as we proceed. Just using UC Merced as an example, I sense in all of the conversations I'm having as to how the campus and the surrounding community are to be developed, that people are very conscious of how this should be done in keeping with the lessons that we've learned, the mistakes we've made, from an environmental standpoint, from an energy conscious standpoint. This I think is the only way to go. I hope we can find ways to do this that are economically feasible as well as environmentally sensitive.

Mildred Mathias

Jarrell: You mentioned Mildred Mathias. In a letter that you kindly sent me, written to you from Ken Norris in 1996 he says, "Dear Rog—" and talks about the formation of the NRS, and about Mildred Matthias. Would you give me a little thumbnail profile of her?

Samuelsen: Well, Mildred, like Ken, was way ahead of her time. For years she was a very prominent professor of botany on the UCLA campus and that's where she and Ken met. She was a distinguished botanist at a time when women just did not blossom in the sciences or maybe outside the home, in many respects. She was able to attain her Ph.D. and go on to a distinguished career even as she was rearing three children and carrying out all her other responsibilities. She was so well respected that the botanical gardens at UCLA are named for her. Several plants that she studied have been named for her. She was just the right person to succeed Ken Norris as chair of the University-wide committee for the Natural Reserve System and served in that capacity for over twenty years. In essence during all my years as director I had two chairs—Ken Norris and Mildred Mathias. I became very close to both of them. Mildred passed away several years ago. She literally had a stroke while she was working in her home garden, near the UCLA campus. She was well into her eighties at that time.

A. Starker Leopold

Jarrell: I'd like to ask you about another person Ken mentioned in this letter to you. He referred to the early days when he drew up the report after his long trip investigating various prospective NRS sites. He said: "It must have been after that trip that I went to A. Starker Leopold at Berkeley, perhaps on Boyd Walker's recommendation, to see what to do next. He was the one who told me to give him the plan for study, to submit it to Clark Kerr and that Kerr would say, 'hmm, you should look at this.' And [Kerr] would say, 'Starker Leopold' and Starker would then tell him it was good." Tell me about Starker Leopold. Another thumbnail sketch.

Samuelsen: Starker was a member of the famous Leopold family. His father, Aldo Leopold, was a renowned scientist and author and all three of the Leopold children went on to very distinguished careers in the sciences. Starker Leopold was on the Berkeley campus and he was a man for all seasons; he was a distinguished scientist, and a member of the Bohemian Club and very comfortable in those circles. He obviously was a very close friend and confidante of Clark Kerr and so when Starker Leopold said something was a good idea you had a pretty good chance of having it succeed.

He also was instrumental in the establishment of the Big Creek Reserve. When the owners of Big Creek were weighing various options as to how to dispose of their property and still hold on to some limited personal rights, Ed[ward D.] Landels, one of the owners, talked to Starker Leopold at the Bohemian Club. Starker asked whether Landels had considered this program called the Natural Reserve System. Ed Landels did not know about the NRS but that led to a luncheon involving Landels, Starker and me. I do not recall whether Ken was there but I have a feeling that if he was in town he would have been there talking about the NRS. Of course that eventually led to the inclusion of Big Creek in the NRS, the Landels-Hill Big Creek Reserve. You asked me about reserves that have the Ken Norris imprint. Of course so many of them do, but I would definitely put Big Creek right up there with the Granite Mountains. Ken was the faculty manager of Big Creek for many years and I think Ken used Big Creek to carry out many aspects of his vision with regard to both the management and the use of the site. Again, it's one thing to acquire a site but it's another to make it usable for faculty and students. So Ken spent a great amount of time drawing up management plans, activating the management advisory committee, improving facilities there that could be used, improving the basic campground where classes could spend the night, and sometimes again he would have to do it out of bailing wire, because there weren't enough funds, but he was anxious to do that.

Jarrell: It seems to me from everything I know about Big Creek that it was sort of the prototype reserve in the sense of actualizing the larger vision: how it was maintained; how it was administered by UCSC; Don Usner and others living down there as caretakers; so many Environmental Field Program publications focused on it, and it was close to home for Ken as well.

Clark Kerr

The other person I want to ask you about is Clark Kerr. Ken went to Kerr with this singular, generative idea and Kerr embraced it. What do you think of that? What do you think of Clark Kerr's role in all of this?

Samuelsen: Clark Kerr was pivotal and he greatly respected Ken's proposal, and appreciated the thoroughness with which the NRS presentation had been made. I think Kerr was a visionary, and still is a visionary, and still going strong. It was a perfect coming together of a scientist of the ilk of Ken and an administrator the ilk of Clark Kerr—two visionaries who saw way off in the future as to what was really needed to make the University of California great. But that doesn't surprise me about Clark Kerr. Again, as I said earlier, I'd known him as an undergraduate at Berkeley and it was Kerr as the chancellor at Berkeley who had the foresight and saw the need for a student center, for dormitories, for adding to the cultural base of the campus, for making Berkeley far more than just a mixture of buildings and faculty and students, to really enrich the institution and that's just a cornerstone of Clark Kerr's legacy. See you're asking me to comment on two of my gurus. It is just incredible that they really came together that way.

Jarrell: I think it's conceivable that maybe any other UC president to whom Ken might have gone, might have said, yes, that sounds very interesting, but might not have appreciated what it was really all about. The NRS was not a run-of-the-mill idea.

Samuelsen: I also think Ken went about it the right way. Where Ray Cowles had recognized the need for preserving some of our natural habitat, it was really Ken who kept talking to a variety of people, and trying to sort through what it was going to take to sell this to the UC administration and to the board of regents. That's where he came up with the idea of a systemwide plan that would serve the entire state and not just the provincial interest of a given faculty member or a single campus. He came up with the idea of setting up a priority listing of acquisitions, realizing that you couldn't possibility acquire everything that you might like, that you really had to have high standards and be selective. He came up with the idea that this couldn't be just for the University of California, that these sites had to be available for other institutions of higher education as well. And so on down the line. I'm just always amazed as I look back into some of those early documents Ken put together—letters, memos, proposals—how far-sighted he was; that almost the entire reserve system we have today is based upon those original documents and his original thinking in every aspect, and I could elaborate, but you get the point.

Personal Impressions of Ken Norris

Jarrell: This dovetails with something else. Although Ken's dreamy, visionary quality certainly was commented on in great detail at the Norris memorial, there was also this idea that Ken didn't care about statistics, all that sort of stuff. Other scientists I've interviewed, including William Perrin, say that Ken was a rigorous, serious scientist and all of this sort of hippy-dippy stuff was exaggerated. He was a very rigorous scientist. I see the way he conceived of the NRS and his strategy was so comprehensive, so bureaucratically adept, so beautifully thought out; it wasn't just a dreamy idea. Before he ever went to the regents he'd done his homework in spades. I get the impression that many people didn't appreciate that about Ken. Even he would make fun of himself. I'd ask him about something administrative and he'd say, "Oh Randall, I don't remember about all that stuff." But you know, he was one heck of a producer.

Samuelsen: That's right. But he also had the ability of involving other people who could fill in the details or do what perhaps he didn't have the stomach for.

Jarrell: But he realized, understood, that it needed to be done.

Samuelsen: He saw that it needed to be done and I think I'm an example of that, where I could fill in and bring whatever experience I had to bear. Ken always treated me as a total partner and gave me the feeling that I was as important as he in our endeavor. I personalize that only to make the point. I think that he did that with many, many other people throughout his career and that was part of his success, that he could encourage and involve many other people and almost at times give them the impression that it was their idea and not his. He never talked down to you. He was never self-absorbed. In fact he was one of the least self-absorbed people I've ever known. He would always cut through and treat you as someone very, very special and give you that "aw shucks, I couldn't have done this without you."

Jarrell: You couldn't have had the NRS without all the legal negotiating. It was essential. You had to make it happen. Ken didn't know about all that stuff.

Samuelsen: That's right. He would write me personal letters, sometimes even sending them to my home, over the years. He was in a very caring, thoughtful, way passing on advice based upon his observations and experience. In one letter I will always cherish he wrote me about the importance of delegating to others; about the process of giving your staff a feeling of ownership and satisfaction and growth. He and I were both aware that there were times my staff felt that I did not delegate enough; that I was too much of a perfectionist and the like. So Ken helped me through this. One of the points he made was that he found during his career that so often he could become even more effective and productive by delegating and giving people a sense of ownership.

Jarrell: And trusting them.

Samuelsen: And trusting them and in the end they felt better and he felt better because he was able to accomplish even more than he would have if he had done it all himself. So often the way they would go about doing something or the end-product would be different than what Ken might have conceived, but he had to recognize that it was far better than he could have conceived.

Jarrell: All by himself.

Samuelsen: Yes, I have so many memories of ways that he would reach out to me on a professional basis. But he would also reach out on a personal side. He would always ask about my kids, about my wife, Jeane. We would share favorite places where we had spent a long weekend with our wives. I would give him a suggestion and he would say, "oh Phylly would love that." That's not the Ken that maybe some people knew but that's the Ken I knew. His lack of self-absorption was so characteristic; he really wanted you, whoever you were, to feel you had his complete attention at that moment, and that was the most important thing in the world.

Jarrell: The new director of the NRS is?

Samuelsen: Alex[ander A.] Glazer.

Jarrell: I've heard excellent things about him. Is he infused with Ken's vision?

Samuelsen: Oh yes, very definitely. He is a faculty member who has been on the Berkeley campus for many, many years. He understands the purpose of the Natural Reserve System. He has the passion of a Ken Norris and also, like Ken, he knows how to work the system. He's been very effective at getting both faculty and administrative support. I think his presentation had a lot to do with garnering this $500,000 that I mentioned.

Jarrell: That's the first of its kind ever, right?

Samuelsen: Right.

Jarrell: That's quite a coup, it really is. Roger, I want to thank you for sharing these experiences about Ken with me. It was a very important piece of his life.

Samuelsen: Thank you. He was a lovely person and I am so indebted that I had the opportunity to know him as well as I did.

Robert M. Norris

Early Life for the Norris Brothers

Jarrell: To start, where and when were you born?

R. Norris: I was born in Los Angeles on the 24th of April, 1921. Ken came along three years later.

Jarrell: Could you describe your career as a geologist; how you first became interested in science?

R. Norris: I suppose for both Ken and me this interest in science developed because of our parents and our maternal grandfather Matheson, who was a merchant in Los Angeles. He had come to California in about 1880, to San Diego. His wide interests were reflected by the library he developed which both Ken and I found fascinating as we grew up. I don't know exactly why, but I think we were both sort of attracted to the books on science in his library.

We were certainly influenced by our parents' background. Pop was an outdoorsman who had a group of cronies in Los Angeles with whom he'd go hunting or often fishing and camping. Since that was an interest of his of course he arranged to take Ken and me and mom on a number of these little short camping excursions, sometimes Sunday afternoon trips, to places like the Santa Clara River. Ken would have been fairly small, but we used to go out there for picnics somewhere near Piru. In 1928 the St. Francis Dam failed, and of course it swept down that valley and destroyed our favorite picnic sites by absolutely reducing what had been willow thickets and little creeks to a big sandy waste. I remember feeling a personal resentment about this. Of course I was much luckier than many of the victims of the St. Francis Dam flood. I don't remember the month that it occurred, but it was in 1928.

My Dad was in business with my grandfather, who had a nursery and a landscaping business. One of the other things of interest to Ken and me was I think, through my mother, who had grown up with Rhoda Rindge, whose family owned the Malibu Ranch before it was subdivided. Pop got a job doing landscaping for Rhoda and her husband, their name was Adamson, down at the mouth of Malibu Creek. They built a very nice house there which is now a state historical monument. We would go out there during construction, because my Dad was involved in landscaping this place. In the course of digging the foundation they encountered some Indian burial sites which were quite intriguing to us. My Dad had the good sense to invite Dr. Harrington, who was at that time with the Southwest Museum in Los Angeles, to come out and have a look at these artifacts. Of course this was long before there were laws and rules—

Jarrell: An awareness of Indian burial sites?

R. Norris: Yes. My Dad realized that this was an important thing. So Harrington came out and made excavations. I remember seeing one of the skulls that they found with a big dent in it. Harrington explained to us that this young Indian had apparently been hit with a club or something and had recovered from it. I found it quite fascinating that an anthropologist could deduce this information from an old skull. The Malibu Ranch then was all rural, just Rhoda's family, the Adamsons and the Rindges had a couple of houses on it. They raised a little bit of hay and lima beans but I don't think they did serious agriculture there. My impression was they were a wealthy family and didn't need to really make any money out of it. They did run cattle. But in any event, my mother spent a lot of time as a young woman before she was married horseback riding around the ranch and getting acquainted with nature. So both of my parents were attuned to the outdoors; they were interested in the landscape, the setting and the animals and the plants. This had an influence on both of us as we grew up. They made sure that Ken and I had a lot of outdoors experiences.

Our first was a long, meaningful trip, particularly to me, but very likely to Ken also, in the summer of 1932. That year my Dad took his Model A Ford nursery truck, put a couple of double mattresses in the truck bed, and we set off for two weeks up in the Eastern Sierra and the Owens Valley. This was our first long trip. We'd made shorter weekend trips to various areas around Los Angeles, but we hadn't done any really long trips. That was a fine and interesting trip.

My grandfather died in 1929 and we fell heir to a lot of his library. So his influence continued in the sense that we had his library after that. Ken's library here today has some of those volumes. I have some also. For Christmas, 1928, he gave us a twenty-volume set of a children's encyclopedia, *The Book of Knowledge*. Ken and I used that all the way through high school for reports and for looking up things and hobbies. By the time Ken finished high school in 1942, it was getting a bit out of date in some areas. But those books were influential for a long time.

In the early 1930s we lived in the San Fernando Valley, a semi-rural area, a lot of chicken ranches and walnut groves and asparagus fields. You can still see something of the same kind of an environment on the outskirts of Fresno except there the emphasis was on fruit groves. But there were a lot of those around the valley. We, in fact, lived on part of an apricot grove for awhile.

So by the time of junior high school Ken's interests were beginning to tip in the direction of zoology. He made collections of lizards. I don't remember him collecting snakes particularly, although now and then he'd find a gopher snake and he'd have that around the house for awhile. Our parents, luckily, were not disgusted by these things.

By high school, we both had some of the same teachers. One chemistry teacher, in particular, Jehiel Shotwell Davis, was a very enthusiastic teacher who fired up students' interests. He had influence on a lot of people in my class too, who went into science or engineering. One ended up being a professor of engineering at San Jose State, for instance, and of course I ended up at UC Santa Barbara in geology. I think that Davis had an influence on Ken, but it wasn't the only influence by any means. Davis also ran the campus science program and was great for organizing these incredible outings for high school students, both girls and boys, and camping out in the desert and kind of keeping them all in shape and getting them back safely. Ken was very active in this club and had a wonderful time.

Jarrell: Do you think these field outings were evocative and later influenced Ken's Natural History Field Quarter classes?

R. Norris: Oh yes! I don't think there's any doubt that both of us got interested in field work in part because of this. It's hard to say what was the defining experience, if there in fact was one. I suspect it was a combination of things, going camping with the folks when we lived at the base of the Santa Monica Mountains, and especially out in the valley. When we were a little bit older we could go up on unsupervised hikes with our friends and often did just to see what was up in the mountains.

Ken and I did those hikes from our home, which was about two blocks from the base of the mountains. Around the Santa Monica Mountains out near Sepulveda Canyon, there were no houses then at all. There were some around the base but not up in the hills. There was a gravel road that went through Sepulveda Canyon, through the mountains in those days, not the 405 freeway. The population was spread out and sparse enough so that you could take your BB gun and go out into one of the washes that ran across the valley and shoot sparrows. Both of us did this. Ken was always I think a little more interested in hunting than I was. I remember one time he went out in one of these washes and managed to hit a sparrow which he brought back home. Nothing would do but he picked this sparrow clean and then my mother had to supervise roasting this tiny little bird that looked like a microturkey in the oven. I don't remember whether I got to sample the sparrow or not, but Ken certainly ate some of it.

University of California, Los Angeles

Jarrell: Where did you do your undergraduate work?

R. Norris: Both of us did our undergraduate work at UCLA. I started out as a chemist, of all things, because of my high school chemistry teacher. What happened was that I went to see what was up on the third floor of the chemistry building. They were having a geology field trip. So I stuck my head in one of the professor's offices and asked him if a chemistry major could go on this trip. "Oh," he said, "that's fine. Bring your own car and—" That trip was wonderful. It was down into the Salton Basin. I came back and changed my major.

Jarrell: Why?

R. Norris: I discovered that I really liked the out of doors as a place for a career, rather than a lab. Chemistry was kind of fun. But I decided I didn't want to work in a lab all my life; I would much rather do something that took me outside. So I changed my major practically as soon as I got back from the trip. I've never looked back since. About the time Ken was just starting at UCLA we got a possum, somehow or other. I can't remember whether it was shot or trapped. But anyway, we decided we would cook that possum. We didn't bother asking anybody how to do this. I remember that possum was edible but it was just sort of tasteless and uninteresting.

Later on, at Scripps, we roomed together for about six months and Ken came home with an octopus. Again, we didn't bother asking anybody how to cook it, which turned out to be a big mistake. We managed to get it skinned and the tentacles looked like little white radishes. I don't know what we did to them, but we at least heated them up. I don't think I have ever tried to eat anything as tough as that. We finally just gave up because our jaws got tired. We did a similar thing with squid; that was a little better because they are more like little strips of electrician's tape, the way we cooked them. Ken went on to try other things. In those days grad students were on a low budget and the cheapest meat you could buy was horse meat. It was excellent and very cheap. So we ate horse on a number of occasions, especially when the two of us were rooming together. And I'm sure he added other things besides squid, octopus, possum and sparrows to his experimental diet. He told me once I think when he worked down in New Mexico that he had cooked a rattlesnake. He said the trouble with rattlesnakes was they had too many ribs.

U.S. Navy

After awhile our careers began to diverge quite a bit. I finished at UCLA in October, 1943, an odd time to graduate. But UCLA during the war years had gone on a year-round operation, a three-semester operation. I had enlisted in the navy, mainly to avoid being in the army, back in 1942.

When Ken came to UCLA in 1942 he enrolled in the Navy ROTC program right away. He started out in geology. I wish I could ask him exactly why. Part of it was that by then he had been on some of our geology field trips. If we could get a weekend, two or three of the students, and Ken and I, if he was available, would set off in our own car and do our own little explorations nearly all out in the desert. I'm sure it was one of the reasons that we both got interested in the desert. He'd had an interest in geology and I don't remember whether I was surprised or not. After awhile I realized that Ken was looking for these critters under the rocks rather than the rocks themselves and he switched to zoology, which is probably where he belonged. But it took both of us a step to find out what kind of science we liked the best, or were best fitted for. I think both of us were attracted to the field sciences, almost from the start.

We had an eagle-eyed mother who was very conscious of what we were taking in high school because she wanted us to be able to be admissible to virtually any good university around the country. She'd gone out and badgered the high school about it, if they thought we should take something else. She wanted us to take all the science and math for admission to Cal Tech if that's where we wanted to go. Certainly that was a good thing for us. We might have done other things with that extra time. When we went out to UCLA we met all the high school requirements, although I can't say that our chemistry course in high school was all that rigorous, but we survived.

Jarrell: So you ended up getting your doctorate in geology?

R. Norris: I spent two and a half years in the navy in the Pacific, and when I came back I had the idea that I'd forgotten all my geology so enrolled in the master's degree program at UCLA with the idea to kind of catch up on things and set the stage for a career. I almost went to work for an oil company. They had such a scarcity of grad students after the war that they recruited everybody to be teaching assistants. I was a TA and I just loved that. I had to do practice teaching and one of the geology professors had some clout with the education people on campus and so he persuaded them to let me do practice teaching by handling a freshman lecture class in geology under his supervision. So I had the whole darn class and it was a wonderful experience, just great. He told me I ought to go on for a Ph.D. UCLA tried to discourage their own students from staying on for a Ph.D. but I was attracted because it was less expensive. By then I was on the G.I. bill so that helped.

My professor was U.S. Grant, IV, the grandson of the general. He was a wonderful guy. He used to have me give guest lectures for him when he had to be out of town. But Grant said that a good friend of his was in charge in marine geology down at Scripps and I should go down and talk to him. I did and he was quite pleased to take one of the students that Grant recommended.

Scripps Institution of Oceanography

Jarrell: Was Scripps at that time an independent entity?

R. Norris: Yes. It was administratively a department of UCLA before UC San Diego was organized. I went down there in the winter, 1949. Having spent two years in the navy, I was impatient about getting on with my career.

Jarrell: And your life.

R. Norris: And my life! Exactly. I did my Ph.D. in record time. It might have been a better Ph.D. But I don't want to think about that.

Jarrell: Right. Unlike Ken, who took a lot longer.

R. Norris: Well, yes. Ken's was much better. I think his master's degree was better than his Ph.D., if you can compare these things. But I was just impatient about this. So anyway, it took me two and a half years to finish it, which is pretty short for a Ph.D.

Well, I was going to go directly to UC Santa Barbara. I'd been up for my interviews and things had gone well but enrollment had dwindled away by 1951; it got down to about 1300 at Santa Barbara. Santa Barbara couldn't obtain a new appointment that year and they couldn't take me on. So I managed to get what we now call a postdoc. My supervising professor, Francis [P.] Shephard, at Scripps, had a nice big grant from the American Petroleum Institute to study near-shore sedimentation processes in the Mississippi Delta and the Texas coast. There were two different field parties and I got appointed field party head of the Texas part. I went down there and worked in the swamps of Texas in the summer which was quite an experience for a Californian. But it was a good experience and I'm very glad I did that. It just gave me a broader background and I've always said that I think it's good for a Californian to go down and live among the Texans for awhile, to kind of find out how they operate, what makes them tick.

The next year Santa Barbara still had trouble getting an appointment but they did have a one-year sabbatical replacement available. By then Ginny and I had gotten married. The following year I finally got an appointment and I've been there ever since. I came up there in the summer of 1952 and have had my whole career there.

Conceiving the UC Natural Reserve System

Jarrell: Now I want to move quite far ahead. During those years Ken was working on his doctorate doing diverse oceanaria projects and working on his Ph.D. Would you discuss your recollections of Ken's interest in what would become UC's Natural Reserve System? You've given the backdrop of these experiences outdoors, camping, going to the Owens Valley, the field work that both of you had done. But while Ken was still at UCLA, by 1963 he had developed his concept of the Natural Reserve System, of ecological laboratories or habitat libraries. Did you and Ken talk about this in the early sixties or the late fifties?

R. Norris: Yes, we certainly did talk about that because having grown up in Southern California, one of the things that you can't escape is the way in which urbanization has overtaken areas, the San Fernando Valley being a good example, but also out through the orange belt, to San Bernardino and even the desert cities like Palmdale and Lancaster. In the 1950s Ken was doing his master's degree under Ray Cowles at UCLA. Cowles was very concerned about this issue, about losing favorite field areas to this encroaching development. I think if there's any one person that perhaps put the bee in Ken's bonnet about this it would be Ray Cowles, because I know it was of great concern to him. He was concerned about broader issues like the world population increase, and very outspoken about that.

Jarrell: That was pretty far-seeing for the time.

R. Norris: Oh, yes. Of course California carried the brunt of this, not only because of natural increase but because of all the in-migration. As far back as I can remember, and we asked about this in school, it was rare that there were more than forty percent California-born kids in any of our school classes up through high school. You know, this is another way of saying that the in-migration has put pressure on California. So we talked about this.

There were field areas in both his discipline and mine where encroaching civilization simply eliminated them. As we got into teaching this became more acute than ever, because these places were our outdoor laboratories. So in the early 1960s I know one of Ken's great strengths was to have a broad vision of how a problem could be attacked on a large scale. I might see the problem but I was much more likely to see a local problem and try to deal with that, rather than seeing a statewide problem. I give him enormous credit for this. Because one of the things we talked about in 1960 was a field area in the

Soledad Basin down near Santa Clarita or Saugus, north of the San Fernando Valley, that was very popular with geologists. I taught field geology there beginning about 1955. I taught it for almost thirty years there. Fortunately it was on property that belonged to the U.S. Borax Company. They had about 800 acres in there. They had very conservative management and they resisted selling any of this. It was a wonderful area for introduction to field mapping and geology. It was not too useful for biologists, probably.

So Ken and I talked about it. And in the early Sixties I wanted to find some way that we could transfer that land to the University and give it long-term protection.

Jarrell: Where did you get the idea that the University could take over or have the land ceded to them?

R. Norris: Well, from teaching down there and seeing the increase in houses each year, as field classes would come up each spring. The University was not in the business of real estate development but I knew they had these agricultural field stations around the state. There'd been a long, long history of that, going way back to the turn of the century. I knew the University did this and by then I was getting well enough acquainted with the University bureaucracy to realize that the left hand of the University never knew what the right hand was doing. You just had to find the right people to talk to, very often, to get this kind of thing rolling. Well, Ken and I talked about this and early on he had the idea that we should make this much more general than just one area. One of the great disappointments in my life, and as we say in geology, I broke my pick on this, I never did succeed in getting that one area into the reserve system because it was torpedoed eventually, ten years ago, I guess, because of legal liability questions. An old borax mine had been up there and it released minute amounts of arsenic into a creek. Well, it was no real problem but the University lawyers were terribly sensitive about exposing the University to any kind of liability. But, they are most inconsistent about this. If you can establish a tradition where the University does something, even if there is a lot of legal liability involved in it, they never question it. But to take on a new one, they get highly upset. I always bring up chem[istry] labs in this; no one is going to ask a first-rate University not to have chemistry labs. But it's hard for me to think of a more dangerous place to turn undergraduates loose in.

Jarrell: Labs are fraught with liability.

R. Norris: Oh, they're terrible! But to assert to me that a field area is dangerous. Anyway, I broke my pick on that one.

Jarrell: It's so interesting that the precedent in your mind was the agricultural field stations which had been established in the late nineteenth century, early twentieth century.

R. Norris: Yes. It seemed reasonable enough for the geologists and the biologists to have something similar to this. Geology has a different problem than biology generally, because a biological reserve can be a fairly limited habitat that will be useful to them, but geology tends to range over bigger areas. Most of the reserves in the system today are not used by field geologists, although they are terribly important for biologists. There are some of the big ones like Santa Cruz Island or Big Creek, where geology is quite important. It doesn't mean that small geology projects aren't done on these sites, because they are. But that didn't matter to me. I can't remember the exact year I became involved in the NRS, but I believe I replaced John Cushing, the UC Santa Barbara representative, in 1967.

Jarrell: So let's just backtrack just a bit. You and Ken were talking about these things and you were thinking somewhat more locally. You said Ken's contribution was that he thought big, he looked at the whole state. Because eventually the NRS ended up with sites in the northern and southern regions of California, comprising somewhere in the neighborhood of 120,000 acres. So, from these original talks, what happened?

R. Norris: Well, of course Ken thought of the reserve as a California-wide thing, that the array of habitats available in California exceeds that of any of the other fifty states, without any doubt. He realized in the southern part of the state, in the Central Valley and other places, urban encroachment was making it harder and harder to take students out to these habitats. Ken saw, much more clearly than I did, much sooner than I did, that we needed to have something that was University-wide, statewide. He put together this thing when he was an assistant professor. I would take very little credit myself, although we had talked about it and managed to get an appointment with President [Clark] Kerr to talk to him about this. Ken did his usual good job and then one thing led to another. Kerr, I think, was taken with this idea. He may have been taken with the fact that one of his junior professors from UCLA had the gumption to come up to Berkeley and make a proposal.

Jarrell: Of this scale.

R. Norris: Yes. Of this scale. I can't help but think that Kerr was intrigued by that. I'm sure Sproul would have been if it happened on his watch. That probably helped, you see. Plus the fact that Ken did a darn good job on this. I can imagine Ray Cowles in the background coming up with a lot of previous experience too, that Ken incorporated into this. Ray deserves credit for some of the early suggestions. I'm sure were Ken sitting here he would be happy to agree with that. I got well acquainted with Ray after he retired. I'd met him a couple of times before. But he retired to Santa Barbara. His daughter was education coordinator at our museum of natural history. I know her very well. So I saw him quite a bit. I was teaching then and so I'd have Ray in to give talks to my classes. He had a theory about what caused the dinosaurs to go extinct and I'd bring him into the geology class and let them see Ray in action. So we had good interactions. Ken just loved him. He was a great, great guy.

Jarrell: When I interviewed Ken he told me such marvelous stories about Ray Cowles. I think he was the most inspiring teacher maybe that Ken ever had.

R. Norris: I wouldn't be surprised. He was a real broad-gauged naturalist and a delightful personality. He wasn't one of these scientists who feels that he has to get ahead by stepping all over his competition, the obnoxious ones in the field. Ken and I often talked about those people. We both had examples from our own experience. But yes, I think Ray had a lot to do with germinating the original idea. But whether Ray was thinking of it in the broad terms Ken ended up thinking of it, I don't know. Probably not, but Ray might have had the desert in mind. I couldn't say.

Jarrell: I would be very interested to know how you became involved in the NRS, once it was established in 1965.

R. Norris: Well, of course Ken and I talked about it quite a bit. I got myself on that committee, each campus had its own management committee. I found it very interesting. It was one of these kinds of committees that they sometimes had to beat the bushes a little bit to get people to volunteer for. But for me it was the most enjoyable committee I served on. Bob [J. Robert] Haller, an expert on the botany of California, turned out to be a long-term member of the Santa Barbara committee. We each served on the committee seventeen years. He's one of these darn guys who has published very little in his life. But he knows more about the native plants than almost anybody I've run across, a dedicated field man. He and I kind of ran that committee for a long time. If I had to be away and leave, Bob Haller would take over for me.

Jarrell: I have a list here of the NRS sites in the southern region and could you tell me about the sites you were particularly involved with?

Santa Cruz Island Natural Reserve

R. Norris: Well, the one I would have to list as number one, because I was the one that made the first suggestion, is Santa Cruz Island. The UC Santa Barbara geology department had run summer field programs out there for a few years. We had what we called the Channel Island Field Station; we had established a little field station at the Santa Barbara campus. I think by then I had gotten on that NRS committee and I thought, now this really should be a unit in the reserve system, not just a Santa Barbara field station. I was the one that started that. Then I got people like Mildred Mathias, who was, I think by that time, the faculty head of the reserve system. Mildred was very efficient about this kind of thing. She knew lots of movers and shakers. Mildred took the ball and ran with it. She deserves a lot of credit, certainly, for bringing it into the system. But the suggestion came from me.

Jarrell: Who owned the land?

R. Norris: The land was owned by Carey Q. Stanton. His father had bought the island in about 1935. He bought ninety percent of it. The eastern end was owned by the Gherini family in Santa Barbara and Oxnard. Pere Gherini was a lawyer in Santa Barbara and his family had owned it, going back a long time. In the 1930s they had sold off ninety percent of it to Stanton, down in Pasadena. Carey Stanton was trained as a pathologist, an M.D. He decided to take over running the island as a cattle ranch. So we had to get permission to put a field station there. He had a love/hate relationship with the University. He loved to have the intellectual stimulation that he got from having these researchers out there. But the University bureaucracy used to drive him up the wall. He was difficult to deal with. When I was director of that field station, if Carey didn't like something that was going on out there he wouldn't hesitate to call the governor, if the governor happened to be a Republican. Then this would filter back down through the governor's office, to the president of the University. Then I would get this call from the president, Sproul, or whoever it was, or Kerr, or Hitch, to do something about this problem. So Carey was a handful, but a very interesting guy.

Somewhere along the line, I think Mildred was as influential as anybody, in persuading Carey that it was a good idea to have the University establish a reserve, and it was on a use-basis, a use-agreement. He didn't turn over title to it, because he eventually turned it over to the Nature Conservancy. Then before his death, he had a falling out with them which was perfectly predictable. This is the way it worked. I used to think that Carey's main hand in life was jousting with major bureaucracies, whether it was the University of California or the navy. The navy had a little base out there, still does, a missile-tracking base.

Because of this he would get all kinds of concessions out of the navy. He got them to take care of the phone hook-up for him; he got them to agree to take his stuff back and forth on navy vessels. When he would come up to Port Hueneme, waiting for the boat out there, he could easily have afforded to fly out, but he would stay in the BOQ out there, the bachelor officer's quarters, until the boat went out the next morning.

Jarrell: So these were his little perks?

R. Norris: His little perks. He spent endless hours negotiating with the navy department. This was his joy in life. He was a very bright man, very interested in the history of the island. He was in so many ways delightful. And yet he could be a pain in the neck, too, for anybody who had to kind of—

Jarrell: Negotiate?

R. Norris: Yes, if you were in one of these great bureaucracies, as I was, the University of California, and I knew by then how the University operated pretty well, it just meant endless hours sitting in Joe's Cafe in Santa Barbara talking to Carey. He died when he was just a little past seventy. I miss the old curmudgeon in a lot of ways, although he certainly made my life difficult for awhile. But Roger Samuelsen— Roger was a master at negotiating with people, and calming down little old ladies. He was terrific about this. So he was wonderful to have the patience to negotiate an agreement, but I was the one that started it, certainly. Then Mildred Matthias and Roger Samuelsen had to bring it to a conclusion.

University-wide NRS Committee

As committee chair over the years I was involved with other reserves in the system that Santa Barbara had. We didn't always accept offers. In fact, frequently we'd had offers of land which we'd turn down for one reason or another. The University-wide committee eventually evolved a very good review system, when new things were always coming on line—people would want tax deductions and to give a nice piece of property. Some of these prospective sites were useless and some were useful. We learned to be kind of hard-nosed about that over the years.

Jarrell: So you developed a set of criteria from the committees on each individual campus. Then you'd come together, in a University-wide committee.

R. Norris: Right. We would screen it first on the campus and if it looked good to us, it would go on up to the University-wide committee. Then a committee would be appointed to go out and look at it. I served on both kinds of committees over the years and reviewed a lot of them. A few reserves that we got were eventually abandoned for one reason or another. Sometimes because of urban encroachment, sometimes because they were too small or remote. There was a little grove of redwoods up in Humboldt County, I think, called Cheatham Grove, that was eventually abandoned. It was rejected. It was one of the early reserves. But it never got any use; it was too small and remote, so it was eventually turned over to the U.S. Forest Service.

Jarrell: Can you tell me how these committees developed criteria for including a site in the Natural Reserve System?

R. Norris: Well, let's see, since most of these were habitats, we had to have an area which was large enough so that the biology people were confident that it was sustainable, for whatever it was. It had to be a site one of the campuses was willing to take on; the campuses weren't all equally enthusiastic about this sort of thing.

Jarrell: What was involved in terms of a campus's resource outlay? Where did the money come from?

R. Norris: Well, some of it could come from instructional money; some of it came out of the Chancellor's Discretionary Fund. You had to have a chancellor on board who was sympathetic to this. UC Riverside had a very good record that way; they had also a person who was assiduous in supporting this, and he was on the very first committee, Bill Mayhew.

It got to the point where the University-wide committee would say, Bill, now you're not proposing yet another reserve, are you? He would come in with these things. Bill did a good job of selling his local administration, and I think in some ways the best job in the whole University system, in terms of convincing them this whole reserve idea was a good thing.

Jarrell: What about department support?

R. Norris: Department support was very sparse. We never were able to get as much of that as we wanted. It came mainly from the field sciences, as you might expect, from geology and biology. Sometimes for the rest of the campus it was a big yawn. At Santa Barbara, we had a real go-round on the Sedgeway Reserve which is one of the latest reserves in the system, because the art department wanted to sell the University's share of that off.

Jarrell: The art department?

R. Norris: The art department. They wanted to build an art museum. Now Duke Sedgeway, who had been the owner and had gotten a seventy-five percent interest in this reserve transferred to the University, was a good friend of our chancellor's. Then there was the twenty-five percent undivided interest, so that the University had seventy-five percent interest in the whole ranch. It took us a long time to eventually get that changed to where the University had seventy-five percent of the land. That involved a lot of legal hassling. The Sedgeway was one rather early on that Ken looked at, I know, when reserves were being organized. It took a long time to get that through. When Vernon Cheadle was chancellor at Santa Barbara he was, I think, pretty sympathetic to this. When Barbara [S.] Uehling became chancellor I was chairman of our campus's Natural Reserve committee. I got an appointment with her, which was hard to do, and told her I wanted to tell her about the NRS and solicit her support. She asked how much money we wanted. I told her that's not why I came at all. I wanted her to know what the NRS did and why it was important to the University, and I really wasn't coming in to ask her for money. We had a hard time with her.

People at UC San Diego had difficulty because there were so few people involved in the field sciences down there. UCLA had problems, I'm not clear exactly why, because that was Mildred Mathias's home campus, and yet it had only been very recently that they had any reserves administered by UCLA. Santa Barbara and Riverside very quickly got four or five, for awhile, but I'm not sure how it is now. I think those three campuses had more than any of the other campuses. I know Ken had some problems at UC Santa Cruz getting them on board with it, too. So it depended a lot on the reception we got from the administrators. Then some of the faculty committees had to review these things, too, and they could either be supportive or they could be a real roadblock. That kind of thing had to be overcome all the time.

The Future of the Natural Reserve System

Jarrell: Do you know if today, in 1998, the NRS is still actively soliciting or open to adding more sites?

R. Norris: Well, I haven't been on the committee for awhile. But at the time just before I went off we had decided we were getting near the maximum manageable number and that there were only a few habitat types in the state that remained really, that were important enough to add to the system, without duplicating them.

Jarrell: Because you were trying to get a representative sampling of all of the different habitats in the state?

R. Norris: Yes, and that's mainly a biological issue. The idea was we were to have a broad sampling. I don't know whether they have, well they do have some redwoods now, but they were talking about say, a Sierran redwood grove. We've looked at several of these and as far as I know none of those have come to pass.

Jarrell: During the time that you were on the committee, did you discover, are there any other campuses, colleges or universities in the United States, or anywhere that you know of, that have a program with this scope? I've looked around and I haven't discovered any.

R. Norris: No. I think that you'll find universities that will operate one or two things. They'll operate, say a summer field camp for geologists in the Big Horn Mountains of Wyoming, or something like that. In the case of Stanford University, they have the Jasper Ridge property up there on the coast range. But they don't have alternative ones and they certainly don't have them scattered around the state. So I'm not aware of any other ones. There are very few places that have the ecological, topographic, variety that California does. So we're kind of a natural for it, in some ways.

Jarrell: It certainly was a great act of imagination to conceive of an enterprise like this.

R. Norris: Oh yes! That's right. I have to make one final comment. You know I have been associated with the University for getting on close to sixty years and the faculty often come up with programs anything from the NRS to a Ph.D. program in the classics. What you have to do in the University is go in and stretch the truth quite a bit about what you can do with a certain amount of money. You finally get the administration to go along with this in a small way and you get your foot in the door; you get other faculty members involved in teaching it. The moment you get some teaching involved in it, even though the University's reputation is not to care much about teaching, it is an important thing. When the faculty begin to invest time in it, then it gets set in concrete. In the case of say, classics, well, they'll stretch the truth about their library resources when they're getting a new program approved. Then they'll come up with all kinds of reasons, some very good, about why they need a program for a Ph.D. in classics at Santa Barbara when the demand is so low that one classics program at UC Berkeley would take care of all the Western United States. The reason for that, of course, is that the University's got itself in an impossible position; if you want a good academic program in any field, you've got to have a graduate program, even if there isn't any need for more graduate students in classics.

To some extent this is true in the NRS. It's now such a part of the University that it's just inconceivable to me that they would ever do away with it. It's completely embedded and it's taken years to do this; it's taken ages to get an adequate budget for it. That's been a pain patching together all of these things and the faculty does a lot of extra stuff, for which nobody gets any credit. But in the long haul it's worth it. That's the way a university's put together. It must drive some of the senior administrators crazy, particularly in the business office, when they know what's about to befall them, another graduate program in classics. I'm picking on the classics people because I sat on one of those committees at Santa Barbara when it was going on and I could hardly keep a straight face sometimes when I'd hear the things they'd say. The same kind of thing happened with the NRS.

It's a wonderful system and the University has plenty of rewards, and I can't imagine a career that would have been more rewarding in almost every respect. It occasionally drove me up the wall. And Ken, too. I mean, we'd sit around the fire talking about this.

Jarrell: I want to thank you so much. I really appreciate you giving me this time. I never got to talk to Ken about the NRS except very peripherally, so I'm very grateful to have this opportunity. Thank you, Bob.

R. Norris: You're more than welcome. You handle these things very well. I can see you're an old pro at it.

Jarrell: Well, thank you. You're very generous.

Lawrence D. Ford

Meeting Ken Norris

Jarrell: When did you meet Ken for the first time and what were your impressions?

Ford: Well, I love to tell that story, because it changed my life. I was an undergraduate at UCSC in the fall of 1974 and this really good friend of mine at Kresge College was walking under my window. He called up and said, "Larry, you gotta come with me! I'm going to go interview for this class." I'd never heard of the class. He just inspired me; I knew that what this friend liked was what I liked. So I said, okay, and went along with him. We went and interviewed to be in the Natural History of California class with Ken on that very day. So I met Ken. He was doing it exactly the way he did it for years afterwards, which was getting a feel for who the students were so that he could craft a group of students who could work together. He had a couple hundred people interviewing for twenty-three slots, plus one TA and one instructor, who could fit in three vans.

I know what Ken asked me about because I have the notes he took on me as well as on everybody else. He asked me about myself and my background. What he picked up on and asked about was this experience that I'd had being a trip leader for kids with a group over in San Jose, the Youth Science Institute, where I had learned to be a bus driver and all these wilderness camping skills. So he asked me all about that. He also noted that I had studied sea otters a little bit, so he wrote that down, too. Then I got in the class. I didn't realize how—

Jarrell: How hard it was to get in?

Ford: Oh yes! But now I know why. I really value and appreciate how he did that. He was trying to make sure he didn't get any troublemakers, any divisive personalities, that sort of thing. My impression of him at the time, I think, was that he was this wonderful, friendly guy. Of course at that time in 1974 he would have just turned fifty that year. Not much older than I am now. (laughter) I had been in Kresge College from 1971 to 1975, I think, and I graduated in 1977 because I took a year off to do some other things. Anyway, I was really into this kind of touchy-feely stuff. So it didn't seem necessarily that unusual at that time. A lot of the professors at Kresge were all into these—we call it touchy-feely, you know, derogatorily, but that's not right. We were—

Jarrell: Experiential, maybe?

Ford: Yes.

Jarrell: You didn't just sit there and listen to somebody tell you what to imbibe?

Ford: Exactly. So I fit right in with Ken. Originally it was a five-unit class each quarter, yet it involved a huge time commitment. We all had to take two other classes each quarter. Ken wanted us to take off on these four-and five-day trips, going all the way down to the desert and other places and so we'd come back exhausted.

Jarrell: And your other classes suffered?

Ford: Yes, and in fact I think it might have been that year when Ken realized he couldn't do that anymore. He had to make it a fifteen-unit class, lasting a quarter, divided into three parts. So he changed the format, or he may have been plotting that as he went along, which was his way. He would get the thing started, and then with its own momentum and with the success that was obvious to others, he could say, well, now it needs to be a Field Quarter. So he got other professors. At first it was Ray [T.] Collett, who taught a course called, I think, Field Biogeography. Then he got Stanley [A.]

Cain, one of the famous botanists of the world, really, of the next generation after Fred[eric] [E.] Clements. Cain came from the Midwest, from that same school. But Stanley Cain was one of those first visionaries, along with [A.] Starker Leopold, coming after Aldo Leopold, also.

In fact Cain was Undersecretary of the Interior under [Stewart L.] Udall for the Leopold Commission, for that year. You may recall, this was very important in American conservation because Leopold defined, or tried to define, what our goal for conservation was, rather than just being some kind of vague conservation thing, you know, of protecting forests. It was no, we have to have a vignette of presettlement conditions. I think those were Leopold's terms. Anyway, Stanley Cain was a very interesting mentor for me because he combined politics with science. I at one time thought I might want to pursue that path. I don't think it would be appropriate for me anymore. But I used to talk to Stanley and his wife Louise about that.

Jarrell: I see you had a biology degree from UC Santa Cruz and one in environmental studies. So you had a double major when you graduated in 1978.

Ford: Which at the time was somewhat unusual. Apparently they do it now, but less commonly. But when the environmental studies board first started I think one of the problems that they faced was credibility.

Jarrell: Because it wasn't very scientific?

Ford: Right. Well, they said it wasn't. A lot of it was because of its social science dimensions. Then there was the prejudice against natural history, which was regarded as a kind of Victorian-era side of science. At that time, even in the 1970s, these blow-hard modernists, or whatever they were, in biology, they would say, oh no, we're moving towards molecular biology and that's the only important thing. Natural history is not even important, which was totally silly.

The Natural History Field Quarter

Jarrell: Ken called you a straw boss or factotum. He referred to you in various ways. When did you become a staff member in the Natural History Field Quarter?

Ford: Well, my graduation was delayed for a number of reasons. Before I actually graduated in the spring of 1975 Shannon Brownlee was in my class and there were a couple of other people, Beth Hird and Nadine Narita. We were all in the same class together. I loved it. Since I had a Class II driver's license I had helped the TA at the time to drive the vans. Anyway, at the end of the class I thought, well, I want to be the TA; I want to be like this guy who TA'd because he had been a student the year before.

Jarrell: Do you remember who that was?

Ford: That was Walter Ward, who didn't show [up at the Norris memorial]. I don't know, somehow he fell through our little net. So the reason why this was an important story for me was because I learned that you had to ask Ken sometimes for things in a certain way. One of them was to be somewhat assertive and the other was that he needed an easy way. A lot of people would write to him and not hear back. Not always, because Ken really tried to always write back to people, but I remember thinking, okay I know how busy this guy is. So I sent him a letter and a self-addressed, stamped postcard with little boxes so he could check yes or no. I said to him that I would like to be his TA, but did he want me? That was for 1976. He sent back the little card and said he wasn't going to teach in 1976 because he was on sabbatical but he'd like me to be his TA in 1977. So I was thrilled! That was the beginning of the professional career that I'm still working on. Because in 1977, I still hadn't graduated that spring and I was working on finishing up my senior thesis. I was working and doing some other stuff. So anyway I went with him on that class. Ken and I just hit it off; we really worked well together. For reasons that I mentioned before, Ken appeared anyway not to be really on the physical plane in some ways. But it was really more like he needed a young guy like me who wanted to help in that way so that he didn't have to worry about all the practical logistics.

Jarrell: He talked in his interviews about needing somebody to kind of lay down the law while he was the good uncle. Here were twenty-three uninhibited young people on the verge of life who were occasionally wild and crazy. So were you sort of like the enforcer? (laughter) I don't mean that in a negative way, but he needed somebody to fulfill that role, to say, okay, let's settle down here. We have work to do, too.

Ford: You know, that was a part of it. But I think there were other dimensions. Ken had an amazing ability to inspire people. Other professors complain because their students all get wild and crazy and disappear. Well, Ken's students didn't disappear; they didn't have time to get wild and crazy because they were having too much fun doing the work that he wanted them to do. That's a really significant distinction. Literally, there wasn't time for that.

Ken took us on a series of trips during the Field Quarter. The very first one was through the Granite Mountains. That was very deliberate. In early spring you can't go to Northern California because it's still raining. He wanted the students to be able to calm down and to get still enough inside themselves so that they could do what he called crossing the threshold of boredom.

Ken Norris's Teaching Philosophy

Jarrell: I was going to ask you about that very Zen concept.

Ford: He was a master. Just from observing how students learned and from himself, he knew this. He had all kinds of concepts: "the window on the world," and the "threshold of boredom," which led to that window. Anyway, he knew that it was going to take five days to a week, and so he didn't want to have anybody with him who would distract students from that. That's one of the things that I did.

So back to your question. I didn't compete with Ken. I also didn't divide the students over issues. It wasn't that I showed them how to be serious. It's that I made sure that there were no problems that developed. I made sure that all the support for the experience was going to work. Not just that the bus was going to be there and that it was going to run; not just that we weren't going to get stuck in a wash. It was that all of these things were going to flow. And they did.

I think the important thing here would be illustrated by a piece of advice that Ken once gave me. He said, these people are not young kids who need to be protected; they don't need to have the shelter built for them so they won't get wet at night. They need to learn what happens when they get wet. They need those kinds of things. So don't go and set up their tents for them, which is what I used to do with seven-year-olds. He said to let them make those kinds of mistakes. You don't want them to think that you're taking care of them so much that they don't have to worry about this. This was just the beginning. Because it was the same with their studies and with their lessons. So I shouldn't set them up too much with how to find materials in the library, how to get themselves over that threshold of boredom, which I'll explain more about later. But anyway, I think that is what I did for Ken, in that way.

The other dimension, as Craig [F.] Schindler said at the memorial, was what he and I had talked about, that Ken taught with love. Half of it is loving somebody enough to get out of their way. So he would set up the situation that gave the students a sense of trust enough so that they could open themselves up to test out being creative. That's really what happened. Then he got out of their way. My job was to get out of Ken's way. My job was to give Ken the kind of support that he asked for and that I knew he needed, sometimes without him even asking, so that he could be creative, so that he could maximize his lessons for these students. I'm not kidding, Randall. This is what motivated me. I could see that this is what made it work, for me. If I could get all these things lined up for Ken, then he would shine. And he did. It worked well. So then he could make these funny jokes. He really appreciated what I did. In fact, I used to think he didn't know. But he did know.

Here's another little insight. I once asked him, what it was that made this work for him. Not only as a teacher. I used to watch him as a boss for the secretaries, like Trish Holter, Tery Drager, and Maggie Drake, who was his secretary at the Natural Reserve System. Anyway, what Ken said basically was the same thing: don't do too much. Let them take responsibility. In fact, he said, he was really good at being this kind of bumbling old professor. It worked for him because then people wanted to take care of him. He said if they love you then they'll do these things for you. So the challenge was to take care of them and to get their needs met and to relate to them in that way. It wasn't really that he was manipulating people. I think it was that he knew how to find that place. Because people want somebody to love and to support and to take care of. So Trish, Tery, Dan Warrick and I, and all these other people who worked for him, we quickly found that we could do that. Then he could take care of us on these other levels. And he could go off and be very creative.

Jarrell: What was he aiming at in the Natural History Field Quarter? What was he trying to set up? What was the goal?

Ford: Well, Ken's book *Beyond Mountain Time*, is going to tell us that—well, maybe not very directly. It will be indirect. But the first element was this very personal crossing of the threshold of boredom.

Jarrell: What did that involve and to what end?

Ford: Crossing the threshold involved unleashing one's own creativity; unleashing one's own personal tools, to be creative in one's own way. The later lessons were to get some experience about the dimensions of ecosystems, about how organisms really work, about how to gain insight into those things, which was another thing at which Ken was a master. I think I can be fairly specific, because each class, although the students may never have known this, had a very specific theme that Ken and I had worked out. In fact, here it all is in my binder. This was my handbook and I've got notes that Ken wrote. It's all Field Quarter philosophy, the announcements that we put out; how we planned the trips. This was my part of it. Then for each trip I have my notes about what our purpose was. The Mojave trip was about observation. The Mattole River trip was about communities and physical processes. The Big Sur trip was about niche-hunting. The Sierra trip was about some of the individual dimensions of the physical environment such as temperature and heat exchange. Then the last trip of the quarter focussed on what Ken called, "mechanisms of integration." I wrote down everything for each class and have collected all the notes since 1977.

Jarrell: Several people we've interviewed said to talk to Larry, that you know everything. How many years were you Ken's straw boss?

Ford: I TA'd in 1977, and then in 1978 he asked me to work for him full time. I came back from Alaska where I had gone off to start a job. He had created the Environmental Field Program by that time, in 1978, and he asked me to come back and help him run it. I was the coordinator. He called me the field logistics coordinator or field coordinator. So then I had really three jobs: to help him with the Field Quarter every year; to essentially coordinate the Environmental Field Program which was giving grants to students and helping them in the field and to keep that whole thing rolling; and then being the manager at Big Creek Reserve. Of course all those things Ken was intimately involved in. I served the same function really. So I did that from 1978 until 1984, although the last spring of 1984 I did not TA the class because I was getting ready to go to grad school. So that was the first year that Don Usner TA'd the class.

Teaching Students Observation Skills

Before we get off it, let me just briefly tell you what all that niche-hunting business was, that kind of stuff. The first trip was to the Granite Mountains . It was so still there that you could hear the blood pumping in your ears.The Granites are so quiet, it's wonderful. That's why he wanted us to be there, really. So we would go out there and that was about learning how to observe. The students needed to learn to be quiet and listen, and to write down their observations.

In compiling the field journals which were such a significant part of the class, writing down one's observations was so important. As you write, and if you're thinking as he tried to teach the students to do, you learn to think through every sentence. Every sentence has to be a complete sentence. The student realizes: I don't really understand that. I think I do, when I'm just babbling in my head. But when I try to write it down precisely, I find it's not quite right. So the foundation of science is observation, and the mental process includes two things. One is the unleashing of creativity, to be imaginative and to think, oh maybe this? Let me take a look. Could that be? And oh, well, that's not quite right and so what else could it be? Or what other things might be coming in here? This is where genius comes out, I think, in a person's life. So creativity is one part. Then the other part, I think, is the discipline of it, the methods of trying to record and to be able to communicate your observations to others.

Crossing the Threshold of Boredom

Usually on the first day of a trip we'd kind of get relaxed and Ken would be talking about things and trying to let people know that everything was okay, they were in a trusting environment. Maybe we'd take a little trip in the afternoon to the Kelso Dunes. Then the students had to spend at least one day trying to break through the threshold of boredom as they observed some object they'd chosen. Literally people would go out and Ken would say, now I want you to go and find a place and find something to observe. He'd give some guidance, and suggest things like watching a bird landing in a cactus or something simple, but sometimes people would propose things and he'd say that it was too complicated. Anyway, they'd sit there and most of them would not be able to cross that threshold at first. One common result was that they would fall asleep. I learned this by doing it many times. You're sitting there watching and you think, I get this, what a cinch.

Jarrell: It's like a meditation. You're just trying to focus on something very, very simple and elemental. Right? Often when people start meditating, they fall asleep. Because it's too boring. (laughter)

Ford: That's right. So you've got it exactly.

Jarrell: They become frustrated and impatient and they nod off.

Ford: Then they would listen to Ken. He would come around to each person and talk to them and he was trying to give them some little nudges, like, just push yourself across. Don't fall asleep. Just push yourself. Some never did. But when they did, there was no stopping them after that. Because after they crossed it—

Jarrell: It's a breakthrough.

Ford: That's right. Look again. Once they experienced this, then suddenly the whole world opened up, but then, as few undergraduate students ever realize, you don't know everything. You know nothing. Then they would realize, my gosh, there's so much out there. I'll never be able to understand this. So then they've learned what it takes. They've crossed beyond their own knowledge. They've pushed themselves beyond the level that they already know that they can understand with their existing tools. Then for the rest of the quarter these students were virtually unstoppable. The only way you could get them back at the end of the day was by dinner. Then we'd have what Ken would call nature notes from all over, and the students would come back. I can't tell you how exciting it was. A student would say, I saw a peregrine falcon and it was doing this and it was doing that—and then we knew that it was working. So the first trip was developing observation skills.

Niche-Hunting

Then these other trips were a little bit more self-explanatory. Niche-hunting was one of my favorites. It was trying to figure out the ecological concepts of habitat and niche. The habitat is the place itself; and the niche is more like the profession of the organisms. So you were trying to figure out, well, what is this thing doing? Ken would usually have people pick things that were relatively stationary. Then he'd say cover this entire property and see if you can find where it is, but also, where it's not. Then try to figure out why. Don't use the books. Just do it yourself.

Let's take an example, say, of some little herbaceous plant. Maybe it grows in the understory of redwood trees. You'd want to then cover the property and try to find it every place that it grows. You might find that it only grows in the understory of redwoods. But you might also find, it doesn't grow everywhere in the understory of redwoods. It only grows in certain places. Then the question becomes why.

So this was one of the incredibly profound things that Ken was trying to do. Some people would say that observational science is not quantitative, not rigorous. Well, I don't buy that at all. This was the kind of thing that the traditional laboratory biologist never got to do. So students by this time had learned about writing in their journals and they knew that they had to be disciplined and write up their observations every day.

They'd discover these phenomenal things. They would observe and find that their problem had to do with air currents that only occurred at certain times of day; these air drainage systems coming down the hill at the end of the day or at the beginning of the day and that's why spiders put their webs in certain places because they're catching this natural flow, say.

Jarrell: And then the insects are going to be passing through.

Ford: Yes, things like that. Randall, it was just spellbinding, the experience, of listening to these students. Because here they were nineteen or twenty years old, and they were telling these stories that were probably not written up in the literature anywhere. They were just as good as other observations. Sure, they were not as experienced and they would need more testing, but it was just wonderful. This is why people still rave about their experience on the Field Quarter. Not only did they bond with these people for their lives, but they really truly did have these profound experiences about seeing nature and learning how to investigate and understand.

Let me tell you about the physical environment theme in the Sierra.

Jarrell: Where did you go?

Ford: We went to a bunch of different places. But in my years we would go to the lower Tuolomne River below Hetch Hetchy Reservoir. Because the High Sierra, of course, was covered with snow in April.

Learning to Think Like an Animal

But the purpose there was, as many of Ken's former students talk about, how he would implore them to think like the animal that they were studying, to try to learn how to be that animal, so that they could get a sense of what the organism was reacting to in its environment, and to each other. A profound kind of thing. So that's what Ken would have us do. He would say, well, let's pretend that we're a little lizard, which of course he knew very well. Where would it go during the day? Well, lizards scamper around on rocks. Well, why do they go to certain places? So then we would bring out these sophisticated thermometers and other things and we would actually measure it. The students would be blown away. This is basically the science of microclimatology. Ken had studied this quite a bit. Students would find that there were maybe forty or fifty degrees temperature difference in the space of a few inches.

Jarrell: In a little tiny locale.

Ford: Exactly. Then they would suddenly see from a different point of reference that the world is totally different for a little lizard that has to be right there on the surface of the rock, or some beetle or something. The temperatures may be unbearable during certain times of the day, when to us, at the human scale, we're getting these nice cool breezes and we think it's a cool, spring day. Well, it's not at all. Like how do lizards find places where they can warm up without cooking? Because they're cold-blooded and they rely on the environment in order to warm themselves up at the beginning of each day. There were all these fascinating questions. The same in streams. He would get people to actually get down on their stomachs. You've probably seen some photos where Ken was in the mud or something. He's lying in it! And he's getting mud caked in his hair and it didn't make any difference. Because he was always covered in seeds and twigs and mud. That was because he would just lie right down into it to get his eyeball at that view—and it was just incredible. (laughter)

Jarrell: What a capacity for imagination, that he was trying to set up the environment so that these students could develop this creaturely empathy. From the beetle's point of view, from the lizard's point of view. Instead of from the point of view of a big, tall, warm-blooded mammal. (laughter)

Ford: Exactly. You know I became a botanist. I often couldn't quite relate to some of these things that Ken talked about because he was more of an organismal zoologist really. But I found some of the same kinds of things. It's harder to relate to being a plant. It's even harder to relate to being a community of plants. But I found the same sort of thing, if I just sort of sat still and sat on the mountain and just tried to think about it. What happens here? What happens here through the year, through long-term time. And that's basically how I came up with some of my own research questions, especially for my dissertation on fire ecology.

Working Relationship with Ken Norris

Jarrell: How were you influenced by being Ken's partner in this Old Blue show, the Field Quarter?

Ford: (laughter) Yes, right. The Old Blue bus. Well, I guess the most important thing was I really learned to love Ken. My relationship with him solidified. Until he died, really, I was in pretty close touch with him and I could always count on him to talk to me. I'd call him up and tell him what I was doing and he always wanted to know and he always had some really great advice for me. He would always try to help me somehow by offering to write letters but he didn't end up ever being on any of my committees throughout my graduate career.

Jarrell: Because you went to Berkeley?

Ford: Yes, right. I didn't really need him to do that. But anyway, that I think was the most profound thing. Another was that the relationships I developed really became almost the emotional foundation of my life. There were all these students whom I got to know really well, and who now are some of my best friends. Like Don Usner and Alisa Fineman, and others. I would probably have never known them if I hadn't worked for Ken as a TA. There were all these really incredible people whom Ken had selected very carefully and we all shared these profound experiences.

Jarrell: In her interview, Shannon Brownlee said that she was 19 years old when she was in the Field Quarter class and that many of her friends and she as well, were looking for boyfriends and had all their emotional *mishegahs* and everything. She said she wished she could do it now, when she's more mature, more present, more centered. She appreciated it then but when she looks back she understands why it was so pivotal. Natural History Field Quarter was transformative for so many students when they look back.

Ford: I think you've got something really important there. I think that's one of the reasons why the memorial was so successful. I think a lot of them realized how much they have integrated that experience into their lives. That it was a good time for them to do it. That they're still living it. In fact a number of people have said things to me like yes, I never gave up my commitment and it was kind of like a renewal for them to go to the memorial. Not so much grieving about Ken. It was more like renewal, seeing each other here again. We are still doing it and we can still do it. He inspired all this idealism.

Another really important thing that I learned from being at Ken's side for eight years was a huge amount about being a professional and about being a teacher, directly by watching him. I know that a lot of my success as a teacher is from that. I mean it's kind of natural for me now, but at this memorial I think I really learned that. I had never really quite put that together. Certainly, Ken taught me all about fundraising, about making programs work and working with employees, how to treat employees and knowing what professional standards are.

Jarrell: You sort of got it by osmosis. You were very observant also.

Ford: I think so. Well, I talked to Ken frequently about those things. In fact, some of my favorite memories of Ken were the times when I talked to him very seriously about my career because I'd been in kind of a mid-life crisis the past few years. The first time I was still in Texas and my job wasn't working at all. Ken said, "You know Larry, you're doing fine. If you had gone off and gotten some job someplace with the government or at some university we probably would never have heard from you again. Instead, you keep experimenting and trying to do these good things that you dream up. And of course some of them are going to fail." Because I had said, "Ken, I'm so sorry that I have to keep bugging you, but I don't know what to do." And he said, "Well, I don't know exactly what to do but don't worry about failing. It's okay."

Of course that's the way he led his life. It's been harder for me to sort of abandon security and stuff. But that was one part of it. Another one, was about six months ago we were driving in the car together, going up to Berkeley. I was asking him some very specific questions about how I could develop the institute that I work with now. He said, "Larry, you know, you're beyond me now. I don't know what to say. I don't have any advice for you anymore." This was really profound for me because I realized, well, I guess maybe I'm launched.

I was talking with my good friend Dave Hart who was on Field Quarter in 1973 and now we're really close. Anyway, I realized that I think about Ken every day. I think about what he taught me about how to do things. I just can't even imagine what I would be like, where I would be today if hadn't met him. (laughter) I'm sure it would be a totally different life.

Environmental Field Program

Jarrell: You were the coordinator of the Environmental Field Program from 1978 to 1984. How did this program get established? Ken talked about it, that there were, I think, five major projects and he would select students who would go out and do surveys and inventories. You were in on it from the beginning, weren't you?

Ford: Well, there are a couple of different ways I can explain this. One is that this program was really essential to Ken's whole teaching philosophy, which was that students needed the opportunity to test their wings, so to speak; they needed to go further than just observing nature and to actually learn how to complete an entire professional project. So he found a way to give them some money to support themselves for maybe a quarter, which is not an unreasonable amount of time to do a project. It fit into the whole senior thesis concept in environmental studies. It helped students to do a project. Of course it couldn't be as much as a master's thesis would be. It had to be appropriate.

So he recognized that what was needed in order to accomplish that were three really important elements. This is something that a lot of people don't recognize. First and foremost, the faculty at a university don't have time to provide the necessary guidance to undergraduate students doing field projects. They need a lot of hand-holding; and they need a lot of behind-the-scenes monitoring and technical support. So Ken realized that meant he needed to have a staff person to make sure that that liaison took place with a faculty sponsor.

Jarrell: Reality checks?

Ford: Right. Exactly. Another dimension of the program was that the students needed some funding support and in order to get that money they needed some kind of a streamlined and fairly effective process of applying, just like the real world. The idea was that more or less everybody was going to get the money that they needed if they had a good project idea.

Jarrell: The students on one of these teams wouldn't be taking other course work. Was it an independent study?

Ford: That's right, although there were all sorts of ways that people did it. They didn't all go just for a whole quarter in a team. Some of them did it as individual students. Some did it over a whole year. We had this small pool of money, sometimes just a few hundred bucks, that would enable them to buy some equipment, gas, or whatever they applied for to be able to do it. We didn't provide any salaries; it was all just for expenses. But they had to go through the process of applying. So it was just like a grant application and they had to apply the same rigor; they had to demonstrate that they had thought through what they were going to do and what its relevance was, all those sorts of considerations. Believe me, and I'm sure you do, plenty of students would come in and say, why should I do this? I just want the money. You should give it to me. But we wouldn't let them do that. There was a faculty review committee. It was competitive. Some didn't get their grants.

The third piece of this was that we wanted to make sure that they wrote up these studies in a professional way. We insisted that they had to have a professional quality product at the end. So Ken brought in Dan [Sheridan F.] Warrick to be the editor. Dan worked then with the team projects and with individual students. We had our own little in-house publications. And of course students were very proud of what they produced. Dan, of course, made sure that it was rigorous.

Jarrell: I have a publications list of the Environmental Field Program.

Ford: Wonderful. Where did you get it?

Jarrell: I got it out of UC's online catalog, Melvyl. Twenty-two publications.[*] I see that you're carrying around Susan Georgette's *In the Rough Land to the South.*[†] I worked with her for several years when she was doing oral histories on the early land-use history of Big Sur.

You said that there were three dimensions. One was that these students needed reality checks, hand-holding, somebody to be a liaison. Because Ken didn't have time to do all that. Would you elaborate?

Ford: Right. No, no way, Ken could have done that, along with everything else. I would go out and visit students in the field and help them with logistical kinds of things, safety, getting themselves set up. I remember Susan Georgette was way off in the North Cascades Recreational Area and she sent me a letter asking if I could please find some documents for her. I went to the

*See Appendix IV for a listing of Environmental Field Program publications.

†Susan E. Georgette, *In the Rough Land to the South: An Oral History of the Lives and Events at Big Creek, Big Sur, California* (University of California, Santa Cruz Environmental Field Program, 1981).

library for her. It was that kind of stuff, in addition to the sort of mechanics of running some studies, you know. So anyway, that was one dimension of it.

The other thing is that Ken was just a master at making that program appear out of thin air. I mean we can talk about how it worked. But the other thing was that it existed. He raised hundreds of thousands of dollars to make it work. It was typical of his strategy for fundraising that he created a sense of the program before funding was found. He had to create the sense of the Environmental Field Program before it existed. He did that by having the Granite Mountains project, which was before the Field Program got started in 1977. Ken got a National Science Foundation grant with Dan Warrick and those other students. There was a whole program at NSF for undergraduate projects and they each had, I think, a thousand dollars for expenses. They often did this. Dan went through the process of editing the *Granite Mountains Resource Survey* and they published it and by the time it actually got produced the Field Program existed. Then Ken was able to show to some donors that, hey, we've already got this thing going and look how successful it is. That was exactly his strategy. So then he could come back to the chancellor, too, and say, well look, the program has produced its first completed project and publication and now we need some more support. He ended up getting, I think, about $300,000 a year from the Hewlett Foundation and from the Packard Foundation, who, of course became his allies. I mean they all loved Ken, too.

Jarrell: Ken told me about a friend of his in Boston whose foundation supported the Environmental Field Program.

Ford: I believe it was a connection with his dear friend Dick [Richard A.] Cooley who was another incredible person whom I didn't know that well. He was Ken's partner and the co-director of the Environmental Field Program. Dick had this connection, I think, with the Kendall Foundation. I think it's Kendall. But anyway, this guy had the discretion as director to be able to dole out money on the order of tens of thousands of dollars. I think that was the connection. So Ken and Dick both had their little cadres of students and Dick was more policy-oriented. Susan Georgette, for instance, was a policy student, not a natural history student. So they were really the main ones in our orbit. But Ken raised that kind of money for the first five or six years until the time I left. About the time I left the donors were getting a little tired of it.

Jarrell: Why?

Ford: They had been supporting it for so many years that they wanted the University to pick it up as a regular program, but Chancellor [Robert] Sinsheimer never did support it. The chancellor was more interested in engineering and other directions for the campus. Ken at one point was prepared to threaten to let the program die. This was another one of his strategies to get support. But he realized that if he did that it probably would fold. So he kept raising money. Eventually, long after I was gone, somewhere in the late 1980s, it did die. That was basically because nobody had the sense to try to make it work.

Landels-Hill Big Creek Reserve

Jarrell: I'd like to move on now to the genesis of the Landels-Hill Big Creek Reserve. Who was involved in giving the land to the NRS?

Ford: The four former owners were very gifted and visionary men, successful, heads of families. Some of their wives were involved, but I mostly knew the men. So the families made up one group. Then there were the Save the Redwoods League, the Nature Conservancy, and the University. The University has rarely had the money to actually purchase lands, whereas with the Nature Conservancy and the Save the Redwoods League, it's their business to raise money. The families recognized that they were all maturing and that their families, and that the next generations, were all going to be just as interested in Big Creek. They saw that what could happen after they were gone was that the families would start to divide up the land and then with high taxes they might end up selling off parcels and it would start to break up. They all appreciated that the integrity of Big Creek's conservation and aesthetic value might be lost and so they wanted a way to permanently protect the site. The families connected with the Nature Conservancy and the Save the Redwoods League came up with a scheme, basically, where the families would designate an in-holding with a limited number of building sites that could ever be built, no matter how much the family fanned out into different groups.

Jarrell: Who were the families? Isn't the Farr family one of them?

Ford: The Farr family was one. Ed Landels was another, although he didn't have any heirs that I know of, and he has since died. Then there was the Stuart family. A wonderful and cantankerous old man was the head of that family. I can't remember the names of the other people. Not all of them chose to build on their little in-holding parcels. Some of them just wanted a campsite.

Jarrell: How many acres are included in the reserve?

Ford: Well, the whole property is about four thousand acres and the in-holding was something like 150. It was strategically placed where the best building sites are, right along the creekside. Their purpose, in fact, was to claim that land so that the University wouldn't build anything on buildable sites; they didn't want the University to build anything. In fact, they didn't even want the University having a resident staff. Of course now there're two families that live down there as caretakers for the University. That's another story. But Ed Landels was one of the partners in Landels, Ripley, and Diamond, a very well-known law firm in San Francisco. I'm not sure where Ed comes from, but he was in San Francisco for a long time, and you still hear about that firm quite a bit.

Jarrell: And who was Hill?

Ford: Kenneth Hill was one of the main people in the early Save the Redwoods League. I think it was his personal contribution. I think he gave a big wad of money because he was never an owner, whereas Ed Landels was an owner. So Ed's financial contribution to the sale was to reduce his price for his share, whereas Hill actually contributed money, probably through the Save the Redwoods League. Hill is regarded by the Save the Redwoods League as one of their heroes, but I don't know a whole lot more about him and I never met him. It is the University's custom to acknowledge such contributors, which I don't favor, but Landels and Hill were the main contributors, so the reserve is named after them.

Jarrell: While you were at UCSC, you managed Big Creek. Was there a period when you lived there?

Ford: No, I couldn't live down there because I had too many other things to do. Also, and this was part of Ken's way of operating, I was hired and paid at the University to run the Environmental Field Program and he tacked on these other jobs that I did. Nobody knew this but he and I knew how that was arranged. But he needed help. He couldn't be manager of Big Creek without help. So it worked and we just got by.

In the first years we were just trying to do things. Ken realized, okay, here we've got this site. Well, we've got to open up some trails so that people can get around. Otherwise they're not going to be able to use it. It was a jungle. So the first few summers I was there I would hire these bands of students, including a whole bunch of Field Quarter students and we'd go down there and spend the whole summer clearing trails, mostly old homesteader trails. We built very few miles of new trails. We fixed up old buildings and basically made it habitable. At first, because it had all been overgrown and there was nothing, anything we did was an incredible improvement and so people were really happy about that. But now people down there complain, "Oh, this building is too old. And mice come in and stuff." From my perspective it's like, what are you complaining about? There's a house there. (laughter) But you know how that goes. That's the evolution of any organization.

Jarrell: You see a vast improvement.

Ford: And all they can see are the current flaws.

The other thing that's important to know is that even Ken didn't want to have any resident staff down there at first. I pushed for it. Because I knew I couldn't get anything done. I came up with the idea to get an intern to go down there and maybe pay them just a few hundred bucks. Just like I was getting students to go off on the field program projects. So I did.

The first person that we got down there was Glenn Browning, a wonderful guy. He lived in this old homestead cottage and I paid him about $600 a month. Of course that was barely enough for his expenses. I couldn't give him a car or anything. He loved it. He had a great time and he did a great job and his role was to help everybody who came down there and try to encourage people and increase our capacity to serve people who wanted to come with classes or to do projects. He also kept the roads open, which was a huge, huge job. Because every rainstorm would bring boulders and fallen trees and stuff and we didn't even have a vehicle at that time. So he would walk around with his chainsaw. By the time that Don Usner became the first resident caretaker we were ready to move into kind of a permanent phase and I had enough for an actual salary.

Having Don there enabled me to take off every spring on the Field Quarter and also to do the support and liaison for the students scattered all across North America and the Pacific, for Field Program projects. So it worked.

Jarrell: What was the relationship between UCSC and the NRS while you were manager of Big Creek?

Ford: It has always been very decentralized. In fact, there has always been sort of an ongoing debate and careful manipulation of what is a central authority and what is a campus authority, for the reserves. You don't want it too centralized because then funds will dry up; you've got to make sure that the campus feels some obligation and responsibility so that they pay for it. At the same time you've got to have a reason for the existence of the central office.

Jarrell: When I asked Ken a question about administrative matters, he'd say, "Oh Randall, I'm not good with this stuff. I don't know."

Ford: Oh, that's not true at all. He was a master at that stuff. He knew exactly what he was doing on that. He knew that if you didn't have campus support that the UC president's office wouldn't support it.

Jarrell: So did UC Santa Cruz give money on behalf of the maintenance of Big Creek?

Ford: Eventually it did. Their first contribution was me. That was unknowingly. It was my part-time obligation to run the place. Then according to Ken's philosophy eventually, before they knew it, they had a successful reserve. It was the number one reserve in the whole system in terms of users. We had more visitor days than any other reserve in the whole system. Ken also started to direct all these Environmental Field Program projects at Big Creek. I think we have seven or eight inches worth of published reports, surveys—archaeology, geology. Then when David and Lucile Packard bought the property to the south, some 3000 acres, they gave us access to essentially annex their property as part of the reserve.

Jarrell: It adjoins the reserve?

Ford: Yes. Right on the southern boundary. They saved it from becoming a hunting lodge. Now the family treasures it. I mean the next generation does, and they're all these wonderful conservationists themselves. So the reserve essentially expanded to 8000 acres, in this kind of loose arrangement. University funds were contributed from UC Systemwide to the purchase of the reserve. The partners agreed that the University would become the manager of the site because neither the Save the Redwoods League nor the Nature Conservancy wanted to get into these big obligations for management. The Conservancy has changed its mind a little bit since then. They have started to do that. They used to give all their lands to some other agency, because they wanted to get on with the business of buying more land which was their critical role. Since then they have realized that there was no good agency to give it to, in many other cases. So now they are in the land management business, and even in the consulting business, which I think maybe has gone too far for them. But they have their reasons.

So the University became the designated manager at Big Creek and therefore took on the responsibility of all the expenses for its management. Eventually the Nature Conservancy and the Save the Redwoods League basically pulled out. They had plans for building a visitor center and all kinds of things and they eventually didn't do that.

Jarrell: You said that of all of the NRS sites, in Northern and Southern California, that Big Creek is the most popular, the most visited reserve.

Ford: It was, during my tenure. I don't know whether it still is. I suspect that it ranks up there. One of the reasons for that is Ken's founding philosophy, which was that he wanted to encourage classes to come there. Also the management of Big Creek was always less focused on research than the other reserves. Most of the other reserves reject many applications for use, they're focused more on their own research and are often not focused on management of the sites at all. This is another problem, from my point of view, that they've focused on theoretical research of various kinds. That's very important, absolutely important. But Big Creek has therefore been used by a lot of visitors for things other than really serious research, and that's why its numbers are so high. For instance, former students of the Field Quarter who love Big Creek can call out there and say they want to come down and check out something and can visit. I think that's a bit of a problem but the current managers don't think so, so I'm not worried about it.

Jarrell: I asked Ken, when he was talking about the Environmental Field Program, how he identified the sites, what process he used. He said he already had the sites in mind long before the program. Were you involved with other sites besides Big Creek for the Field Program projects?

Ford: I was involved in all of them and that's right about Ken. Part of his agenda was to take care of any needs of the NRS sites, in case a survey was needed. He wanted to make sure that he would do that. He had the discretion to propose and build a group of students to do these surveys. We sent students out to all kinds of places. For instance, putting ten students for three months on a project was very effective. We did projects all throughout the

Mojave Desert area, the San Sebastian Marsh, and the Kingston Range. These were all priorities for the Bureau of Land Management [BLM]. But not necessarily for the NRS. But we did other projects for NRS sites and had hoped to do more. In fact, at one point we were hoping to actually build a whole program that would help support the NRS by sending students out, but that never materialized.

Jarrell: I see. It seems that you never suffered from a lack of students?

Ford: Oh no, never. If we'd had more money we would have been bigger and I'm sure we would have been even more popular.

Natural Reserve System

Jarrell: Okay, we're going to move on now to the NRS, the Natural Reserve System of the University of California. Larry, you were a member of the Chancellor's Advisory Committee for the NRS.

Ford: That's because I was a grad student at Berkeley at the time. I knew all these professors at Berkeley when I was at Santa Cruz, because we were all going to meetings together and I would often accompany Ken to meetings. When I got up there they knew I was there, and so they asked if I would sit on this committee as a graduate student member. So it was a very different role than when I had actually been a manager.

Jarrell: Different campuses, I've noticed, oversee different sites. So what would Berkeley be overseeing and you were on the Chancellor's Advisory Committee, and you were no longer a manager at Big Creek. This was a totally different hat you were wearing.

Ford: Okay, many of the UC campuses have a set of reserves. So Berkeley has Hastings Reserve in the Carmel Valley.

Jarrell: How come Santa Cruz wouldn't oversee that site?

Ford: History.

Jarrell: Not geography?

Ford: Right. Hastings preceded the NRS; it was a field site of UC Berkeley, of the Museum of Vertebrate Zoology, for years. In fact, Berkeley has some other sites, like Morea in French Polynesia, that station out there. But that's not part of NRS. It could have been but they decided not to include it. In fact Ken went out and surveyed it before Morea was accepted from the Gumps. They decided to bring it in but they decided to leave it at Berkeley. Berkeley also has, or did have, what's now called the Heath and Marjorie Angelo Coast Range Reserve, which used to be called the North Coast Range Reserve, something like that. It's up in Mendocino.

The Hans Jenny Pygmy Forest Reserve is under the Berkeley campus; Chickering American River Reserve, up in the Sierra, is part of Berkeley. The Bodega Marine Reserve used to be Berkeley but it's now UC Davis. That's it.

Now that committee was mostly faculty and then rotating graduate students. We would meet and review the various problems and go off on field trips to the different sites and try to deal with problems. During my time Chickering was a real problem; the family was threatening to pull it out of the NRS. They wanted the land back and the NRS was threatening to give it back to them because there were disagreements with the family. So, we were trying to find some happy medium. The family didn't want students staying there; they wanted them to stay in motels, and not stay on the site overnight and not to walk through their lands. They had visions of these hordes coming in causing trouble and leaving trash and stuff, which were very reasonable concerns. I'm not sure that it's ever been resolved. But this is one of those things. The NRS is held together just as best it can. And it can't be too strict with rules or anything. It has to try to make it work.

Jarrell: After Ken launched the NRS he joined the faculty at UC Santa Cruz. I never had the opportunity when I interviewed him to ask him to what degree he was involved in NRS policy after the regents founded the NRS in 1965.

Ford: He was fundamentally involved until the day he died. Absolutely no question about it. One of the things that Ken used to tell me was that he could not give up his vigilance. Because whoever it was, the faculty and the administrators who were running it, it was like entropy. They would start dealing with the nonessential problems and they'd start making decisions that were not advancing the vision. To maintain the vision he had to keep harassing the faculty and the administrators, including NRS director Roger [Samuelsen]. Roger will tell you that Ken was continually haranguing him to do certain things such as making sure that the University administrators didn't withdraw funding and say that the NRS had to raise it all from outside sources.

Jarrell: When you say faculty to whom are you referring? Faculty members on the board of directors of NRS?

Ford: Right. They don't call them directors; they call it a faculty advisory committee whose members are drawn from all the campuses, even campuses like UC San Francisco that don't have any reserves. This was basically an advisory committee. But other things that Ken would often complain about would be comments that would come up, such as doubts about needing any new NRS sites or the giving up of sites. Ken worked to see that these things didn't happen.

There're two dimensions about the NRS that are very important to understand. One is that the origins and the real sort of fundamental motivation for faculty and for campuses to participate in the NRS is the need for faculty to have sites nearby their campuses to take students and to do projects and to make studies where they have reasonable access and that are not being overrun by the public. You cannot find those kinds of sites on the public lands, because there're too many people, too many human impacts, too much vandalism, really. So with that in mind you can imagine that Ken, as a graduate student and a young professor at UCLA, used to take his students out to find lizards and look at plants and things and gradually those sites started to get lost.

Jarrell: Encroached upon by urbanization?

Ford: They got developed. So that is still one of the biggest motivations today. But the other dimension of Ken's vision was the need to look centuries into the future. We need reserve sites like this throughout California. I mean the new UC Merced campus is not going to be the last UC campus. There probably will be someday another one in Northern California, who knows where.

Jarrell: Way up north?

Ford: The population doesn't really justify it yet. So who knows, Marin, Sonoma, farther north. But anyway, the same needs will be there for the public to have the resources for solving environmental problems. The kind of support UC gives to agriculture ought to be recognized for environmental sites; we need these environmental sites just like all the agricultural field stations that UC supports, we now need and will need these in the future. That was Ken's first vision, back in the 1960s. That's what he talked about. This is why he wanted to stay involved. Because, you see, the status quo doesn't really have that need. Ken's vision was that these sites would have a staff, libraries, study equipment, and on-going research. It's been hard to get the current leadership of the NRS to buy into it, because it's expensive, and there are more sites to buy. Ken had in mind two large-scale reserves for Northern California. This is one of the saddest things about Ken's death. We were planning to work on this. His death, his illness—we didn't expect it; it just happened so quickly. Everything was on hold. We stopped. We didn't have a meeting of the Norris Fund committee for six months or so.

Jarrell: So during all of these years, since he conceived of the NRS and got the support of President Kerr, and established the system of reserves, he was plugging away at this and he never lost touch, he never let go of this. The NRS was abiding in his life.

Ford: Absolutely.

Kenneth S. Norris Fund for the Natural Environment

Jarrell: Tell me about the Kenneth S. Norris Fund of NRS, with which you became involved in 1990.

Ford: Okay, in 1990, the year, I think just before Ken retired, or maybe it was the year he retired, I wanted to do something special for him. My co-conspirators and I planned a big retirement reunion party for him. We invited the 440 or so students who had taken the natural history class, including Dave Hart from the class in 1973. About 240 or so former students came back to Santa Cruz for the reunion. They came from Europe, from Australia, from all over. It was an incredible party. And of course we had speeches and all these things. And Ken—oh, he loved it! He did a Dr. Van Denburgh skit.

So anyway, as part of this reunion party we wanted to give Ken this gift. My thought was what better gift to Ken than to give him a big pile of money with the instructions to spend it as he wished. As former students, we had a few ideas. We suggested that he fund projects related to the NRS, to Big Creek, or to the Field Quarter class. We had a bunch of ideas. Anyway, Ken was thrilled. We raised something like $6000. Wow. Including $1000 Ken himself put into it. We named it the Kenneth S. Norris Fund. Because we thought if we didn't do it he wouldn't. So he loved that, too. Because he could say, "the Norris Fund." (laughter) He was very proud. We started thinking about what would we want to do. At first we thought about supporting some student projects from Santa Cruz, Big Creek Reserve and these sorts of things.

Jarrell: When he saw something that was worthy, that he'd be able to dole out the money?

Ford: Yes. What we had in mind was that Ken would just be able to fund various little projects. If someone said we need a new roof or something Ken could say, I'll pay for it. That's what we envisioned. That's exactly what he wanted to do.

Jarrell: Some shack down at Big Creek or something?

Ford: Yes! You know, a couple of hundred bucks, he could do it. And we all thought in the next ten years while he can still do it or whatever, let him be able to. Ken came up with the idea of well, why don't we see if we can get the NRS to oversee it. What do you think the NRS said? Of course! Of course! We'll get right back to you about how we can set it up. The next thing we knew we had the Kenneth S. Norris Fund for the Natural Environment. They told us we had to set up a board of directors and so we wrote some bylaws and we did it and brought the money up and they've been managing it and we haven't spent more than a few tens of dollars from that. Now it's up to $12,000, just from accruing interest. They have some control over it, but that's the way you have to do it.

Packard Foundation Grant to the Natural Reserve System

Jarrell: Could you tell me about this really remarkable donation that was made to the NRS in Ken's behalf and in his memory by the David and Lucile Packard Foundation?

Ford: Well, let me tell the true story for the record. Because this has gotten dissipated and changed over the two years or so that it's come about. Two years ago, after I had come back from Texas, I was able to rejoin Ken on the Norris Fund. We sort of decided to ramp it up a little bit. Ken was really worried that the NRS might disappear out of administrative atrophy, basically. If additional money wasn't raised, the endowment would basically disappear and leave the NRS with virtually nothing to fall back on. At the same time the University was going through this cut-and-run kind of thing and were motivated by the legislature's cutbacks. So Ken realized we had to rebuild an endowment; we had to give the NRS a built-in future so that administrators couldn't just let it go away.

So we started to cultivate this idea: why don't we launch a major fundraising campaign for an endowment? But further than that, we wanted, number one, to give the NRS a future that nobody could deny. We wanted to have the endowment directed towards activities that would be towards that future, too. That is, this endowment could never be used for basic operating expenses. In fact it would explicitly not be for that. It would be focused, in part, for example, on a semi-annual conference that would be among other things, about the future, about the contributions of the NRS to society's needs for environmental science, focusing towards this future. Ken wrote the first draft of the proposal. It was never going to be called the Ken Norris Endowment. It was just—we were going to do it. Ken had personal connections to the Packard family, and in fact had been invited by Nancy Packard Burnett, and also by Julie Packard, to submit a proposal, to develop it. So he wrote the first proposal, and then the rest of the Norris Fund board, of course, we were all behind it, and we all worked on subsequent drafts. It eventually went to the NRS. They had to submit it. But in the first submission that went to the Packard Foundation it said very clearly that this grant proposal was submitted by the Norris Fund. There's absolutely no denying that.

Subsequently, with that first draft Nancy Burnett had specifically said, "Don't send me a bunch of material. Just send me the nuts-and-bolts proposal. We want to do this." Subsequently, as is typical in organizations, the staff of the Packard Foundation said we had to send all these details; they needed to have the details. It couldn't just be some thing where Ken Norris outlined what the problems were. Of course the NRS didn't want it to go in with all the crisis language because their attitude was to show how great the NRS was, to highlight their accomplishments. Whereas Ken's real motivation was, Yes, fine. But we're in this serious crisis; if we don't get an endowment, if we don't do something major like this, the NRS is not going to survive. But the NRS people didn't hear that, they didn't really hear it; their political interests were to downplay that.

Anyway, along came the new director, Alex[ander A.] Glazer, who was incredibly successful and sharp. He came in at the tail end and I don't think he realized what had been done with that proposal. He just saw it as basically this piece that was incompetently delivered in the first draft. The Packard Foundation people came back and said, look, it's got to have all this other stuff, of course. So Glazer, being quite familiar with what was needed, added all that. He saved the proposal.

But what I don't think was sufficiently appreciated was that if Ken's friendship with Nancy Packard and the other Packards hadn't been there in the first place it never would have even come up. Without Ken's persistent communications with those family members, it would never have flown. But it did. So then the NRS named the endowment, in fact, while Ken was on his last legs in the hospital. They named it for him, which he knew. He heard, because I was there when he got the phone call. He was quite proud of it, but over that, I remember him saying after he hung up the phone with Alex Glazer, "We have got to make sure that this goes through." His commitment was always for providing this future and staying vigilant about this for the NRS.

We had originally asked for eight million dollars. We got four. This was another thing we were going to do. We had all these plans for additional fundraising. Because four wasn't enough. At first we estimated that we needed sixteen million; then we were going to reduce it to eight. We were going to try to raise this other four million through some other mechanisms. I guess it will never happen now. But, it's there. I don't know what restrictions were placed on it, but the original intent was, as I said, that it could never be used for operating costs and stuff. I think Alex Glazer has some great ideas for how to use this NRS endowment. So it's basically out of our hands now.

The future of the Norris Fund is uncertain. We're trying to decide that right now. We all jumped in to try to help the Norris oral history project and the memorial project. We may have some role in the future, but I don't know yet. But it served its purpose. I'm very proud and happy about what we did because we gave Ken that happiness. I heard him many times say, "the Ken Norris Fund." And he loved it. (laughter) It gave him a vehicle. I mean he was the chairman and it gave him this vehicle to not just do these little projects, because he made it much, much more than we ever imagined that it would be.

Dr. Van Denburgh

Jarrell: To end on a humorous note, who was Dr. Van Denburgh?

Ford: He was a herpetologist at the California Academy of Sciences in San Francisco, sometime in the Victorian era. He was very proper and formal. He wore a bowler hat and a tie and so did his assistant, even when they went out to do field work, according to the stories Ken told. So they'd go out and they referred to each other as Dr. Van Denburgh and so-and-so, whoever the other guy was. Well, Ken decided that this guy was the patron saint of natural history field trips and Ken didn't even believe in patron saints. But anyway, this was a convenient way for him to get some laughs and to appear to have supernatural powers. When we were out on these field trips there would always be these sightings of Dr. Van Denburgh. And Ken, of course, was the only one who could interpret them. Ken kept changing the rules about what these sightings meant just to bug people and to keep them on their toes. But, the main thing was that anybody with a gray beard could be Dr. Van Denburgh. So driving through some town on our way someplace, if you saw some guy with a gray beard, pretty soon all the students would be looking out, "Is that Dr. Van Denburgh?" Ken would pronounce, yes or no. Ken would usually come back with some incredible story. "I just saw Dr. Van Denburgh and he was riding a bike! Do you know what that means?" (laughter) "No, what does it mean?" "Well, he was riding it fast and he had on a green shirt so therefore it means we're going to have good weather."*

---

*In the mythology of the Natural History Field Quarter, the name Dr. Van Denburgh is frequently mentioned; his mysterious apparitions and visitations enlivened the class as it traveled throughout the state and were a constant source of merriment. Ken Norris invented the mythical character: a proper Victorian scientist, with bowler hat, furled umbrella, and impeccable suit, but he was based on a real figure. According to the Norris mythology, Dr. Van Denburgh was found dead one morning, curled up in the carapace of a Galapagos tortoise in the basement of the California Academy of Sciences, his umbrella placed carefully beside him. The Academy received its first herpetological specimen in 1853—a Galapagos tortoise carapace. John Van Denburgh was appointed in 1895 as curator of the reptile and amphibian collection at the California Academy of Sciences. During these early years he collected mostly in the San Francisco Bay Area and the desert regions of California and western Arizona. He developed collections from the Galapagos, the Philippine Islands, and the Far East as well. Van Denburgh's numerous publications culminated in his two-volume monograph, *Reptiles of North America* (1922). He died in 1924, the year Ken Norris was born.

Jarrell: So it was just like a running joke from year to year, from class to class.

Ford: Oh totally. And so *Beyond Mountain Time* has a couple of stories of some of the most incredible Dr. Van Denburgh visitations. Like, one time up on the Mattole River, Dr. Van Denburgh actually got on the bus and actually sang a song. The funny thing about it was that there was this nice, lonesome guy who lived near the campground that we stayed at. Perfectly harmless. But he didn't realize why Ken was walking around with these expressions, of, "Hey, that's Van Denburgh! And my gosh, we're being visited by a saint."

Jarrell: (laughter) The patron saint of the Natural History Field Quarter.

Ford: You may remember at the Norris memorial that people were walking around with buttons that said, "Dr. Van Denburgh Lives," with a picture of Ken in the center of it. Those buttons came from the 1990 reunion, where we were claiming that Ken was really Dr. Van Denburgh.

Jarrell: I see. What does "woof" mean?

Ford: I have no idea. It came after I departed from daily operations with Ken.

Jarrell: Right. Everybody was wearing buttons and little things on our name tags at the memorial, it would say, "My name is Larry Ford, Woof, woof," at the top.

Ford: Well, I think it happened when Ken was on sabbatical or in Hawaii for awhile, maybe he came back from a summer and somehow he had picked up this term. This was typical of Ken. He was just continually coming up with these hysterical things. Of course everybody just jumped on it, you know. Because they all wanted to participate. So pretty soon everybody was saying woof, woof.

Jarrell: Well, Larry, thank you so much. I've really learned a lot talking to you today.

Donald J. Usner

Reti: To start, Don, could you tell me how you got involved with the Natural History Field Quarter? You were a TA for Field Quarter, and before that, a student of Ken Norris's.

Meeting Ken Norris

Usner: Yes, I was just very lucky. A friend of mine from New Mexico, Bruce Bannerman, had come to school out here [at UCSC]. And he said, "Oh, you've got to come out here. It's a fantastic place; there's this wonderful group of people, and this guy Ken Norris, and you'd love him." I dropped everything and came out at the end of spring quarter 21 years ago. Bruce had just done the Field Quarter class. I went to school and at the end of the quarter he invited me to the class's final party, although I hadn't been in the course. I had no preparation for what was going to happen. It was their final get-together at Ken's house. Bruce felt like it was okay to invite me. I don't know what got into him. I was at a time in my life, like a lot of students and people who came into Ken's world, really searching and unsure of myself and basically on the verge of being lost, and not knowing my direction very clearly.

We went to this party and there was this wonderful group of people and Ken, and the other teachers. Craig Schindler was there. The energy there was unbelievable. People were so happy and having so much fun. Ken was just the craziest person I ever encountered. He immediately welcomed me with open arms, focused on me, and didn't make me feel that I wasn't part of the group. My first feeling when I got there was, oh God, I'm out of place. But the whole class was welcoming. And Craig was that way. I just became part of the Field Quarter class for one night. We went tromping around the woods. Ken had a little walk he liked to take people on down through the woods and he had these silly games and just the novelty of it. To have a professor who was crawling through redwood trunks, and rolling around laughing and everybody jumped in the creek, and a bunch of us just took off our clothes and jumped in the creek, and Ken was completely comfortable and loved it.

At the same time he was so intimately engaging on a personal level. I think everybody probably felt that. But to me it was an immediate feeling of being accepted and beyond acceptance, having him be very, very interested in who I was. He wanted to know more about what I thought and it was not like a professor's dominating or dictating presence. He was eliciting from me. It was a complete flip-flop in my whole conception of education and teachers and mentor relationships. I guess he was really my first mentor, in that respect. I was immediately swept up and determined to come back to Santa Cruz in the fall of 1977 and to get involved more with environmental studies. The following spring I didn't do Field Quarter. There was also UC Extension then, which was kind of a similar thing.

Reti: The Sierra Institute?

Usner: There was the Sierra Institute but UC Extension had a one-time course, Springtime in the Rockies. We did a trip up to the Northern Rockies. That was ecstatic and just whetted my appetite for more. I came back in the following spring for field quarter. Then for the following one I was TA, I think. I can't remember the exact sequence, but I did field quarter and then subsequently was a TA twice.

The thing with Ken, from the first moment, and it never abated, was always this intense interest in knowing each other more. I always had the same feeling of such delight with this person whom I admired immensely for his intellect. His intellect was so powerful and perceptive, and I always felt honored to spend time with him.

Reti: So it wasn't just that he was wild and crazy and fun.

Usner: No. Not at all. It was really balanced by, for me, an awe at his intellect is one way to say it, which is true, but more than that it was his awareness and his perceptiveness; his ability to perceive and to observe in everything, which especially he brought to bear in natural history. He was so focused. To me it was a way of being present, so present. It's so rare to find anybody who is present. All of us are so busy. Our minds are worried. He was able to be present, with an individual, with a class, with a plant, with a rock, with a seal. I remember when I first met him the way he looked at me was so unnerving at first. Did you ever have a talk with him?

Reti: No I saw him lecture a couple of times but unfortunately I never got to study with him.

Usner: What I experienced was he would look at me and his eyes seemed to be scanning, really looking right into my eyes. But he was looking for something. Somehow he was picking up a lot of information when you were just talking with him. He would listen so carefully and he would always bring it to your level, to your turf. He wanted to know what you thought, as a student. He wanted to learn from you, as much as or more than he wanted to impart anything. That's the feeling I got. He was always viewed as an icon and a fountain of information and stories. But when you were with him one-on-one he was willing and able and enthusiastic about engaging in whatever you were interested in, whatever was happening with you. At least that's the way it was with me.

I think what made him so wonderful as a teacher was that he made everybody feel that way to some extent, that they were important, that he cared about them; he wanted to know what each individual was about, and what was worrying them. What kept him so alive and interested was that he loved to engage; he was really trying to understand what was going on with young people, and always trying to learn from them, trying to be informed by all these different young minds. He talked about that a lot, how with his own work he found it very important to keep his perspective fresh by listening to young people. He said many times that they kept him honest, kept him looking at what he was doing from a new perspective. I think it was a two-way street. He was getting a lot out of it. He was so nurturing, and so kind and willing to give praise. I don't know what his relationship was like with other people, so much. I know that students lit up around him and felt inspired and driven to excel. Because he was tuning his mind in. He was paying attention. He was actually reading the Field Quarter journals. He would write little notes in the margins. You could tell that he wasn't just scanning them, checking things off. He was listening to your thoughts. Having that kind of engagement with somebody like him whom you admired, and who had so much experience and capacity for thinking, felt like you were engaged with his mind personally. He was extremely generous about giving out praise, finding out what it was that you liked and what made you tick as an individual and saying yes, that's wonderful. Look at that! Look at what you did! Look at your uniqueness and go for it in that unique way you have to offer. It was a completely new experience for me as a relationship with a teacher. I never felt it in the same way with anybody else.

Reti: Did he have ways of challenging you?

Usner: I think of challenge as an affront, or a direct, confrontational thing. It was more of an encouragement; he would affirm you, and say, "take this work or idea a little further. This is wonderful. Keep going." With him it never felt like, "what do you mean? I don't get it. What are you trying to say?" He didn't have an agenda about where you should be going or what you should do or how you should see the world. I came out of the end of the whole beat poet era and all that stuff. But I still came from that place, and I think a lot of us did. There was a fascination with Eastern ways of thinking and the whole notion of trying to be present.

Reti: Yes, I remember very well talking about that in environmental studies in Craig Schindler's classes.

Usner: Oh you were with Craig. Yes, Craig was great. He was great in looking at this stuff. But to be with a person like Ken who was completely immersed in a Western way of thinking but was also completely capable of being present and letting that intellect work, all that rational, analytical stuff be there, but it wasn't the only thing there; that was in the service of being present. Whereas most of our educational experiences just cultivated nothing but that kind of analytical, rational thinking without ever stepping back and looking at its purpose or being apart from it. I think Ken was able to suspend all that intellectual machinery and be present while it was running in the background. That was one of his strengths as a teacher and a researcher. He was able to learn from everybody and everything interactively.

The Natural History Field Quarter

Reti: When you were a TA for Ken what did he pass on to you in terms of how to teach, how to work with students?

Usner: Well, you know not as much as to Larry [Lawrence D.] Ford. Ken very carefully and deliberately, from what I understand, imparted techniques and ways of doing things to Larry. At least this is what Larry told me. He would tell Larry stuff about the mechanics of the class and what his intention was behind creating this space for students. For me it was less that. My relationship with Ken was very personal. We were usually engaged in talking about whatever was on our minds. There was the logistics in directing, in trying to keep the class functioning, in creating the right atmosphere.

He was such a social person. I still can't believe I'm saying was; it's still very odd to think of the world without him. But he was so social and he wanted to always make sure that everybody felt included, everybody felt safe, and that people wouldn't isolate and ostracize others and develop little cliques. He was always working to try and keep the group experience positive and nurturing. That was what we did talk about. It was such a great adventure that occasionally we had to say, "Okay everybody, now we do have to do some work here." (laughter)

Reti: Right. I was going to ask you about that. How do you keep twenty-three young students who were totally excited, on this bus going around California, how did you get them to not go wild? It seems that would be a real challenge in terms of the group dynamics, and in terms of students not just looking at it as a giant backpacking trip.

Usner: Yes, well, Ken commanded enough respect. People were basically in awe of him. I think he used an old way of teaching, and I say old because I don't know if it's used anymore. He gave people responsibility for their own motivations. Sometimes it didn't work. I remember one incident in particular. We used to have the students do presentations in each field locale on geology or flora and fauna and so forth. There was one time down at Big Creek where he felt that people really slipped on their presentations. So he said something to me, we had a meeting, and he gathered everybody together. He told the students that they weren't cutting it; that they had to learn more and to present it more clearly and he specifically cited some individual presentations. It was a little tough. But that was pretty rare. Usually people were so anxious to excel, so anxious to do the best because that was just part of what he created. It was to have the most fun. Be yourself. Be as zany and as out there and as original as you can possibly be and really learn what we're here for, too. Everybody just kind of got it. It was very rare that somebody didn't get onto that wavelength and really want to do their best. That was what was so wonderful about it, too, you realized that it was not all fun and games. There were some really important things going on.

Reti: So the students were expected to do presentations and keep a journal?

Usner: That was basically it. Presentations and the journal. The presentations were very, very challenging because of the fact that the students wanted to let Ken know that they did get it, that they did care. People would invest a lot, work really hard.

We'd have a traveling library we called the Parnassus. Ken and Larry made two special boxes. For each trip we'd take one set of standard books, and on each trip there'd be different specific books and papers and journals. Then when we returned there was time between trips to work in the library and find materials. So it ran the gamut. You'd find some people who just did fantastic term papers on every trip, they would do incredibly deep research. Others would take it more lightly. But still, there was rarely anybody who really slouched. It was all without any enforced discipline. It was just like, you got with the program because you loved it. It was fun. It was exciting. And you got to celebrate a lot.

A Typical Day

Reti: So what was a typical day like on Field Quarter? Did you get up at the crack of dawn and head out with your notebook?

Usner: Let me see if I can characterize it. On a typical day students would be getting up and having a time to take a walk, to stretch, to sit and write in their journals. Then came breakfast, usually fairly early, seven or eight. Then they would have their plan for their day. There were four sets of exercises in each location that you did.

Reti: Was there a syllabus or something like that?

Usner: Not really a syllabus. I don't remember if we handed out a syllabus but we would work on specific exercises related to natural history at each location. So we'd get up and it would be a day for species accounts, for example, at the Granite Mountains. The whole field quarter was pretty carefully choreographed; for all its looseness and spontaneity, there was a pretty clear idea of what was going to happen at each place we went, and it was all building. It all had a place in the whole structure of the course. It wasn't just let's go hang out and look at birds. I would have to dig out my notes to be specific about it. Larry could tell you just off the top of his head because he was TA for many years.

But the Granite Mountains in the Mojave Desert was a far away, totally different environment, a big long trip of ten days and we were at Ken Norris's family retreat cabin.

The Bunny Club

Reti: That was the Bunny Club?

Usner: Yes. He had found that place in the forties when he was driving around in a jeep doing his research. It had a little spring. He leased it from the Southern Pacific Land Company and he and his brother built a cabin where they would go sometimes. This is where we went with the class. It was a perfect way to start because everybody was out of their element, away from the coast, away from the school, out in the desert, and we were at Ken's place. It was very personal. He had created this wonderful place built into the rocks. It was so magical. You couldn't escape the grip of that place. It was so powerful, the feeling of that place, and the desert. It would completely blow people out of the water and they'd be ready, wide open.

Crossing the Threshold of Boredom

There was a lot of work going on there, students bonding; creating, setting the stage for the whole quarter. I believe that's where we started an observation training technique where each student would have to take a specific species. You could pick anything, a bird, a plant. You can imagine the environment. You'd have to spend the entire day with it, with your journal.

Reti: With that one species?

Usner: With that one species, yes. You'd just have to look at it; you'd have to watch it and keep notes and write in your journal. One of the topics that I got the most out of was this idea of the threshold of boredom that Ken developed. It was very important to come prepared with water and food, to stay warm and dry, to get comfortable, and then to watch and watch. Every time you started feeling bored, and thought you'd seen everything this species was going to do, you'd watch it some more. You kept writing. You kept going past that threshold of boredom. At a certain point you broke through and you suddenly saw a completely new species. Suddenly you had an Aha! A breakthrough. You saw that you weren't just looking at a bird sitting on a branch, but the bird was actually engaged in a very deliberate mating display, for example. If you watched closer still, you'd see the pattern of this display. If you watched closer still you'd see how far the other males were and where the females were and each time you pushed that threshold of boredom, there would be this incredible—wow!

The fun thing about that was that we would come back in the desert evening, to this beautiful cabin. There would be a fire going and we'd be making food and people would be drinking beer, and playing music. It was a great atmosphere. Then we'd have time either that night or the next day to share from our journals. People would really wake up to how magical and wonderful nature is. You just cannot get this awareness if you just pass through, or just spend half a day hiking. You really have to tune in. So that was the introductory thing, to sharpen your skills, to start working on observation, to keep a journal, and learn this thing about patience and pushing that threshold of boredom.

Reti: You're talking about being present, and tying that to observation, about Ken's approach to teaching people to see. I didn't quite have a sense of how that worked and you're giving me much more of an idea.

Usner: It was a very intuitive process that was filled with wonder. To see yourself as a student, and watch other students have that experience. They would be so excited. It's like, wow, look what I've discovered. A lot of times it was stuff that nobody had ever noticed before about different species as far as anybody knew, including Ken. He'd say, "you know I never knew that about this plant or that animal, and let's find out more." Then people would come back to campus and dig through the literature and find out if anybody had noticed that before. It was really a neat experience.

Reti: That's extraordinary.

Usner: Yes, I mean ten days was a long time to be out. There was always so much celebration, so much joy.

Singing Sand Dunes

We'd go to Kelso Sand Dunes, big sand dunes down there, close to the Bunny Club. And they're, I forget how many feet high. A big pile of beautiful sand. We'd hike up the sand dunes. We'd go to the top and Ken would give his lecture on geology, and how sand dunes are formed, a general geological overview from this perspective at the top of a sand dune, and you are just looking out across the Mojave Desert.*

Most of the the kids were pretty wild. We were having so much fun. By this time we'd figured out it was okay to have fun. (laughter) So we would jump on the sand dunes, roll on the sand dunes, and usually we would all take all our clothes off and get in big lines and jump. Ken had this ongoing interest in singing sand dunes and these were one of the few singing sand dunes in the world. When they move they vibrate and you hear this *oooo* sound. It sounds almost like a [musical] saw. Clearly audible. You can get different frequencies, maybe not different frequencies, but different volumes, depending on how much sand you can move. We would line up, all of us, twenty-three students, stark naked, on top of the dune. Ken would get down in the sand and he had headphones and a microphone buried down in the sand. He'd say, "Okay!" And we'd jump over the dune and he would be recording it and listening to it. He was trying to figure out where the sound came from and how it worked. So it was community in the service of science. It was so much fun.

I remember the first time I was down there, Ken—you know he was a little overwhelmed sometimes with this wildness and there's twenty-three naked, howling students running around.

Reti: Yes, I can see it would be overwhelming. (laughter)

Usner: But the first time I remember, he stripped down to his boxer shorts, just to be kind of in the spirit of things. We all gathered around him, and

*The Kelso Sand Dunes, about forty miles south of Baker, California, between Interstates 15 and 40, are majestic 600-foot high dune structures. When one slides down the steep face of the dune, it sings or booms, and a deep harmonic resonance is set off. When a group of people synchronizes their movements, the sound is amplified.

we're all naked, and he's in his boxer shorts giving us this lecture. This is really teaching. This is how it should be! That was just the beginning. From there each trip had a different kind of focus and set of exercises and they kind of grew and grew and grew. There were always new additions and variations. But it was always the desert first, the Mojave Desert. And God, I'm forgetting now. Was Big Creek next? But the idea was that we would go to the desert and then to the mountains, the Sierra, and we'd always camp in the White Mountains, which was fabulous. Then the North Coast and Big Sur and when Steve Gliessman came on board, Santa Cruz Island, where he'd done a lot of work. He and Larry would be able to tell you a lot more about Field Quarter, because I only taught with Ken twice.

Personal Relationship with Ken Norris

Ken and I had a very amazing personal connection. It was really life-changing for me. Basically he cultivated me. In his earlier years we would talk about our projects at home and our water systems and this complete other side of him that was just as important to him as all the academics. We would talk about his family, and his home and his sheep and his little projects up there, and building things, and watching his grandchildren. He was so interested, always, in whatever I was doing. Even when it was totally non-natural history, non-science. He was completely supportive, completely engaged, encouraging, and so thoughtful. In a way my relationship with him was a lot more time on that level than it was on the school level.

Reti: So you've really kept in touch with him all these years.

Usner: Yes.

Reti: More than kept in touch, you've had a friendship.

Usner: It's been really hard for me the past few months. I felt real bad to see him go. He was really a mentor in many ways, the least of which was academic. When he met my wife, he came out to New Mexico to our wedding. He was so great. We had a picnic the next day and he and Larry came and we played guitars and sang all those Field Quarter songs. It was just wonderful that way. Then he met my wife. She's a social worker. He was instantly completely engaged in wanting to know about what she did, how she did it and what it was like, and who was involved, and every ramification possible. And he was there. Phylly was the same way. Phylly and Ken were just like that. They were totally two parts of the same whole. They always opened their doors to me. I was not the only one. A friend of mine said they adopted strays. Not that I felt like I was one of their dogs. (laughter) But they would sit up with me at night. Everytime I'd come we'd sit by the fire. I always had this feeling that I should hurry or that they didn't have time for this, that I shouldn't be there. They had busy lives and [more] important things to do. It was never that way. I felt like part of the family. It really made a huge difference in my life, what they did for me.

It's kind of hard. I haven't even talked about it since he died. I haven't been around here. I haven't talked with anybody about this. (pause)

Reti: So it's intense to do this. I appreciate you doing this. So you would come and visit, periodically?

Usner: Yes, whenever I could. It wasn't enough. I really wish I could have come more.

Reti: When did you actually leave Santa Cruz? Right after you graduated?

Usner: No. There was a very wonderful thing that Ken did for me. First of all, he was an adviser for my thesis. He was the main reader. That was another turning point for me. He had so many nice things to say about my thesis, about my ability as a writer. He was particularly interested in writing. That was one of our main shared interests. He was a fabulous writer. It doesn't come through in a lot of his published work, just how eloquent he could be and how much he loved the craft and art of writing. But on my thesis he told me that I could really write, and really encouraged me to keep writing. Just to have that voice say, hey you can do this. It's like a little kid, you know?

You think you're so grown up and you're in college and I certainly wasn't. (laughter) I don't think anybody else was.

Reti: (laughter) I was such a baby when I was in environmental studies, God!

Usner: Yes, he basically did just what you or I would do if we were teaching a first grader: I would say, "that's a very good little mud pie. That's a beautiful one. You should do more of those." He did that for me with my writing and it really got me going. He was the key person who encouraged me. That's basically what I've done for a living since then, is writing and photography. And teaching.

Landels-Hill Big Creek Reserve

So he did that. Then I'll never forget, one of the most endearing things that I'll never forget Ken for, one of thousands, was at Big Creek on our Field Quarter. We were hiking out on our last day. It was day five and we were coming down a big, beautiful grassy ridge with the ocean down below us. We were all just high on the place. Ken, as usual, took time to walk with me. He'd do that; he'd take individuals and take time and be with them. I was walking with him down the ridge that day and I was telling him I was so overwhelmed with how beautiful this place was. I was just stunned. We had a conversation during which he said they had just bought it from the Nature Conservancy and it was going to be under University control.

Reti: In the Natural Reserve System.

Usner: Yes. I said to him, if you ever, ever need anybody just to be here, for anything, to take care of it, work on it, just write or spend time here, I would be just so delighted, so enthralled with that possibility. I graduated not long after that, in 1981. Then I got a letter from Ken. I had been a fire lookout in Idaho and then went back to New Mexico. I was working with this biologist in the middle of winter in Colorado, tracing mountain lions. It was a great job. I got a letter from Ken and Larry: "hey, remember you mentioned that you would like to go to Big Creek. Well, come on out. We've got a job for you." So he gave me my first real job. I really appreciated it. I was caretaker at Big Creek. Larry was the manager for a couple of years, too. Part of the reason for Ken's motivation in doing it was because we'd had that conversation. He remembered. I was stunned. But even more remarkable than that was the fact that I was very confused and torn at the time because I had lots going on in my life and I had another job offer for the summer to be on a fire lookout in Idaho. I couldn't decide. Big Creek was the dream of an entire lifetime and I'd already told them I'd be in Idaho. There were other factors involved. My girlfriend was going to be in Idaho, too. But I couldn't decide.

I have this craziness, or used to have it worse, of not being able to make decisions. Ken was so patient. I kept saying, I don't know what to do. He kept saying that they had to have a decision. I kept saying I couldn't decide, I can't decide. He never got impatient. He finally just said they had to know because they had to hire somebody else if I couldn't. I told him no, I said I had to go to Idaho. He said that's fine.

I was driving to Idaho and he'd already hired somebody else. I stopped at the last pay phone before the fire lookout. I said, "Ken! Ken, I don't know if I really want to do this." At that point he should have just said, "Look, stay out of my life!" But he said they had already hired somebody else and not to worry about it. There would be other opportunities. I was so devastated. Well, luckily, the next fall this guy quit. Then Ken and Larry called me again and asked if I was still interested.

Reti: So it worked out okay in the end.

Usner: I ended up staying at Big Creek for four years, six years total in Big Sur, working with Ken and Larry. Part of Ken's generosity included that the position came with very few strings attached, some minimal things to do, but I was free to do whatever I wanted with it. I ended up doing a lot of photography and writing and co-authored a book on Big Sur with a friend of mine down there, which was my first publication, *The Natural History of Big Sur.** Ray[mond F.] Dasmann wrote an endorsement for the new edition,

*Paul Henson and Donald J. Usner, (Berkeley: University of California Press, 1993).

which was great. It really helped us. It was because of Ken that I was there and because of what he taught me that I did that book. I owe a lot to him in that regard.

Old Blue

Reti: What was it like being on the bus?

Usner: Well, you know, I grew up at the tail end of the Sixties, about which I was always very fascinated.

Reti: You mean getting in a VW bus and going around the country?

Usner: Yes, and Ken Kesey and the whole thing. I always had this incredible feeling being on the bus. It was partly related to having read about and fantasized about being on the bus with Ken Kesey and all those guys. It was like that feeling. You were being involved in an experience that was—for me at least, it was so different. Once you got on the bus you were plugged into a whole different reality. You left all this stuff behind, and Santa Cruz and whatever you had going on in your life. You were on the bus with Ken [Norris]. He loved being on the bus. We had a microphone and loudspeakers on the bus and Ken would get up in the front and do a monologue about what we were going through, the natural history and the history of the places. It was usually so funny that sometimes I almost died laughing. The things he would come up with were just hilarious. It was like a comic on stage sometimes. But at the same time, what was wonderful about it was that it was all connected and engaged with the whole experience of looking at natural history. But it diverged into sometimes completely fabricated falsehoods that he would tell just to see how long he could string you along. Then people would catch on. Somebody else when it came their turn, they would do the same thing. Weaving parallel fantasies was almost as important as being present and observing reality; coming up with really hilarious, funny twists on natural history and natural selection and just bizarre, impossible things. But sometimes you couldn't tell if they were true or not until you got to know Ken. (laughter) He told us once that in his Ph.D. thesis he had written a couple of paragraphs that were complete gobbledygook, just using words and terminology that were typical of that kind of writing. None of his advisers caught it.

Reti: Just to see if they were reading carefully?

Usner: That's right. Exactly. (laughter) That was the kind of thing he would do sometimes; he would just start weaving some impossible tale that wasn't always even related to natural history. He had ongoing fantasies too. Like Dr. Van Denburgh.

Dr. Van Denburgh

Reti: What is this Dr. Van Denburgh thing? I was reading the *California Journal* that Michael Arenson put out.* You had a piece in there that was really wonderful.

Usner: Oh yes. I forgot about that.

Reti: And Ken had a piece. People were talking about this Dr. Van Denburgh and I thought, what is this, I thought Ken was Dr. Van Denburgh? I couldn't figure that out.

Usner: Well, you have to get the whole story from Larry, because I don't really remember it. But the point was that there was this mythical person named Dr. Van Denburgh and there were sightings of him on each trip somewhere.† The idea of the game was to find Dr. Van Denburgh. We would always see him, inevitably, someplace. We'd be at a truck stop buying food or something and then this old man with a beard and glasses would walk by. He'd always have a message for us that would be relevant to the trip or some kind of guiding bit of wisdom. So we had to watch for Dr. Van Denburgh, because what he was wearing would tell us things; what kind of vehicle he was driving

---

*Michael Arenson and Kevin Kilpatrick, eds. *A California Journal: A Selection of Essays and Images from the Journals of the Natural History Field Quarter Program* (University of California, Santa Cruz, 1988)

†See earlier footnote for information about Dr. Van Denburgh.

would tell us what the weather was going to be. If you actually got into a conversation with him, that was awesome. (laughter) So students were always trying to find Dr. Van Denburgh. It was great. There were those kind of ongoing things on every trip.

Reti: I bet you guys were quite a sight traveling around California in this bus, pulling into these little towns. Did you get weird looks?

Usner: Oh yes. We would get off and buy groceries in Barstow and everybody would be staggering around the parking lot, sleep-deprived from driving and playing hackeysack and buying granola. (laughter)

Reti: You really stuck out.

Usner: Ken was right in there. He led that whole experience. He would usually be really tired at first because he'd be trying to finish all this bureaucratic University stuff before he got on the bus.

Reti: Wasn't he the head of the department at that point?

Usner: He was for a time there. I remember he used to sleep in the aisle of the bus. He'd bring a pillow and a foam pad and he'd just lie down in the aisle and go to sleep.

I think at the Norris memorial celebration we'll hear a lot of really good, hilarious stories; and details about field quarter from Larry, who did it a lot more than I did. He's probably the most important person because he knew Ken and worked with him more closely and longer than anybody.

New Mexico

Reti: You live in New Mexico now?

Usner: Yes, north of Santa Fe.

Reti: In Chimayó.

Usner: That's where I came from. After ten years I went back, armed with all this stuff that I learned.

Reti: You went back to the community and landscape that is home.

Usner: Yes, it's been a real interesting experience. Hard in some ways, but I needed to get back to my roots. Ken was very, very fascinated and in love with New Mexico. In fact, I'll just tell you one story that really got me. It was one of these stories I was telling you about that he sometimes fabricated. But the true part is that his first job out of graduate school was to go to New Mexico and climb every high mountain and sample vegetation, because they'd done the nuclear testing and the cloud had drifted north and east. They were trying to see if they could trace the cloud by radioactive elements in vegetation on the moutaintops. He was seeing what was left in the residue in the vegetation. So he climbed all the peaks in New Mexico, thirty five, or something. He completely fell in love with New Mexico. We had this ongoing conversation because he was enchanted by it. He really related to me. A whole group of us from New Mexico came out here to Santa Cruz and became his students. Bruce Bannerman and Paul Rich, who is a biologist now at Kansas, and Sydoriak, and Tom Ribe and me and a couple of others came out and became friends with Ken and worked with him. We had this ongoing thing about New Mexico. Because he loved it tere.

He told me a story when I first met him that part of that research as a graduate student besides going up on peaks, was they had to determine if the cows had ingested radioactive grasses, and were concentrated in their gut. But if they went out and sampled cow pies they'd be getting radiation from the grass and not necessarily from the cow. They wanted to know how much was in the cow. So he had to go around and try and get samples of cow pies before they hit the ground. He said he followed cows around for an entire summer and had some kind of little tray. He said he studied and learned cow facial expressions so he could predict when they were about to drop one. And he would run over and quickly place this tray— (laughter) For the whole summer he only got one sample. I think that story was probably 90% fabricated. But I was like, really? Wow! What an interesting research problem. (laughter) He said, oh yes, and also, that this was top secret. That was why they didn't want the ranchers to know what was going on. He had a specially designed jeep that would come to fences and it had a device on it to cut the fence and the jeep tool would put the fence back together and twine it so it was virtually undetectable that you'd been there, see? But it was difficult because all these ranchers noticed jeep tracks going right across their property right through the fence lines.

Reti: (laughter)

Usner: Yes, the whole thing was totally made up. But I was—really? Wow! Another example was one time we were driving by Soledad Prison on our way to the desert. He was doing one of those monologues. He said everytime I drive by here I look over and I just imagine Sirhan Sirhan leaning over the fence waving at me. One of those crazy images he was always coming up with. One of the things I learned about him was that he was never morose or despondent about the destruction of the natural world. He was just the opposite. Be enthusiastic. Do good work. Be who you are. One of the things he would always say to me when I would say goodbye to him was, "Think good thoughts." That always stuck with me. One of the things that can happen to you in environmental work is that all you can think of is all the bad things, all the horrible stuff that's devastating the world. He wouldn't convey that kind of despair, which was really healthy. He was always engaged, and working towards understanding and doing something about it, not being despondent about it. Hard to do.

Reti: I wonder how he was able to maintain that. Because he must have seen so much of what he loved being threatened. He was obviously very aware.

Usner: I don't know. I guess he was so enthusiastic about doing something about it he overcame despair about it. Yes, he was a lot of fun. It's a much different world without him, for me, it really is.

Reti: Well, he's passed on a lot of that to all of you.

Usner: Yes, maybe. But I can't imagine not being able to go talk to him. It still doesn't make sense that he just could be gone. But it happens. To all of us.

Reti: Is there anything you want to add?

Usner: I was trying to think beforehand what I would say about Ken. He was so many things to so many people. I think what impressed me most, that I'll take with me more than anything else, was his heart. It's so ironic that that's what failed. Because he had the biggest heart. He was so generous. It just boggles my mind to think about. When I think in my life about the children and kids and people around me—I don't have any of my own kids, but my nieces and nephews—how he found so much time to give is just amazing. He had a life busier than mine by a factor of ten, yet he really reached out and took so many people under his wing, engaged with them and gave them his time. Phylly was such a part of Ken; as a unit they were just the most big-hearted people I have ever known. All the science, all the academics, all the teaching, were just a tiny subset of a great, warm, and giving humanness.

Reti: Well, thank you, Don.

Usner: Thank you. Thanks for doing this.

Shannon M. Brownlee

Meeting Ken Norris

Reti: To start, Shannon, would you tell me how you first met Ken Norris?

Brownlee: Well, I was his undergraduate student, to start with. I think Ken was the first adult person I met at UCSC when I came as an undergraduate in 1974. My father had met Ken and Gregory Bateson at Sea Life Park [in Oahu, Hawaii] when Ken was there. He said, "There are two people you have to meet, Ken Norris and Gregory Bateson." I only got as far as Ken Norris. I walked into his office about the second day of school, after orientation, and there was Patty [Patricia W.] Poodry, his former secretary, and her dog Tash, under the desk, and she made an appointment for me for later in the day. I walked in and I said, "Hi, I'm Mick Brownlee's daughter." He said, "Oh, that's wonderful. You'll have to be in my natural history class." I had no idea that this [class] was very competitive; it was very hard to get in. I just thought, oh, okay. And I got in. That was the beginning. Ken was just so welcoming, so quickly, it was clear that he was a very special person.

Reti: When did you go on Field Quarter?

Brownlee: I was on Field Quarter in the spring of my freshman year. I was the youngest person in the class. Of course I had no idea what I had stumbled into. I was a real pain in the neck because I didn't want to write anything; all I did was draw pictures in my journal. I did not write. Ken decided that that was okay, because I was expressing my observations of the world.

But what was really funny was I quit [school] my sophomore year, for a year, and then I came back. When I came back I decided that I wanted to find out more about dolphins. So I went to Ken and said, "I'd like to do an independent study. I don't know what I'm going to do, but what I want to do is come up to your house and read scientific papers, and I'll design an experiment at the end of the quarter. I'll come up with an experiment to test something about dolphins." He said, "Okay."

He didn't think I could do it because he thought I was an artist; he thought that I couldn't think scientifically. But I came up with an experimental design to test a piece of acoustic acuity in echolocation in dolphins. So he suddenly said, "Gosh, you know, you can think this way!" It was really a lot of fun to be allowed to come up to the house and spend time with him and with the science as well.

Natural History Field Quarter

Reti: Please talk about what it was like to be on Field Quarter.

Brownlee: It was incredibly fun and incredibly silly a lot of the time. I was saying to a couple of friends last night who were in the class with me, that we wish we could do it now when we are more awake to the world. Because then we were so busy being filled with emotional stuff, like, can I find a boyfriend? Those sorts of things. We weren't paying perfect attention, and Ken was always paying perfect attention; Ken was so still inside that he was able to perceive what was going on with each of his students and tailor the way he talked to you and the way he encouraged you, that really fit each student. But we were filled all the time with these internal dialogues that kind of obscured our ability to experience this amazing, amazing man, and these incredible trips. But, I blame Ken for the fact that I love California as much as I love my home in Hawaii, where I grew up. That was another connection with Ken, that I grew up in Hawaii, and in fact I was in the same class with his daughter Nancy. We didn't really know each other then. I love California in the sort of visceral way that I love Hawaii. No other place on earth compares to either of them.

Reti: Now you get to be homesick for two places.

Brownlee: And it's Ken's fault. It's all his fault.

Ken Norris as "a Basin of Attraction"

Reti: Yesterday, you were talking at the [Norris] memorial about the basin of attraction? I was really interested in that.

Brownlee: Well, it's a concept in physics that I don't even pretend to completely understand, but it's called the "basin of attraction," and it has to do with elementary particles. I always thought of Ken as a basin of attraction that you fell into; that if you were a little graduate student electron or undergraduate student electron, rolling around on the surface of the earth, you would all of a sudden tumble down the magical hole into Ken's world. It was a magical world with Ken. It was fun. It was incredibly fun to be around Ken because he was always silly. But he was also, always thinking about how the world worked. We would have these grand arguments about how, why, animals behaved the way they did; or whether sound propagates in a particular way, all surrounded with a lot of sort of silly stuff, on top of the science.

There was this freedom to express yourself with Ken. He could disagree with you without making you feel like he thought any less of you, and that was incredibly liberating for students. You didn't feel like you had to bow down to the ideas of the professor. Really, he was the first man, besides my father, who really took me seriously as a mind, as well as a woman. That was really, really wonderful. He was very, very unchauvinistic in that way. He adored women's ways of thinking about things as much as he adored men's ways of thinking about things.

Reti: In his oral history that we completed a couple of months before he died, he talked about how he conceived of himself as a caring uncle. He was really careful about boundaries with students, especially women students.

Brownlee: Yes. That was very liberating for women students. That here was this person who obviously cared deeply about you, but there wasn't a hint of anything that was threatening. I always thought of Ken and Phylly as sort of an extra father and mother. And a very good father and mother. They were sort of a magical father and mother because they were completely approving and completely nonjudgemental. You don't get that with your own parents.

Reti: That's so true. So you were on Field Quarter and then you went on to be a graduate student working with him?

Brownlee: Yes, after I did that design of the experiments. I never actually did the experiments. I would have had to procure a dolphin to do them. I never intended to do them. I simply wanted to learn how to think about an experimental design. I designed the experiment, laid out the protocol for the experiment, laid out the hypothesis and then didn't do it. But on the basis of that, Ken asked me when I graduated if I would come to Hawaii to work on his spinner dolphin project as a research assistant.

Before that, in my senior year, I did another project under Ken's auspices. I don't know if the name Roger Luckenbach has come up. Well, Roger was a former student of Ken's. I had taken a class with Roger and a couple of students and I conceived of this wacky idea that we wanted to go to the southernmost island in the Sea of Cortez and study a very rare endemic lizard. We wrote up this project proposal, got Ken to sign off on it as one of our advisors, and got some money from the President's Undergraduate Fellowship. Then we got in a Volkswagen van, drove the length of Baja, and did these observations. Now one of those students has gone on to be, I think, a professor of herpetology at Berkeley.

While I was there I got totally bored with lizards and decided to study vultures. Ken really liked the way I had put together this natural history study of vultures. When I graduated he asked me to come to the research project to do the acoustics in Hawaii, which was really insane, because I didn't know one end of a tape recorder from another. But he had this trust in people and he let you figure it out yourself. He basically gave you a broad goal and then he never micromanaged you. At least he never micromanaged me. He'd let me figure it out myself. That was part of the trust that he had in people. You know, he had misplaced trust, occasionally; he would have a student who just was a disaster and couldn't finish anything, and he would have judged wrong. But with the students that he judged right, he let us have our head.

Reti: Then did you go on and do your thesis with him?

Brownlee: Well, what happened was I came back from the research project and I was working as an illustrator and a computer programmer to support myself while trying to analyze the data, because there wasn't any more money on the project. I thought, this is ridiculous: why don't I just get a degree out of this stuff? So I entered the master's program. Then I found out that not only did I have to support myself, I had to take courses as well. So I analyzed the data while I was here, and that turned into my master's thesis.

Reti: You said something yesterday, I don't know if it was a joke or what, about how difficult it was to get him to focus on your thesis. You would go up to his house to discuss your thesis and you would end up moving rocks at the ranch or—

Brownlee: It was impossible. He loved to talk about science but when you had a real knotty problem that was not very interesting but you had to somehow solve something, I think he knew that you could do it yourself. So he would be very happy to talk to you but then pretty soon it would turn into a project where you would literally would be down at the creek helping him rebuild the spring box or up in a tree pounding nails, rebuilding a tree house, with Ken standing below saying, "I'm afraid of heights. This is what you have to do up there."

Reti: (laughter) Would you be talking about science while you were doing that?

Brownlee: Sometimes. But not a lot. Then eventually the evening would come around, you know, and after dinner you'd get around to talking about your thesis. It was just wonderful. I think some of his graduate students were frustrated by the lack of guidance. But I was the kind of student that if you guided me too much I got restless and chafed. So he dealt in a very perfect way for me. He let me do it myself. I have a three-year old now who says "I do it myself." And my mother says it's revenge.

Reti: How did Ken teach you to be an observer, a naturalist?

Brownlee: He didn't. I knew. I grew up in a family that was very artistic and very scientific. We always had aquariums. We always drew. My father's an artist. One of the things my father used to teach us was how to sit still by a tidepool in Hawaii and wait for the animals to come out. With Ken, on the Field Quarter, we learned how to be more sophisticated about it and also to think outside the boundaries of human experience.

Learning to Think Like an Animal

I think that's the thing that I really learned from Ken in that class, is to think about what it's like to be a bug and to be down in a little crack or a crevice in a rock when the wind is blowing. Now what is it really like for the bug at that level? Ken really taught me a very important principle about getting inside the animal to get a sense of what it's like for them, so that you can then ask the right questions from the outside. It's very interesting because in writing —this is translated into my work very perfectly. In writing about science, one of the things that really helps me is to think at the level of the molecules that I'm writing about, and what the world must be like if you're a molecule. Then I step back and write it as a writer. But for a minute I have to sort of get inside the cell and look around the cell to be able to then describe what's going on.

Reti: So you've gone on to be a science writer.

Brownlee: Right.

Personal Relationship with Ken Norris

Reti: Did you keep in touch with Ken?

Brownlee: Oh, very much. Every time I came to California I made the drive up Back Ranch Road and came to see them. I've been very close to the family for over twenty years. Well, I met Ken when was eighteen, so it's been twenty-four years. A long time, my whole adult life. I wrote to Phylly, and said to her that they have been incredibly important in my life, for more than half my life. So, they were pretty special.

Reti: Do you feel that Ken had anything to do with your ending up becoming a science writer? I mean obviously indirectly.

Brownlee: Well, indirectly. But unfortunately in a somewhat negative way and through no fault of his own. I quit science because I didn't think I could make it; at that time, I couldn't hear all the people telling me that I was really terrific at what I was doing. Including Ken. I couldn't really hear that very well. But Ken wasn't a woman. There were very, very few female professors at UCSC at that time. I didn't really like most of them. I mean there were really only three or four and I didn't want to be like any of them, even the one whom I really liked. I didn't want to be like her. I couldn't imagine how you could be a woman and be a scientist. I didn't think I had it in me to do it, to withstand the emotional difficulty of doing that. So I kind of chickened out of science.

At that time my father was very ill. I thought, even though he couldn't speak—he'd had a brain operation and he couldn't speak—I thought that he wanted me to be an artist. So the combination of not feeling like I could make it as a woman scientist, and this perceived pressure from my family to go into what my father did, made me decide not to go on in science.

Ken once said to me something. Later it was very funny. He said to me when I was a graduate student, "I don't know if you really should be a scientist. You're not monastic enough." I mentioned this to him about five or six years ago. And he said, "I wonder what the hell I meant by that?" But it really made an impression on me. It's interesting. Those kinds of comments can be very important in your life as a young person.

I decided to go to art school. I went to New York. I got a job with *Discover* magazine, oddly enough, and never went to art school. I just kept writing. I kind of fell into it. But in a lot of ways I was really prepared well by my experiences with Ken.

Reti: I find it interesting that you were the person who was drawing in your field journal, rather than writing, and now you are a professional science writer.

Science with an Artist's Eye

Brownlee: I find that interesting too! But one of the reasons that Ken and I had this really wonderful, special relationship, is he had the same sort of dichotomy in himself, where he was an artist at heart but he had to decide on art or science. We talked about that a lot, that the fact that we looked at the world with an artist's eye, had a great deal to do with being able to observe. Ken and I were able to stand in a boat and identify whales and dolphins from an incredible distance. I think it's because we both saw the animal as a gestalt, and could tell by just the movement and the blow and a little bit of fin, which animal it was. I think it was the artist's eye. Because you had to observe, you had to be able to observe it that way to draw an animal. It was second nature. Ken had this really wonderful artist's eye as well.

I'll tell you something about feeling as if you're the favorite one. I think Ken had an ability to make everybody feel as if they were his favorite. I always thought that I was his favorite graduate student. But I think that there are a lot of people who think that they were his favorite graduate student. That was really a knack he had, to make each person feel that they are absolutely precious to you.

Reti: Do you have friends whom you knew from that time of working with Ken, whom you've kept in touch with?

Brownlee: Oh, yes. It was really old home week yesterday at the memorial. There were lots and lots of old friends. I haven't kept in close touch with a number of them but here and there and Christmas cards and things like that. We've kind of dispersed. It's been a diaspora from Santa Cruz.

Reti: Many spoke about how Ken lives on in all of the people in that room who worked with him.

Brownlee: Yes. We're not a patch on him, but we carry little bits of him.

Reti: I think it was you who said that he didn't want little carbon copies of himself.

Brownlee: Yes. He absolutely didn't want carbon copies of himself. Ken's ego was not bound up in his students. Ken's ego was so solid; he knew who he was. He was quiet on the inside. He didn't have to bolster his ego with making his students be just like him to reinforce and reaffirm him, his goodness and greatness. He didn't need that.

"Sweet and Lumpy and Full of Nutty Surprises"

Reti: Would you talk a little bit about what you said yesterday about the rocky road ice cream?

Brownlee: I wrote this in a letter to Phylly and I stole my own phrase. Ken was so amazing. The phrase that I used was that in a world full of vanilla, he was rocky road. He was sweet and he was lumpy and he was full of nutty surprises. Without him, everything is a little blander. You know? He was (pause).

Reti: It's emotional, yes.

Brownlee: You know sometimes I wake up and I think he's there, and then I realize he's dead. It just seems impossible that somebody so full of life could not be alive.

“The Play Just Kept Him Going.”

His stories were so wonderful. And he was such a good liar! It was the pranks. You know, there was another scientist who was very much like Ken, Richard Feynman, who was a great physicist. There was a series of books he wrote. *Surely You're Joking, Mr. Feynman*, was one of them. He was an incredible practical joker and a prankster, always a prankster. He was the scientist who figured out that it was frozen “o” rings that brought down the Challenger shuttle. And this practical joking and all the silly societies. Ken had more silly societies. I was a member of the Santa Cruz Geographic Society, where our main aim in life was to transnavigate Nevada. Since Nevada doesn't have very much water, what we were going to do was carry water in a raft and pour it out in front of the raft; and then drag the raft along and then pour out a little more water in front of the raft and drag the raft along. We never did that, but they did navigate Elkhorn Slough, the wild and raging waters of Elkhorn Slough. You had to choose the name of a real explorer and then sort of twist it around. My husband became Sir Edmund Bill and Hillary. You had to think up things for the society to do. It was sort of like the regular geographic society without the money, and without the seriousness of purpose. Another one that he had was the Society to Inform Animals of their Taxonomic Classification, which is just silly. (laughter) I don't even know what that society did. I just saw the letterhead he had printed up for that one. He used to write me letters on that letterhead.

Ken didn't think authority and pomp were good enough reasons to respect anything. He was incredibly irreverent. He had a great respect for people as human beings and not much respect for the pomposity and little social structures that we erect to maintain our self-importance. If I really wanted to annoy him in an argument I would call him Dr. Norris, in a very sarcastic way: “Oh please, Dr. Norris. Explain that to me.” And he'd say, “Oh, I'm not a doctor. Nobody's got a broken leg!” His favorite story on himself was about a student who came up after one of his lectures about whales or something, and said, “Who cares, Dr. Norris? Who cares?” (laughter) He popped his own bubble as readily as he burst other peoples' bubbles.

That was part of his charm, but I really do think that the silliness and the play and the practical jokes and the incredibly outrageous stories that he used to tell were all part of his genius. Because he had a mind that could range anywhere. The play just kept him going. It kept his mind working all the time. It opened the door to bizarre possibilities. No idea was a stupid idea. There were wrong ideas, but there were no stupid ideas. That was an incredibly important part of how brilliant he was. He really was a genius. I made fun of him in my talk by saying that he liked to give talks without slides because he wanted to be unencumbered by data. He really was terrible at statistics, because mostly I think he was impatient with it. But he was a brilliant scientist. It was really extraordinary to be in his presence. It made you more confident of your wacky ideas. Because you never knew when a wacky idea would be the right one.

Reti: Sure. I mean, who would think that dolphins navigate by—

Brownlee: Right, by sound! Who would think that they hear through their jaws? Who would think that a spermaceti organ in a sperm whale was partly for amplifying sound to blast away at giant squid? I mean, who would think any of this? Who would think that clownfish would coat themselves in slime so that they could live in the tentacles of a sea anemone? There were just no boundaries to Ken's thinking. Just the way there are no boundaries to a child's play. I watch my three-year old son and anything can be anything in his world. A piece of lint can be a telephone, if he feels like it. For Ken, anything could be anything. The natural world was so astonishing that why should you limit the way you think about things, according to some sort of standard, human ways of classification, or of knowledge of the way things work. All kinds of things are possible. This is what all scientific breakthrough is made out of, is that somebody thought the unthinkable. And Ken was thinking the unthinkable all the time.

Reti: You said something yesterday about how the world often told Ken that he was full of beans.

Brownlee: Well, it did. Everybody thought that he was absolutely cracked when he told them that dolphins hear through their jaws. Everybody thought he was absolutely cracked when he told them that the sound came out of their foreheads. He said a lot of things that were just ridiculed by the standard scientific community.

Reti: And now everybody knows dolphins echolocate.

Brownlee: But see, that's always the way it is with really brilliant ideas. When you come up with a truly innovative thought you are by definition breaking down the carefully erected edifice of thinking and of science. Ken was constantly, constantly tilting at the windmill of science. The thing that allowed him to succeed is that he was an incredibly stubborn person. I think that people working for him found him impossible sometimes. He was wonderful to relate to if you were a graduate student because you didn't have to actually make him do anything, or keep him on a budget or anything like that. But he said, I want to do X and I'm going to do it. He had a saying that I never heard until last night but it absolutely comes out of Ken's mouth, "It's easier to beg forgiveness than it is to get permission." As every three-year-old knows. He just set his sights on what he was going to do and what his ideas were and he barreled through all obstacles. Now, he also was wrong a lot. And he was very quick to say that he was wrong.

I know how stubborn he could be. He would get ideas into his head and it was very difficult to shake them loose. But it wasn't because of an emotional attachment to his ideas. It was because he just really thought that he was right. If you proved him wrong he admitted he was wrong; if nature proved him wrong, he let go of the idea instantly. Nature always had the last word. And he let that be, he always let that happen. He always went back to nature and said is this right? Is this idea right? That's what every scientist has to do. But an awful lot of scientists get so emotionally attached to their ideas because they don't have very many. So they have got to prove the one that they've got, the one little precious idea that they've got, come hell or high water. Well, Ken knew that ideas are a dime a dozen. He always knew that he could go back to the drawing board and get a new one if he was wrong. You just had to work pretty hard to convince him he was wrong.

One of the lessons that I took away from him I had also learned from my family which is: ability and talent and brilliance will always take you through. So just be good. Just be good at what you do. Do your best and don't worry about anything else. Don't worry about getting tenure if you're a professor. Simply do your absolute best. Publish a lot and your abilities will shine through. Now I don't think that that's actually true, but that was Ken's philosophy, and it absolutely worked in his case.

Reti: Well, as you were saying earlier, being a woman involved a different set of challenges that he never faced.

Brownlee: Right, in an era where there was infinite money. He started in science when the space program had made science king. Vannevar Bush had made his big push to fund a whole series of science agencies. The National Science Foundation sprang up in the 1940s and 1950s. Scientists were flush with money in those days. He lived in this wonderful, sort of rarefied world at the very beginning. It got more difficult as he got older, but he had established himself by then.

Natural History Field Quarter

Reti: Can we go back and pick up on the Natural History Field Quarter? How formative an experience was that for you? Or was it more working with Ken as a graduate student over a period of time?

Brownlee: Well, it was all formative.

Reti: I know you wrote me when we first talked and said, "Be warned. I was only on Field Quarter in 1975."

Brownlee: Yes, spring of 1975. Yes, it was a long time ago so it's hard to remember. Just being with Ken was formative, more than anything.

Reti: It was the whole picture.

Brownlee: It was the whole ball of wax.

Reti: There're all these little Field Quarter jokes, like Dr. Van Denburgh.

Brownlee: I never knew about Dr. Van Denburgh. That was after my time. Well, Dr. Van Denburgh was before my time in that Ken and his pals had seen Dr. Van Denburgh. But it wasn't that big a part of our field class. It became a part of later field classes. Because we were one of the first in 1975. We were really very early in the evolution of how the class worked. It wasn't really the Field Quarter, although we ended up taking all the same classes. We took the Natural History of California with Ken; California Geography with Ray Collett; and then a class with Stanley Cain. And in fact the Field Quarter ended up being constructed of that.

Reti: Was Ray Collett also involved with Field Quarter?

Brownlee: No. He didn't come on the Field Quarter. Ken took these various resource people. One of the people he took was a psychobiologist whose name I forget who I think was really shocked by the behavior of students on Field Quarter. Because we were pretty wild and loose in those days.

Reti: I heard some stories yesterday about running naked down sand dunes and—

Brownlee: Well, yes. I have this image of Ken standing buck naked along the Tuolomne River with his fishing creel and his boots, his fishing creel in a strategic location and his boots. That's all he wore. That's all any of us wore was our boots, to avoid getting bitten by snakes. It was a really amazing time. You wouldn't find that now, in many places.

Reti: No, I don't think so.

Brownlee: I think you'd still find it on Field Quarter. But it's a rarity that you find that in universities anymore.

Reti: Yes. Did you guys have a reunion?

Brownlee: We did. We had this wonderful Field Quarter reunion that Larry Ford organized, of course. Larry is really, really stricken by losing Ken. He's been instrumental in organizing this tribute to Ken.

Reti: Was there anything that you want to add?

Brownlee: I think I didn't recognize how special Ken was until I was out of graduate school. I just kind of took him for granted as an undergraduate and as a graduate student. It was only later when I went off to work that I started to realize how special a person he was. It was really funny because it was only when I read Ken's obituary in the *New York Times* that I suddenly realized that this man whom I adored, and had so much fun with, and was just so close to, was also an incredibly important person. Phylly and I were talking about the fact that we don't have any pictures of Ken. You don't take pictures of fixtures in your life.

Reti: You don't think they're ever going to be gone.

Brownlee: No. I have almost no pictures of Ken except when he married my husband and me. We have these pictures from our funny little wedding ceremony up at the house.

Reti: I heard that he married a lot of students.

Brownlee: Oh he did. He married a lot of us. He got worried about it, because a lot of us got divorced. But by the time I was ready he knew I'd waited long enough. I'd found the right one. But I never really acknowledged, I never really formed in my own mind, the image of him as a very important person. And that's partly his doing, because he really did break down those kinds of barriers between himself and other people at every opportunity.

Reti: Right. He didn't want to be Dr. Norris to you.

Brownlee: No. He just wanted to be Ken. And I was Shannon-san. Because in my field class there was another girl from Hawaii, Beth Shiki. She was Shiki-san and I was Shannon-san. We danced the Tahitian. And we were the members of a dance troupe in our group called the Trashettes. We made Ken an honorary Trashette, even though the only dance he could do was the hokey-pokey.

Reti: That was so great yesterday, everybody at the memorial doing the hokey-pokey.

Brownlee: Yes. We did the hokey-pokey at my real wedding. We had the little private ceremony when Ken married us and then we had a public ceremony and we did the hokey-pokey and Ken participated at the big ceremony.

Reti: That's fabulous. One of those pictures on the board yesterday, I think was of the hokey-pokey. There were a bunch of people dancing in front of the bus.

Brownlee: Oh yes, we did the hokey-pokey everywhere, in front of the bison, we did it for the bison. We did the hokey-pokey at every opportunity.

Stephen R. Gliessman

Reti: To start with, Steve, how did you first get involved in teaching the Natural History Field Quarter?

Coming to UC Santa Cruz

Gliessman: Well, I think it was Field Quarter that had a lot to do with me even getting hired here at UCSC in the first place. I was working down in Mexico at the time, teaching in a school of tropical agriculture. Some friends had seen an announcement for a job at UCSC for a plant ecologist, a specialist in California vegetation, which I had been trained in, working with some of the best folks in that area, down at UC Santa Barbara, where I did my undergraduate and graduate work. They sent it to me. I'd been out of the country for almost ten years. I think they got me into coming back. I looked at the job description and I thought, well geez, that's not what I've been doing for the past ten years. But down at the bottom of the announcement it said something about experience in managed ecosystems. Since I'd been doing agroecology for almost ten years I figured, well gosh, maybe they'll see that and see my past and it could turn into something. So kind of on a lark I sent it in.

Reti: This was in what year?

Gliessman: That was 1980. I guess just after Ken had completed a couple of years as chair of the board of environmental studies. I think he had a lot to do with the job description and was looking for somebody to help him on the plant side with the Field Quarter class. The field class was in its third or fourth year with the fifteen-unit structure. He tried different people on campus and off campus, and hadn't been totally satisfied. So he finally got a job description that he thought could help fill that position. I'm not exactly sure how I got chosen for an interview. Partly, I guess they saw my background in agroecology and at that time, too, the [UCSC Farm and Garden Project] Farm was kind of struggling. They were very close to shutting the whole thing down, from what I understand. So I guess several people on the board saw that maybe I could kind of cover both things.

I came up and I remember my interview seminar was actually a talk on agroecology. I got real excited about that. I remember talking to Ken during the interview process and he kept questioning me about, well would I be able to help him on the focus with teaching and natural systems and Field Quarter and all that. I said, well yes, I'd love to do that stuff. I'd be interested in continuing agroecology as well. Well it wasn't yet called agroecology here; it was just The Farm.

Reti: There was no pathway in agroecology at that point?

Gliessman: No. There was a course offered in principles of small-scale agriculture, and ecodevelopment and those kinds of things.

Reti: Ray Dasmann was doing a little bit of that.

Gliessman: Yes. But there was nothing else. I think the other thing that really swayed Ken was who my advisors were, and their recommendations; they were some of the best-known plant ecologists and botanists in California. So I guess that helped a lot. They offered me the job. As soon as I came here—I got here the first winter quarter 1981—I taught my first agroecology course. Then the second quarter I taught my first Field Quarter class, but actually Ken was on sabbatical, so I taught it with Maggie [Margaret H.] Fusari, who'd never taught it either and our TA was Larry [Ford]. He had been a TA for the course and kept us all headed in the Ken Norris direction. I know that teaching it that first quarter, I just fell in love with it. It had the focus in botany and ecology that had gotten me into that field originally as a student. So God, I thought, Yes, I could keep being a student and get paid for it. (laughter) The next year I switched agroecology to the fall and kept Field Quarter in the spring.

The next year I taught it the first time with Ken. It really went well. From there on we did it together every year, for gosh, I guess ten years, until he retired in 1990, which was his last year.

Reti: So you're the main Field Quarter person now, still teaching it?

Gliessman: Yes. If I weren't teaching it I know we wouldn't have it any more. Every year it's a struggle, getting the funding together, organizing the logistics of moving twenty-three to twenty-six of us around the state, making sure the field stations are open and the vehicles are available and the gear is all together and all that stuff. Pretty limited budget. It's gotten more difficult since they retired our bus.

Reti: Yes, I was going to ask. You're not using the Old Blue bus?

Gliessman: No. It got retired; the campus just decided that they weren't making enough money on it; there wasn't enough use. We used it all spring quarter and paid a lot for it. But they said it wasn't enough. It sat there too much of the time and it was too hard to maintain. It was getting old. I said, okay, if you're going to get rid of it, then let's get another one. But they used a couple of different arguments. First, the Americans with Disabilities Act, and the fact that if they got a new bus it would have to have all this expensive access stuff on it; and second, there wasn't enough use. I think it's mostly the lawyers, as Ken always used to say, worries about liability and all that stuff. I worry about the liability. We used to be together in one vehicle with me driving, because I had a bus driver's license from the very beginning so we didn't have to pay a driver, because that's the main expense. Larry always had his bus driver's license. TA's always had their bus driver's license. [W.] Breck Tyler, with whom I now teach Field Quarter, he has his, so we could drive the buses.

Reti: So now you have a couple of vehicles?

Gliessman: Now we have to get three or four vans and sometimes the drivers maybe aren't all that alert. You always worry when somebody else is behind the wheel. We're transporting ourselves around the countryside. But we do it. We get there. Even though we don't have the bus, things carry on quite well.

Working Relationship with Ken Norris

Reti: So how did you and Ken develop your working relationship? Did you split up Field Quarter as to what your roles were?

Gliessman: Yes, because it was really fun for me, my specialty being plants, Ken's specialty being more the animals, although he was truly a natural historian and very knowledgeable about all parts of the environment. Yet I could bring that plant side in much greater depth, and I had my own way of doing it that seemed to complement the way he did it. Our styles were kind of complementary too, in that Ken's was much more—he liked to call himself sometimes the uncle figure.

Reti: Yes, he referred to that in his oral history. He said he was the caring uncle.

Gliessman: Yes, I was more the younger kind of faculty member. I had to go through my process of getting tenure and setting up my research focus and doing all that kind of stuff that you've got to do around here. So he would kind of be the more fun spirit. I always had fun, too, but I'd hang back a little bit, watch, observe and at the same time be there to complement, to be a counterpoint. I was very comfortable in that role. Being able to observe Ken on the Field Quarter and soak it in and absorb it and watch how it worked over the years affected my whole approach to teaching as well.

My approach had always been more of a sharing with the students what I knew and what they knew, back and forth. Ken was a master at that. I think this came out of the upbringing I had as a graduate student, especially where my faculty advisor was a lot like Ken although he was not nearly as joyful. He never told me what to do; he just sort of helped me figure out what I wanted to do. So when you chose what to do you felt like you'd made a real choice which was really important. That's something I've always tried to do in how I teach; I direct and advise by asking my students what they're interested in, what are their passions. I hoped to encourage and help and stimulate people to follow that, as you do so much more when that's what's tied together. That was always Ken's approach and our approach in the Field Quarter. A lot of times I would be the one worried about logistics. Had we made our reservations for here? What time were we supposed to be there? Did we have the vehicles? You know, who was going to take care of this that or the other? I kind of carried that role so Ken didn't have to worry about it. And I'm not sure he ever really did anyway.

Reti: There definitely needs to be somebody who's got his feet on the ground about that kind of stuff.

Gliessman: It made a lot of difference to make sure everything worked and stuff was there and we didn't have to worry about it, so the rest could just happen.

Reti: It seems like a tremendous endeavor to take twenty-three students around California.

Gliessman: You have to make sure everybody's safe, that nobody falls off a ledge or whatever. You constantly think about it and worry about it but we've learned ways over the years, too, to caution folks, to let them know just how privileged we are to be in this course, and how important it is not to jeopardize it. There're a lot of little internal things about safety and communication and responsibility and all that we keep hammering in. If somebody blatantly disobeys some of that kind of stuff, well, those were some of the few times I could really see Ken get sort of a little steamy under the collar. He could really get upset when somebody jeopardized themselves in a way that then would jeopardize the whole group and even the ability of the whole Field Quarter to continue. Because we were out there on the edge. Yes, but thanks to Dr. Van Denburgh it's all worked out over these years with all these different groups.

Dr. Van Denburgh

Reti: I have a little bit of an idea from Don Usner about who Dr. Van Denburgh was, but—

Gliessman: Well, he's the patron saint of Field Quarters.*

Reti: You would look for him wherever you went and see him in different forms?

Gliessman: Yes, you don't have to look. But you have to be aware. Because he shows up at the most unusual times and he usually carries some message of something to be watching for, to be careful of, or to be alert for. Something new you might see. Often times he helps keep us from getting lost. He helps us with the weather. A bunch of different things. It's pretty remarkable what happens. He was in his own way, early on, quite a naturalist; he worked all over the western United States and sometime in the 1920s wrote a two-volume book on the reptiles and amphibians of the western United States. It was such a thrill when I finally I discovered his books. We were on Field Quarter over in the northeastern part of California in Modoc County and through there. We were actually over there looking for a new site for a reserve, doing resource surveys, looking at habitat types scattered around because that was a part of the state that didn't have a reserve at that time. I think it was 1985 or something like that. We went to Eagle Lake. At that time there was a little field station on the east side of the lake that belonged to Chico State University. They would do field trips up there. There was a little research station, too, that had a little library in it, things related to the area and California. That was one of the places we spent a couple of nights. I was wandering around in the field station and here was this bookshelf and I looked right in the middle and there it was, his two-volume set, *The Reptiles of Western North America.* That was really something to see that. I didn't even know that he had published. Ken had known but he hadn't said anything about it. I'm sure Ken had read a lot of his work because he had worked so much on the same kinds of things, and was a specialist on the reptiles and amphibians of the western United

*See earlier footnote for information on Dr. Van Denburgh.

States. I guess he'd read some of the earliest observations on distributions and patterns and where these things occurred and all that, were done by him. Hence, Ken being a naturalist as well, must have read a lot of his work and carried on from that.

I'm not sure how the story evolved of how Dr. Van Denburgh went to the next level of wherever we all go after we leave, wherever Ken is now. But he told us a story about how Dr. Van Denburgh in his later years had continued to work at the Cal[ifornia] Academy of Sciences. That's where he'd been employed. He was curator of the part of the museum that dealt with all those kinds of creatures. Every day people saw him come to work, and he was a formal person, almost English in the way he went about things.

Reti: Like one of those old English naturalists?

Gliessman: Yes, with the suit and coat and vest and bowler hat and a little umbrella cane kind of thing that he carried with him in case he got caught in the rain. All that stuff. They just noticed that for a couple of days that he wasn't showing up, and he was always there every day. Never failed. I guess somebody happened to go way down into the lower reaches of the collection, down in the basement somewhere, the place where they kept things, like a canoe and some big tortoise shells and stuff like that. They noticed his bowler hat and cane sitting in a corner and started looking around and of all things, inside one of these large land tortoise shells, they found his remains. He was inside there, all curled up and when they lifted him up out of there he was almost weightless. There was nothing left except the shell. Ken always said that he hadn't really died, he'd just etherealized. He'd moved on to another world and left behind what he couldn't take with him.

He began appearing in different forms to us in the Field Quarter. At first, according to Ken, nobody could see him but Ken. After awhile he began to make himself known to others. Ken would always say you need to watch real carefully. He was always in a different form. It wasn't the formally attired Dr. Van Denburgh that he'd been in true life; the form he took in his new state was usually an older man with a white beard, white hair. Sometimes his beard could be very white and short, sometimes it'd be very scruffy and dirty and streaked with tobacco juice, or whatever. There was a range. He could be fat; he could be thin. Dressed in different ways. But all of the ways he made himself known was the way he communicated to Field Quarter. If he was all bundled up and wearing a rain jacket, that was the message to watch out for rain. If he was wearing a red hat and a red shirt, you could count on some pretty hot weather ahead. I remember one time we were up north of Chico trying to find a road to take us up into the mountains. We were going down a highway and on the other side, hitchhiking in the other direction, he was standing there, all dressed in blue, with a long white beard. I looked over at Ken and he looked back at me and he said, "Yes, we're going the wrong way." So we finally found a place down the road to turn around and headed back. When we got to the spot where he had been hitchhiking he was gone. But sure enough we had been heading in the wrong direction and that was his way of telling us that we were.

Reti: And then you found the road?

Gliessman: Yes, then we found the road we were supposed to be on. Things like that.

Reti: Is he still appearing even though Ken's not teaching the course any more?

Gliessman: Oh yes, most definitely. Sometimes you'll see him several times, sometimes you might only see him once. But as I mentioned, I think we'll probably start seeing him in pairs now.

Reti: I bet you will.

Gliessman: Anyway, that's the story.

Miss Prim

Several times in the manuscript of his book, *Beyond Mountain Time*, Ken mentions another person who was part of Field Quarter, Miss Prim. She was our librarian who traveled with us. We have a mobile library that goes with Field Quarter; it's several big field locker-type wooden boxes full of field manuals and guides to the regions. We have some things that travel with us all quarter long and other things that we take out or put in, depending on where we're going. Resource surveys, maps, floras, faunas, guides to this, that and the other. It's all kinds of great stuff to have in the field. We used to carry a camping tent we would set up at each site where we'd set up the library. Miss Prim took care of the library. Again she was a person you referred to, but you never actually saw, although Ken said he would see her occasionally. Very proper, hair up in a bun, typical kind of old librarian.

She finally retired. I think it was because the tent finally wore out and we didn't have a place to keep the library anymore. He always made comments about her; he'd say you better take care of that book or she won't let you check it out anymore. She's watching. Or he'd say she told me you'd left the book out overnight in the dew or the rain, whatever. He'd always refer back to her as an important person in the group.

Field Journals

Reti: Tell me about the students' field journals and what the requirements were for keeping them.

Gliessman: Yes, we better get serious here soon.

Reti: At the Norris memorial Dan Warrick sang a song about how you would get mud and bugs and everything on the journals.

Gliessman: Well, before we talk about how the journals— There was a part of Ken's teaching that I found wonderful. Sometimes he would really in all seriousness explain something, and this was especially towards the beginning of the course, he would talk about, say, why a particular geologic formation was where it was, or some historical fact about the landscape or some little town that we drove through, what its history was and the little bar he used to go in there when he was doing his field work, or something.

You always believe what your teachers say. He would do this in a very serious way so that it sounded very, very reasonable and truthful. He wouldn't let on a lot of times, at least at the beginning, that he wasn't telling the truth. He was just telling a story. He would do it on purpose because he wanted the students to not just accept everything he said. This was a way of getting them to realize that, after a while, that there would be another little phase, a little later on, where sometimes they couldn't tell if he was telling the truth or not. The things that were truthful were just as outrageous as the things that weren't, which is how nature can be. The only way to find out was through observation. Going back and testing it with further observation and then interpreting it. I always found that was a wonderful way of giving the students more responsibility for what kind of information they would take in and believe. It was a way for them to test, to become critical. He'd then reach a point later on in the quarter where he'd start backing off. He didn't have to be as outrageous as he was. But he'd still do it. It was always great fun. I loved it. Some of his stories were great. I get to tell some of them now.

He was always very serious about wanting the students to do their best on the journal. Because the field journal really was the core of the course. We didn't have exams. There wasn't a term paper. But the journal was something that grew and developed and evolved over the quarter. There is a systemic way to do a field journal.

Ken was brought up in the Grinnell school of natural history observation and journal taking, which had very strict rules, prescribing the size of the paper, the line that separates the margin from the text, the heading and what's in the heading, where you put your date and your location, and whether it's an observation or a species list, or a specific place where you stay for a period of time. When traveling across the landscape, the field notes helped you to capture what you saw. Ken would keep stressing over and over again how important it was to capture it all.* Because the journal was your way to then go back and see what you'd seen, to evaluate it, to interpret it, and then ask more questions about what you'd seen. So you could then, as he would say, go back to the organism for more answers. But the organism is always the authority and the only way you can get at those answers was through observation. He really worked hard at letting people know that you had to let down your blinders of how you saw nature. You weren't filtering it through your own way of seeing; you were trying to place yourself in that organism or on that mountain side, in that place, at the same pace of time that that place was experiencing. So that you saw through what you were looking at, rather than through your own eyes. It's a real fine art. He and I would learn if students were doing that by reading their journals, and then giving them feedback constantly. Collecting a journal at the end of the first trip, sometimes even halfway through the first trip, we read and commented on it, made suggestions on what to develop, what to look for more, how to keep from getting too intellectual about what you were seeing rather than actually seeing it.

A lot of things just take time. At the beginning students struggled with it; they tried to capture everything and ended up capturing nothing. It's important too, to keep a chronology, a log, of where you go and what you see. But it's also important to just sit down and spend a period of time with an organism.

---

*Larry Ford wrote about Joseph Grinnell: "He was Director of the Museum of Vertebrate Zoology at UC Berkeley in the early years of this century. He is regarded as one of the fathers of modern zoology, especially mammalogy and ornithology. His field work and efforts to directly observe nature are legendery, driven by the desire to discover and record the animals of California. Among his many conservation efforts, he is known for his searches for hard-to-find species and his writings against the introduction of non-native mammals. Ken Norris described to his students Grinnell's meticulous methods of recording field notes, and demonstrated why these methods helped to both clarify the process of field observation itself and enable accurate reference to those observations in the future. Grinnell's legacy includes the discipline required of the many subsequent naturalists and field scientists, including Norris's and Steve Gliessman's natural history students, to take careful notes and spend their evenings catching up on their daily journal entries. Many brilliant careers in writing and natural science were born of those first few lessons in Grinnell's methodology in UCSC's Natural History Field Quarter."

We stressed with them, too, that our course was a little difficult in that we are covering a lot of distance. We were doing a lot of things that made it a little more difficult to capture it all, to get it into the journal. A lot of times at the end of the day, sitting there for a couple of hours around the lamp, or whatever light one had, students were trying to catch up. If you didn't catch up that night, then you had two nights to catch up on. If you didn't write for several days you might get a a week behind. We kept stressing with them how important it was to capture their observations in the moment. Because what you capture while you're looking at something is so different than what you capture later thinking about what you were looking at. It just changes it completely. Students go through a transition: at the beginning it's more important just to get the structure of the journal down, to get the discipline of writing in the journal down, rather than exactly what they write about. Once they get that part then we started moving on to the actual way of writing, what they were seeing and how they were interpreting what they saw, and what it all meant. So it's a process.

We'd also do the journal notes and then an observation series in which the student spent a couple of hours in one place with an organism or one location and this got the students to, again, as Ken would say, move beyond the threshold of boredom. And all of a sudden, once you were able to do that, time is irrelevant; all kinds of things started to appear that you weren't seeing before.

Reti: Yes, I would imagine that one could get overwhelmed once you start seeing in this way. I'd be afraid my journal would just be this wild description of everything.

Gliessman: Yes, and sometimes it can be that way but then sometimes it's really interesting to train yourself to look at one organism. That's again where Ken had an uncanny ability of always putting himself inside that organism.

That's another way of saying, getting beyond the threshold of boredom: because suddenly you're not bored anymore because you are that organism. Then you can't be bored. And it's not easy to stay in that place, especially if the thing sits there and doesn't move for a half hour.

Reti: It seems like a kind of meditation.

Gliessman: It really can be. You're capturing a lot of things. You're spending less time with any one thing and spending more time with all of the stuff that's out there, and capturing it. And there's a time for that. And there's a time to sit down and, as Ken would say, one of the first steps of being a good naturalist when you're in the field is to get comfortable.

Reti: How do you do that?

Gliessman: Well, each person does it differently, I guess.

Reti: Do you mean physically, in terms of how you are sitting and whether you are cold?

Gliessman: Right. You can't be barely hanging off a cliff and make a good observation because you're worried more about whether you are going to fall off the cliff, rather than what the organism is doing.

Reti: How do you think that Ken had that ability? Was it something he was born with?

Gliessman: I think Bob [Norris] stated it well, yesterday, you know about how they had been brought up and the effects of both of their parents on them. I remember him talking a lot about that. Because it was just always from when they were the smallest kids. These folks would just walk the Santa Ana River bed, or wherever it was, just looking at things. They went out to the desert a lot, as a family. They would just pile into this old car and go out there where most people never went. Ken showed me the place and the old fire scar on the rock where the family camped when they first went out there for several years.

Reti: In the Granite Mountains?

Gliessman: Yes. It was just around the corner from where the Bunny Club ended up being. But they didn't know then that the spring was there, so they didn't camp there. They were at another place where it became their family spot. It was unusual to just go out and camp in the desert then. It was something Ken grew up with. How he developed his sense of observational ability and all that, being able to see nature, I don't know. But I've seen other people develop it, train themselves to do it.

Reti: That's what you were trying to teach?

Gliessman: That's the whole point of the course, Yes. It's something that can be learned.

Reti: Maybe it's something we know as children.

Gliessman: Curiosity is the foundation of it. Ken used to talk about that, how important it was to almost become a child again. It was real easy for him to do that. He did it all the time. He would encourage the same thing. Sometimes I would feel, almost too much. In some groups we'd get carried away with it.

Reti: With the playful aspects?

Gliessman: Yes. And I'd kind of have to say, "Ken, it's time to get back to work." He'd say okay. But he himself knew when it was going too far and would just say, "Okay. It's time to get serious again." Before you knew it Field Quarter would be over, and all of the opportunities that you'd had were over as well, so you wanted to take advantage of as much as you could the whole time. It is an interesting balance between just plain having fun and learning, but again, it was always Ken's feeling that if it wasn't fun it wasn't worth doing. No matter what it was. That was really the philosophy of his life and it was the philosophy of Field Quarter.

Reti: Did you ever have problems with students thinking that they were going on Field Quarter to just have a great time, travel around, spring quarter?

Gliessman: Sometimes. Yes. But we wouldn't just let that happen. If we saw it happening we'd pull them aside. We'd talk to them, explain what we were seeing. They'd hear it. They'd get it. Today we learn pretty well how to judge if someone's going to work out or not, when we do our application process. We always have more people apply than we can take.

Reti: Do you have an interview as part of that?

Gliessman: Yes, a lot of times we have interviews, we'll find out what the students are interested in, what their background is, where do they want to go with it, all that kind of stuff. Generally I think that works pretty well. I think our sense now over the years has developed pretty well as to who would be a liability out there.

Reti: I was talking to somebody who'd been on Field Quarter awhile ago, and she was saying that for her it was really difficult to be in a group for ten weeks, with twenty-three people. She loved Field Quarter, but she was going through a lot of that insecurity.

Gliessman: Oh, everybody's different in a group. Some people are right out in the front, making a lot of noise. Other people are in the background listening. I read a piece yesterday from a student from last year's Field Quarter, but it could have been from any Field Quarter. The opening paragraph was that she started out worrying that I wouldn't remember who she was, because she wasn't one of the boisterous Field Quarter students who was always right out there in front. She sort of hung back, was quiet, but wanted to share this experience she'd just had with me. Of course I remembered who she was and recognized that that's who she was, and that was her style. Something that happens in Field Quarter is that, and I learned this from Ken, too, we really developed some sort of connection with each of our students. In a way that brought out the ones who were hanging back and reined in those who would have a tendency to take off. Part of it was maybe an aspect of collaborative learning, cooperative learning, of how you share, how you learn in a group. It's very important, and in fact, by the end of the quarter you realized you've learned as much from each other as you had from the instructors. That's a pretty powerful realization too, the way we organize it.

So writing the journal really was a big piece of the class. There was lots of feedback all the way through the quarter, between Ken and me and the student. The journal was divided up into sections. One section was always a log, the chronology, setting the stage for each day's entry. Students answered questions such as, what are the conditions? what's going on? where are you? what's happening at that place? what do you see?

We also asked them to do an observation series. On each trip, two or three times, we made sure they had an opportunity to sit down and spend time in one place with one organism and really to go into detail, which is a different experience. We also asked them to keep a species list for each site, of what they were seeing. Students' references to different species as they first appeared in their journals ended up as species logs, a whole collection of what students had seen in a place such as the Granites, a species list—all the plants and animals. In those lists we asked them to write the common name, the scientific name and some key characteristics distinguishing each species. To be able to make those entries the student had to be able to identify them. You couldn't just ask; you had to learn the skills of identification, which come from close observation and the use of guides to the flora of California, field guides to the birds, to the mammals, to the reptiles, whatever. The students began learning what particular aspects to look for, in order to distinguish between species, which is all wrapped in the observation process as well. So observation and identification really are linked, they have to be. But the goal was not just to be able to identify, but also to observe behavior: what is it and what's it doing? Why is it doing what it's doing? Why is it where it is?

What's it going to do next? And on and on. The students got wrapped up in asking questions about what they were seeing. Rather than asking a question and then sitting there and trying to answer it, the student couldn't answer it until he or she went back out and did more observation. In that process the organism became the authority; it had the answers and then it revealed those answers through further observation. Ken always believed that that kind of training was essential for being a good field biologist, a biologist of any kind, that you had to ask the questions in the context of the organism in its whole environment.

Reti: In its environment, not divorced from it?

Gliessman: Yes, and you can very easily miss what's happening, or not ask the questions that are most important. But I think it became pretty clear in some of the presentations yesterday at the memorial how Ken used that in his own work.

Student Presentations

Reti: Would you talk about the students' presentations?

Gliessman: The presentations were part of our goal of getting them to realize that they were as much authorities as we were. They could learn things in an area that they hadn't worked in before and learn to share information with others in the class who didn't have that information. So for a moment they were the authority. It taught them how to gather information, condense it down to a ten-minute presentation, and have it come across well. They would get experience in standing up in front of the group.

Reti: Ken said in his oral history that he was shocked that there were students who had never done an oral presentation in their university career.

Gliessman: That's right. But by the time Field Quarter was over you wouldn't believe the quality of most of the presentations and the confidence that they'd built up and how so many of them could go on doing things like that when they'd never done it before. It's an amazing skill to develop. It's an important one too, if students are going to be the change agents we need to speak for the environment, to be stewards of it, and to help create change so that we can protect it. They are the ones who are going to do it and a lot of them are doing it. Most obviously. We would work with them after a presentation and try to explain ahead of time what to do and how to do it. It was always information that helped increase people's knowledge about the place we were in. Rather than just have an assignment in a reader—okay, here's the reader for the Mojave Desert and there's a section on geology and a section on plants and a section on animals and issues and all that. Read it. No, we wouldn't do that. What we'd do instead is we'd break the class up into four groups. One of them was a cook group for that trip.

Reti: All they would do is cook?

Gliessman: That's all they would do. They'd buy the food, prepare the menus. They'd cook. And oh, that was always a great adventure. Wonderful stuff.

Reti: I heard some of the food was pretty bad.

Gliessman: Oh no. Rarely. Rarely. Ken always—

Reti: I guess it was Ken who said it was the dreadful food. (laughter)

Gliessman: Well, Ken always used to like to joke about the vegetarian fare.

Reti: So it wasn't really bad?

Gliessman: Oh no, he used to just like to make noise about it. Sometimes it would flop. I mean cooking for twenty-five people is not an easy task if you've never done it before.

Reti: Oh no, you could burn everything or—

Gliessman: Yes, sometimes it didn't work or didn't cook on time, or whatever. But those were the exceptions rather than the rule.

Reti: So there'd be one group that would just do the cooking.

Gliessman: They wouldn't have to do presentations. They'd do everything else.

Reti: They'd still do their journals.

Gliessman: Oh yes. They did everything else. Sometimes it was a challenge to be the cook group. But we always set it up so that they would get up early in the morning, have the breakfast stuff all laid out, which was usually not something you had to cook unless there was hot cereal—it wasn't eggs and bacon and all that kind of stuff; it was stuff you could put together very quickly. And then at breakfast, all the fixings for lunch would be laid out as well. You'd make your lunch in the morning, along with breakfast, and then carry your lunch with you. There would be no food put out the rest of the day and so the cook group could be in the field all day. But they'd have to be back in the late afternoon, or early evening and put the dinner together for that night. But then that would be the only time they'd do it because we would usually divide the cooking group into four sections during the quarter. So each group would get it once. The other three groups would be divided into presentation topics. They'd vary a little bit but it was usually a flora group, a natural history of animals group, and then a group that talked about the environment and the history of that area. So there'd be presentations on the geology, or the geologic history, or the Native Americans or the history of how the reserve was formed and what were some of the current problems or issues they faced and how they're trying to solve those and manage them in the future.

Reti: I need to clarify. So each time in the field would you be at one of the [UC] natural reserve sites?

Gliessman: Usually. Especially for the first three trips. The desert, Santa Cruz Island and then right now—we used to go to Big Creek. But we've switched now. We go up to Mendocino. Ken started going up there. A new reserve was formed. It's got really excellent facilities, on a river, old growth Douglas Fir forest, spotted owls, all kinds of good stuff that you get down at Big Creek too, and it was kind of a hard choice to do one or the other, but over the years we've ended up, probably for budget purposes more than anything else, going to fewer places but spending more time at each place. When I first started teaching, gosh we'd go to six or seven places. And often times a couple of days just out and back down to the little barange or the bolls on the San Benito Mountains down behind Hollister. Just for the day or two days or three days. Well, it got to the point where getting vehicles together for all that, it just got too expensive. We couldn't do it anymore. If we could just get to a place and stay awhile it was a lot easier. At the same time the facilities at some of the reserves were changing and evolving. When we first started going to the desert, the only place to stay was the Bunny Club. There was no reserve. It hadn't been established yet. All it was was the Bunny Club. The main reserve headquarters was a private ranch, as was the camp that's now named after Ken. We were stuck in the middle of that. We had to be careful we didn't go onto the private property when we wandered up into the mountains. The rest was BLM land, open land that they were part of. Thanks to the fact that the Norris family had the Bunny Club the Field Quarter class had a place to stay in the Granites.

But meanwhile, of course Ken was negotiating with the BLM and the ranchers and doing all this stuff to get the reserve set up. Every year was a little different. And finally, there was a six-thousand-acre chunk of land that belongs to the University, the reserve research center, all kinds of stuff. So we ended up with really nice places to be able to stay that we didn't have before.

Santa Cruz Island has always had a fairly nice operation. It's a University reserve and we've used that. We started going out to Santa Cruz Island the first year I taught because I'd done part of my thesis there as a graduate student, knew the reserve manager and the island. So we started going out there and it became an integral part of Field Quarter after that. We've gone every year since. We also camped down at Big Creek and hiked around and it was our only real backpack trip.

Reti: Oh I see. So it wasn't always camping. Somehow I got the idea that it was all camping.

Gliessman: No. Not always.

Reti: So when you're talking about facilities you're talking about some kind of a lodge.

Gliessman: Oh, I'm talking about a bunk house, places to sleep, a kitchen, maybe even some hot water for a shower. That kind of stuff. Because that evolved too, and this was happening even before I came, but continued to happen after I got here. Ken used to say that it was important to get to a place, to get comfortable, and then get to know the place, rather than having to worry every day about packing up your stuff and where you were going to camp. You ended up spending so much time just taking care of yourself that it actually took away from your ability to do the natural history you wanted to teach. Not that you can't do it that way, and we always tried to have some opportunities for that. But it was a lot better just doing day-trips out from a central place where we could return at night. It just worked better. When they finished the reserve up there on the Eel River, up at Branson, it was an old summer lodge kind of thing for folks from the Bay Area, taken over by the Nature Conservancy, and then handed on to the University as a reserve. We go there now. Now the last trip of the quarter has always been one that has more camping. By that time we're ready to camp; we've formed a group, we've developed the skills, all that kind of stuff is moving. We used to go and camp just below Hetch Hetchy Reservoir on the Tuolomne River and then go over to the White Mountains and stay at the Forest Service camp.

Reti: At Grandview? But you don't do that anymore?

Gliessman: Yes, we're still going there. And again, when I first taught Field Quarter, the first year one of the students in the class had worked with the [Save the] Mono Lake Committee in its early days and they had camped at the property belonging to a woman above the lake, called Dejambeau Ranch, Dejambeau Creek. She had refused to sell to Los Angeles. So it was still one of the last little pieces with water running through it and aspens and meadows and everything. There was an incredible view out over the lake. You could see the sunrise coming up over the White Mountains. It was just a wonderful, magic place. So we decided to take her up on her offer for us to come there whenever we want and we've gone there practically every year since. We stay there for five days. We also go to the reserve location at the Sierra Nevada Aquatic Research Labs (SNARL), which is near Mammoth, across the highway from the air strip, if you know that area. On Convict Creek. It's an old USDA fish lab that they took over in the late seventies. The manager, who has been there ever since, has done an excellent job of fixing it up; got money from the National Science Foundation and built a bunk house, a kitchen operation, so we started staying there. But we usually stay there for just a couple of days in between Mono Lake and the White Mountains. Then we go from there up to the White Mountains where we stay for five days, doing all kinds of neat things up there. That's traditionally where we ended. That last picture of Ken and me that I showed [at the memorial] was taken up there on the mountain above Grandview. That was actually taken on the last night of the last Field Quarter we taught together.

Reti: I was looking at the book A *California Journal: A Selection of Essays and Images from the Journals of the Natural History Field Quarter Program.* You have those pieces written at the Grandview campground.*

Gliessman: Right. Yes, it was nice that Michael [Arensen] did that book. Then we'd take the bus home after that. We've experimented the last few years, sometimes going to the White Mountains first and then coming back to Mono Lake and ending there instead. It's actually a little more comfortable now being at this little ranch there on the lake because we're alone. We're not in a campground. We're not surrounded by people. During the last few years the White Mountains have really become much more heavily used.

Reti: I noticed that. I was up there just a few weeks ago and I was shocked at how many people had been up there since the last time I had been there.

*Michael Arensen and Kevin Kilpatrick, eds. (University of California, Santa Cruz, 1988).

Gliessman: Did you go up to Schulman Grove and see the Visitor's Center they put in?

Reti: Yes. That's new, isn't it?

Gliessman: Oh, it's brand new. It's been open since the spring of 1997.

Reti: Oh, I didn't realize that. It looked really new. I hadn't been up there for about five years.

Gliessman: Oh, it's a just a lot more people. It makes it a little more difficult for us to be alone up there for our closing few days, which is kind of important. So the last couple of times we switched it around. We'd go all the way to the White Mountains, a long drive. But then we'd work our way back and end up at Mono Lake. As long as the "no see 'ems" aren't too bad at Mono Lake, it's a good place to end up.

By the end of the class I noticed Ken always became more reflective, more observant of the students, how they'd evolved and changed during the quarter. They were ready to launch forth. They were eager to do it. But it was always hard to break up the group.

That gets me back to something I was thinking earlier on, about Ken being that uncle figure. That's part of it, but I don't think it's all of it. I think a lot of it was the relationships he developed with the students that created such trust, such caring back and forth, that allowed a lot of things to happen in a normal teacher-student relationship. All that good stuff could take place because that trust was there. Ken always valued and treasured that closeness because it created a different learning environment where the process of learning was being shared rather than directed.

Reti: Is that something that you've brought to your more traditional kinds of classes?

Gliessman: Yes. I know I have. At least I've tried to. The damn place is pushing us towards numbers. It's so big that you just can't develop these relationships as easily. I teach agroecology now with a hundred students. I go to the labs, all four of them, with twenty-five students, because I need to get that closer interaction with them that I can't get in the big lecture room. So gosh, I'm doing twelve hours a week of just labs. But that's all right. That's what's important—to bring that in.

Reti: It seems that UC Santa Cruz really was founded for that kind of faculty-student relationship.

Gliessman: Yes. That's changed considerably. But it is a key part, not just to Field Quarter, but to teaching in general, it's part of it. You see Ken did it all the time. He gave me lots of opportunity to learn how to do it, too. It was always fun how Ken would stay in touch with Field Quarter students. He had an uncanny ability. I treasured it. I wish I could do it but I just can't remember people's names years later. He had ways of connecting them to something in his mind. And it was always fun at the beginning of the quarter how quickly he would learn the students' names. He had ways, either a nickname or a feature, or a characteristic that allowed him to connect to that person. Then it stuck. I try and I try and I try. And some do, but a lot of them I can't. I think partly it's just because there are so many of them.

Reti: Well you've had eighteen years of this now.

Gliessman: Ken did, too. He had eighteen altogether. I guess it was in 1975 or 1976 when the Field Quarter became a fifteen-unit class. It had been going on for maybe four years as a fifteen-unit class when I got here. It was already in that mode.

Reti: You've got an entire generation or more of people who've gone through Field Quarter.

Gliessman: Yes. It was interesting at the memorial. There were some folks from some of my first Field Quarters there and, yes, they've changed.

(laughter) Of course I have, too. There were some pictures that I would not have dared show in that group yesterday that catch the more free spirit side of Field Quarter.

Reti: Yes, well I can imagine. I mean there were some pictures there in the display that were pretty wild.

Gliessman: Oh, I didn't get over there to see those.

Singing Sand Dunes

Reti: The running down the sand dunes naked stuff. Don Usner was telling me that story yesterday. It's a great story.

Gliessman: It's a wonderful story. Climbing up on the dunes, getting a sense of the dunes and then how much fun it was to get them to sing. But the experience of making the dunes sing and having your skin completely in contact with the sound while it was happening—there's nothing like it in the world! The effect it has—you're immersed in the sand while this hum starts.

Reti: You can actually hear it?

Gliessman: Oh yes.

Reti: So you don't need the tape recorder.

Gliessman: Oh no. No, you not only hear it, you can feel it. It's a vibration and depending on how fast the sand's moving it will be at different pitches. You can hear it from a distance. I've actually been sitting on the dunes in the midst of a big sandstorm, where the sand was just pluming over the top and then down the slip face on the other side, in such amounts that it was creating these big slips of the sand, and as it would start to slip, it would start to sing. It's just fascinating, fascinating stuff.

Reti: Why is it that those particular sand dunes sing?

Gliessman: Oh, Ken used to just explore that one forever.

Reti: There's probably an hour-long explanation there. (laughter)

Gliessman: Lots of things about stacking order and shape and composition and all this kind of stuff. Yes, neat stuff. Not all dunes do it. Kelso was one of those that did.

Reti: It's fairly uncommon?

Gliessman: Yes. But what an experience. It was always planned we wouldn't go out there the first day we went to the desert and do that. We had this whole process of getting the group to form, to become comfortable, to become trusting. Then the opportunity was there and usually, not everybody, would jump in the sand. It was fun. It's not something you can explain.

Environmental Politics

Reti: Getting back to the human side, I was thinking about the coming together of cultures. Here you were with this group of UCSC environmental studies types, and you're out there in some areas of California where maybe people are very different than who you might encounter in Santa Cruz, at least for the most part. How did you deal with the cultural differences? So often in environmental studies the question comes up: does the environment include human beings and how do we deal with those differences?

Gliessman: Something we always tried to do at those sites, and we still do it, is whenever possible to have people from the different organizations or institutions, those responsible for managing or protecting or using those areas, to have them come and talk to us around the campfire in the evening. We'd hear from the forest service, the Nature Conservancy, the Bureau of Land Management, the Natural Reserve System, or others from the areas we visited. Each one of them presented their different viewpoints about what needed to be done at a site.

Before that happened we'd already educated ourselves about the history of the area, the changes that had occurred over time in setting up a reserve and managing it. We'd learn about the weaknesses and the strengths and what became clear very soon was how much impact an individual can have. Like right now, out in the desert the park service is a big player, because they've created the Mojave Desert National Park. The University Reserve sits right in the middle of it, when before it was surrounded by BLM land. Dealing with BLM people was very different than dealing with park service people. In fact sometimes we think maybe we'd like to go back to dealing with BLM people. (laughter) For instance, right now the director of the national park out there seems to be on this personal campaign to make this her crowning accomplishment and seems to be very unwilling to talk to or deal with the University and make UC a partner in protecting that land. Instead she has her own ideas as to what the University ought to be doing out there. The reserve managers have worked really hard and it's very frustrating at times to try and maintain the things that we feel are important for the integrity of the reserve itself, within a national park. So getting students aware that that is the way it is, and that this person may transfer, may retire. You may suddenly be dealing with a different superintendent and the whole thing could change. You hear that from the reserve managers and begin thinking, this is a human thing. The park service has a different mandate than the Nature Conservancy or the BLM or the U.S. Forest Service or whatever, as to what they believe it is they are supposed to be doing, and how it's legislated. The park service emphasizes use by the public while the BLM encourages grazing and mining. The park service's mission is to protect, but to allow people in. You run into the same stuff on Santa Cruz Island right now. We deal with the Nature Conservancy, the park service, the University, the private sector, etc. So we always give the students an opportunity to think about that.

I've watched our students role-play, trying to put themselves in the position of some of those different points of view. It's one of the things we encourage them to do in their presentations. When they're talking about the management issues in this area they take on the role. Take it honestly. They try to understand why those people take the positions they do, and to be honest about it, even if they don't agree. They try to represent another point of view and by doing that, it's amazing what they learn about their own ways of thinking.

Reti: Kind of like putting yourself in the place of that bug.

Gliessman: Same kind of thing. It was always one of Ken's major strengths. I know I'm not as good at it as he was—his ability to communicate with just about anybody. It was that same skill. It was why he was so successful at convincing people to give money for a reserve or for a marine station or to trade a piece of land, or do something. Or even convince the administrators of the University that a reserve system was a good idea in the first place. Sometimes out on the mountainside you'd hear him really say what he felt. He could do that, too. (laughter) But he'd just say it and then move on.

The Future of the Natural History Field Quarter

Reti: Well, is there anything else you want to add?

Gliessman: Yes. I remember when Ken retired, he expressed to me concern about whether the Field Quarter would be able to continue. He had a little bit of worry, a concern whether the class was too dependent on him and he didn't want it to be. He never wanted anything to be dependent on him, which was another wonderful trait he had, of being able to let things go and let other people take them on, even if they didn't do it exactly as he had. He was a little worried that Field Quarter would suffer the same fate. He'd had a real hard time with the Environmental Field Program and not being able to get the University to take it over. He tried and tried to get funding, to get other people to take it over so that it could keep going. That whole program got funded under graduate research. The Environmental Field Program was a wonderful program. Finally he just had too many things on his plate and decided that was one of the things he couldn't do any longer, and it shut down. I guess if I hadn't been so wrapped up in agroecology I might have tried to take it on, but I couldn't. I had other things I was doing. He was concerned that that might happen to Field Quarter as well. But I was, of course, committed to keeping it all going and to do whatever I had to. I remember the second year I actually taught it all by myself, all fifteen units, and Breck Tyler was the TA.

Reti: The second year after Ken retired?

Gliessman: Yes. The first year after Ken retired Maggie Fusari and I did it together. And it worked pretty well. It's just that Maggie wasn't as comfortable in whatever roles we'd set up and I guess, maybe I was learning to move from being in the background to being in the foreground of the course.

The second year I did all fifteen units and Breck was TA. But he actually was a teacher, or at least I became aware of just how wonderful a teacher he was and how he was in that same tradition as Ken. So after that year he became the other faculty member, and has been, pretty much ever since. A wonderful, wonderful teacher. I feel lucky to be able to work with him.

But I did have Ken. He was in the desert doing some other stuff that second year, while we were out there with Field Quarter. He came to the group and spent a day in the field with us and a night around the campfire, talking. Everybody was sitting around listening and saying, oh gosh, there's Ken Norris. It was wonderful. I could see that Ken would like to have stayed with us. He was just being himself like he always was, and it was just great. At the end of the quarter, we always have a party, kind of a farewell. Kind of like we did last night. It almost felt like a Field Quarter party. Ken was there. I had asked him to come. He was wandering around, talking to people about the quarter and how it went and watching them, and seeing the dynamic of the group after the whole quarter long. It was like all of them had always been before. Ken came up to me and I remember him saying this—just looking at me— (pause)

Reti: It's a really emotional thing for everybody.

Gliessman: Yes. He came up to me and said, "Hey Steve-o. It's working."

Reti: Oh, that's great.

Gliessman: Yes.

Reti: You're carrying it on.

Gliessman: And it allowed him, too, to be able to walk away feeling good, to say, hey this thing's got a life of its own. It's going to continue and work. We did kidnap him one time a couple of years after that, and hauled him out to the desert so we could stay at the Bunny Club with the class one time. That was pretty fun. It wore him out, but it was great.

Reti: Well thank you, Steve.

Gliessman: Yes, thank you. So it will continue, as long as I've got anything to do with it. That spirit will continue. When I was in Mexico I got to know an older ethnobotanist whom everybody called *maestro*. If you translate maestro it means teacher. But it was rarely used to address a person as their name. Oh, he was a *maestro*. It was one of respect, of awe, of trust, of all kinds of things wrapped up together. A true teacher, through not just the way they taught, but who they were, what they did, how they lived. Well Ken was one of those types. A true *maestro*.

Photo by Norden H. (Dan) Cheatham

Appendices

APPENDIX I:

Remarks from the Kenneth S. Norris Memorial

UC Santa Cruz, October 24, 1998

Lawrence D. Ford

Fifty years ago at the other end of Monterey Bay John Steinbeck asked, "what are we going to do without him?" upon the tragic death of Doc Ricketts, the legendary marine biologist and eccentric character in Steinbeck's books. Refer to the appendix, "About Ed Ricketts," which was originally published in the 1951 edition of *Sea of Cortez* by John Steinbeck and E.F. Ricketts. Now I wonder the same about another great biologist and eccentric on the shore of the bay: what will we do now that Doc Norris is gone? How will we fill the great void in our hearts and imaginations left by Ken Norris? Who will offer that cheering advice, the reference letter, the amazing idea, the far-sighted initiative, the illuminating observations of nature, or that hilarious story and song?

Many years ago, I thought I was one of perhaps ten people who regarded Ken as their most important mentor and colleague. I soon learned otherwise, but it wasn't until I helped plan the memorial celebration of Ken that I discovered there are hundreds of us. How could one professor have such profound personal impact on so many, and nearly at the same time? How did he make the time for all of us? Ken's personal mentoring represents one of the most enduring measures of his greatness, perhaps greater than his teaching, research, and institutional successes.

Once I asked Ken how to be an effective teacher and leader. We often had deep conversations about such subjects as we piloted the bus on long trips with the Natural History Field Quarter. Ken gave me three answers. Ken's first answer was simple: the secret is love. He said that love is the ingredient that transcends method, dogma, and other tricks; love means that the students and assistants feel trusted and free to explore their own creativity. They respond with love and will perform creatively.

Ken described how he nurtured creativity in his students and assistants by carefully crafting the learning or working experience to be safe, fun, and free of divisive forces. All that before the "sermons," detailed lessons, and high expectations. Students can also provide that nurturing environment for their teachers, and colleagues for a creative leader, he thought. To cultivate creativity and effectiveness, we should get out of the way of the creative person—let him have his foibles, listen to him, honor his choices, let him express his ego and ideas, and "clear the decks" for him with trust and competent help. Ken maintained that this was the most rewarding approach to teaching and to creative collaboration.

The third answer was about staying focused on the most important goals. A look around at Ken's great influence on the lives and accomplishments of his students and colleagues, at the many wonderful people he collected around him, and the great university institutions he built, shows just how this strategy worked. Ken never stopped making time to advise me on professional decisions or reassessments. I remember many times while I was employed to help him manage the Environmental Field Program and Big Creek Reserve at UCSC when I complained like a child that Ken did not appreciate my work enough. Then Ken would patiently explain how to improve another professional skill, how the bureaucracy worked, how donors could feel engaged by our projects, and how valuable I was. Soon I learned that Ken relied on me to take responsibility wherever I saw the need, which included making mistakes. Ken ignited in many of his students the creative motivations to cross the "threshold of boredom," which marked the internal transition from known worlds to exciting explorations of unknown worlds. I hope to keep the flame lit. Recently when a major job did not work out for me, Ken offered some poignant advice. He said that taking risks to achieve great goals meant exposure to "peaks and valleys" including difficult problems. He encouraged me to keep taking those risks and to need help in doing so.

In 1990, on the occasion of Ken's retirement from UCSC, his former undergraduate students established a fund for Ken to use in support of the great learning opportunities that he had initiated. The fund grew to be the Kenneth Norris Fund for the California Natural Environment, which supports the UC Natural Reserve System. Ken was immensely proud of the fund, and he used it to leverage strategic planning and successful fund-raising for an endowment that will help to assure the future security of the NRS in its roles in nature conservation and the field sciences for California.

I think we know the answer to Steinbeck's question. Doc Norris lives on in his inspiration of us and the many happy memories we carry. Ken left us several challenges: to have fun in our work; to creatively engage our colleagues as he did with us; to nurture the habits of curiosity, critical thinking, and caring that he practiced so faithfully; and to build and advance great institutions like those he founded Ken's happy model is to build our unique lives in our own ways so that we can be as creative and devoted to great purposes as he was.

M.R.C. Greenwood, Chancellor, UCSC

I stand before you today, feeling an array of complex emotions. I am personally honored and deeply moved to have been asked to begin this tribute to Ken, who gave so very much to this campus and community. But I am so very saddened by our great loss. Today we want to draw strength from each other in our recollections of this extraordinary man. It is most appropriate that this tribute occurs on the campus that he helped to shape during his twenty-five years—years that were his most productive as a researcher, scholar and builder of programs. Indeed, Ken put his body, soul, enormous energy and personality into shaping many of the UCSC programs that we all enjoy today. Only seven years after the first class arrived on the campus, Ken was hired by our biology department to help shape its programs in organismal biology and ecology. He did this with great creativity and wisdom and helped to mentor and guide the careers of a multitude of graduate and undergraduate students as well as faculty colleagues, many of whom are here today to share in this tribute.

Realizing the great need for an academic program in environmental studies, Ken then turned his efforts to helping to develop this program. He was keenly aware that the development of this interdisciplinary program required the cooperation of faculty from both the sciences and the social sciences, and he worked tirelessly to assure that these groups became symbiotic.

Part of his efforts focused on establishing the Environmental Field Program that has provided unparalleled opportunities for undergraduate research experience in ecology and environmental biology. During his time here at Santa Cruz, he continued to help develop the UC Natural Reserve System that he helped begin while an assistant professor at UCLA.

Today, Ken's dream of establishing and protecting land tracts throughout California for the study of ecological systems, has resulted in an unparalleled system of thirty-three reserves, encompassing over 120,000 acres. In recognition of his role in its inception and development, the David and Lucile Packard Foundation recently awarded 4 million dollars to the UC Natural Reserve System to establish an endowment fund that has been named the "Kenneth Norris Endowment for the California Environment."

But a dreamer and doer's work is never done. Recognizing the importance of UC Santa Cruz as a world leader in ocean science and marine biology, Ken was one of the driving forces for the creation of one of the first UCSC Organized Research Units. This ORU was originally named the Center for Coastal Marine Studies and only later expanded its scope to the open oceans and assumed the title as the Institute of Marine Sciences.

This vision of Ken's has led to one of the best marine research programs in the world, which includes over thirty-six faculty, thirty postdoctoral research and more than a hundred graduate students. Its research facilities and instrumentation are some of the best in the world, including the on-campus analytical laboratories and the world class Long Marine Laboratories.

Ken was a catalyst in conceiving the vision of what is today one of the most important marine laboratories in the world. Along with other faculty and staff, he hammered nails into dry wall, did electrical wiring, and plumbed the early seawater tables to give birth to the first humble laboratory.

Ken's ability to share his vision of what this humble marine laboratory might one day become, inspired its benefactor Joe Long (whom many of you remember) to endow this laboratory. Now, nearly twenty years after inception, Ken's marine laboratory will be supported by a wonderfully generous gift by the Packard Foundation. This gift will establish a Center for Ocean Health which will help consolidate many of our educational and research programs and provide them the space and infrastructure required by modern science. I only wish that Ken could have seen the completion of this project, as well as the opening of the Marine Discovery Center. Ken so generously shared all his visions and himself with all of us—and we, and generations to come, have been shaped and improved by him in so many ways.

Robert M. Norris

Despite what Ken may have told you, he wasn't born in Angkor Wat, but in downtown Los Angeles. The family lived at the time in a duplex on 2nd Avenue just off West Adams Street. Our parents both had an interest in the out-of-doors and they surely conveyed an interest and some knowledge of nature to both Ken and me. From the time Ken was quite small, but able to take short hikes, Pop would take us on short walks in the nearby Santa Monica Mountains at Griffith Park. We had moved from the 2nd Avenue house to a new house adjacent to Fern Dell in Griffith Park and had many chances to see and hear about animal life in the relatively undeveloped mountains. Later on, when Ken was a third-grader, we moved out to the San Fernando Valley to a house almost at the foot of the mountains, so there were still more opportunities to get acquainted with nature.

When Mom was a young woman she spent a great deal of time with her close friend, Rhoda Rindge, whose family owned the Malibu Ranch. Mom and Rhoda rode horseback over the ranch hills and canyons and got well acquainted with the plants and animals of the still rural ranch. Pop, for his part, was a dedicated camper, fisherman and hunter and often went on outings with his close friends. Both parents taught us outdoor lore and how to identify many plants and animals we encountered on our explorations. They were never upset when we bought snakes, lizards, or bugs home.

In addition, our maternal grandfather, John Matheson, who ran a clothing store, had a fine library and very wide interests. His library included classic literature, philosophy and the sciences. When he died in 1929, we got much of his library and among the books Ken and I found most interesting was the three-volume set on introductory physical and historical geology by Chamberlin and Salisbury, then the standard college text. Another of his books had a drawing of a giant octopus wrapping its tentacles around a rowboat full of terrified fishermen and shortly before his death, Grandpa gave us a twenty-volume set of the *Book of Knowledge* that Ken and I used all through school. No matter what the scientific subject that interested us at the moment, be it astronomy, geology, reptiles, butterflies or electricity, we could find something of interest in the books we had. The semi-rural nature of the San Fernando Valley in the 1930s gave us many opportunities to learn about everything from raising chickens and ducks to collecting butterflies and shooting sparrows with our Daisy BB guns in a nearby wash.

Another shove toward careers in science was provided by a wonderful character who taught chemistry at Van Nuys High School, one Jehiel Shotwell Davis. Mr. Davis and his wife would take the Science Club on extended outings as far away as the Salton Sea. Ken loved these trips and caught some of

Mr. Davis's great enthusiasm for science. On one occasion, which Ken often laughed about in later years, was a report he did for Mr. Davis on mineral crystal systems. Ken had read something about minerals crystallizing in six different systems, each characterized by plane faces but different geometry. It then seemed to Ken that there ought to be a spherical system as well, so he included that in his report. Mr. Davis evidently accepted this notion without question. Later on, when I went to UCLA as a chemistry major, I became aware of some lack of rigor in my high school course, but there was never any doubt that that course inspired enthusiasm for science and nature.

During his junior high years, Ken collected lizards and brought them home. On one occasion he decided to keep his lizards in his dresser drawer. Clothes were removed and a layer of sand was put in the drawer. For a time all went well and Ken tended his lizards, but eventually, he began to forget about them until one day, when he was out of the house, Mom came down the hall past my room where I was studying. She said she had smelled something funny in Ken's room and enlisted my help to find it. In due course, the drawer with sand and two or three decomposing lizards were discovered and some new rules about keeping pets in bedrooms were instituted.

After Ken graduated from Van Nuys High School in 1942, he went off to UCLA as a geology major and enrolled in the Navy ROTC program in order to get as much college work completed as possible before being called to active duty. I don't remember whether he switched to zoology or not before he was called up, but he went on active duty as a junior officer on a big navy personnel transport in late 1944 or early 1945. When he returned to UCLA in the fall of 1946, he was a zoology major. He continued after getting his bachelor's degree as a grad student under Ray Cowles and did a major study on the sand dune-inhabiting lizard *Uma* that Ray Cowles said would have been a good Ph.D. project.

While I was doing what is now called a "post-doc" at Scripps in the fall of 1951, Ken came to La Jolla to work under Carl Hubbs and moved in with me and my roommate Dave Poole. I will close with one of my favorite "Ken" stories. Dave and I had gone north to the Los Angeles area to see our respective girl friends over the New Year holiday. I had left Ken with the keys to my 1928 Chevrolet so he could attend a big party somewhere near Escondido.

After he started out, in this old car, it began to rain heavily, and while driving very slowly on a country road, he was followed by a highway patrolman who eventually pulled him over. The cop came to the car after having watched Ken traveling about fifteen miles an hour. Ken was dressed in a suit and tie which further puzzled the officer. "What are you doing?" asked the cop. "Before I tell you, give me a sobriety test," said Ken. "Okay, you're sober, now what in the hell are you doing?" "I'm looking for salamanders that come out during the first good rain of the season," said Ken. "And just what are salamanders?" said the puzzled patrolman. After Ken told him, he shook his head, and dripping wet, got back into his car and drove off to find a real drunk.

William N. McFarland

We met at an intellectually exciting time of our lives, as beginning graduate students at UCLA. Ken was enthralled with reptiles and working toward his master's degree under Professor Ray Cowles. I was into fish. In looking back I realize how fortunate I was to cross paths with Ken at the formative stage of our careers—for it led to a long-term friendship and scientific bonding that was most significant to me, and I hope also to Ken. Ken to me was "Kenuto," and I to him was "McFoo," our handles being symptomatic of the gentle irreverence we both felt about aspects of society, having both just stepped out of World War II. Reverence about society clearly was directed at science, for at the time it was the answer to living life. Ken's master's thesis, "The evolution and systematics of the iguanid genus *Uma* and its relation to the evolution of other North American desert reptiles" was published in 1958 in the *Bulletin of the American Museum of Natural History.* The study is insightful in that it reveals early on how Ken would approach scientific investigations throughout his distinguished career. Although the title implies an evolutionary approach to the fringe-footed lizards of the southwest deserts, the work is filled with comments on the natural history of the sand dune ecosystem, a topic on which Kenuto continued to think deeply about at least until New Years Eve day of 1997, the last time we were together. Even though Ken focused heavily on the animal under study, he always wanted to know how the animal meshed with its habitat. He was thus as much an ecologist as naturalist.

After finishing his M.A. at UCLA Kenuto moved to Scripps Institution of Oceanography to work on his Ph.D under Dr. Carl Hubbs. His chosen topic dealt with how sea temperatures might play a primary role in the life history of the California opaleye, *Girella nigricans*. It was during his stay at Scripps that Ken met Phylly. I guess it was love at first sight for they were soon married and moved back to L.A., when Ken, as a grad student, was offered a job as the first curator at Marineland of the Pacific, then under construction. I emphasize that there were few assistantships available to grad students in that period, (1953-54), so one had to look outside the University to make ends meet. Ken hired me as biologist-chemist.

At Marineland our friendship blossomed. There he built the icthyothermatron, a very long fish tank separated into adjoining compartments held at different temperatures. Opaleye were introduced and then their temperature preferences at different growth stages determined. It became his Ph.D thesis and was published in *Ecological Monographs* in 1963 under the title, "The Functions of Temperature in the Ecology of the Percoid Fish *Girella nigricans* (Ayres)." For the excellence of his research on fishes, as exemplified in that paper, Ken received the prestigious Mercer Award from the Ecological Society of America. The paper truly represents how one can synthesize information by using well-documented field studies with the experimental approach to tease out the interaction of animal and environment. Ken was, if not ahead of his time, certainly a leader in the flourish of comparative environmental and physiological studies that issued in the late 1960s.

Marineland of the Pacific was a telling experience for Ken. As a scientist and unusual persona, what developed in Ken during those years at Marineland? What hidden strengths were honed into sharp focus? Can anyone really characterize Ken the scientist and person in a few words. I think not. But each of us can emphasize, at the least, what we saw in him and what we learned from being with him. From my perspective Ken was first and foremost a "functional naturalist." He had a driving curiosity about *what* each animal did, and *how* it managed to *do it*. When we were watching an animal in nature—say a dolphin or whale—he would say "McFoo, think like that whale, be that whale." Ken could do that, blessed with the vivid imagination and sound intellect that he possessed. Ken in an uncanny way just understood what his animals were doing and why they did it. With his marvelous gift for writing he transposed those insights into the beautiful scientific prose we all have come to know. Although I am sure that somehow a "naturalist gene" snuck into Kenuto's genotype, it was as a graduate student, and especially due to his experiences at Marineland of the Pacific, that his particular flair for natural science crystallized into the scientist and person we all know and cherished.

Ken loved life and was fascinated with the people who surrounded him. He had a strong influence on his colleagues, but drew strength from each of them as well. One such individual was Captain Frank Brocato, head collector in the early days of Marineland. Frank's experience as a commercial fisherman gave each of us an understanding of marine life that we could never have learned at the university. The knowledge Ken assimilated from interacting with Brocato and Ken's management of animals at Marineland mostly was applied and gave him a real feel for practicality. In my opinion, Marineland was the underpinning experience that Ken later translated into developing the University of California's land reserve concept. If you have not read *The Porpoise Watcher*, do! For in it Ken describes his formative years at Marineland, with a flavor that describes both his reverence and irreverence for the world that surrounded him. Certainly we will miss him and, for me especially, the glorious discussions about "meaning." But his writings live on, and a bit of his spirit resides in each of us who had the privilege to be around him. For me what began as the camaraderie of graduate students, flourished as a life-time friendship. We shared the creative joy of simply doing science—asking questions and trying our damnedest to "be that animal."

Samuel Ridgway, Senior Scientist, Navy Marine Mammal Program

Three score and fourteen years ago, the Earth was given Kenneth Norris. I would like to say, Phylly, that I was privileged to know him for almost half that time. To me he has been colleague, advisor, collaborator, and hero. He has been so to many others in the marine mammal field.

Already the leading cetologist, Ken Norris, along with friends Carleton Ray and the late Bill Schevill, tackled the whale problem in 1971. Leading up to that time, Ken had discovered the vaquita porpoise with William McFarland; discovered with his Ph.D. mentor, Carl Hubbs, that the Juan Fernandez fur seal was extant; with Tom Lang first demonstrated the swimming speed of a trained dolphin in the open sea which made the cover of *Science*; along with John Prescott and others, Ken proved dolphin echolocation; and with Bill Evans, its directionality. Ken also established the first measurement criteria for small cetaceans. With his experience at Marineland

and after, he established the scientific basis for observing small cetacean behavior at sea. This work has been carried on and expanded by Ken's disciples such as Pryor, Gentry, Wells, Würsig, Johnson, Dohl, Connor and others.

Ken loved his sheep, the males and females, the large and small, the black and white and spotted. He told me, "Sheep don't soar like eagles, but then they don't get sucked up in jet engines either!"

In 1963, Ken chaired the "1st International Conference on Cetacean Research" for the Office of Naval Research, the conference from which came his *Whales, Dolphins and Porpoises*, a book still cited today. Attending this conference with no credentials save the backing of my mentor F.G. Wood, I listened to Ken Norris, in effect, telling this group of renowned cetacean scientists that I was a veterinarian who would erect cetacean medicine and that they should all send any information of medical bent to me. What generous support to me at the outset of my career! How generous Ken Norris was to so many others in the marine mammal field.

How can we say enough about Phylly? When Bill Perrin and Bob Brownell and a group of us went over to China with Ken to help save the most endangered whale, the baiji, I fell and broke my arm in the first week of a three-week stay, and had to have a cast done in a Red Army hospital. Phylly and Ken were domiciled across the hall from me and she gave me Motrin and sympathy to help me through the painful ordeal. Because he knew Phylly would make it possible, Ken could write to Carleton Ray saying,"The Experimental Gopher Ranch is always open, and what we must do sometime, is to take the better part of a week and go out to our desert place and chase lizards."

Ken was a man of foresight. Ken Norris was influential in framing the landmark Marine Mammal Protection Act. Ken served on the Scientific Advisory Committee for the first Marine Mammal Commission. A founder of the Society of Marine Mammalogy and its first president, Ken headed a commission to tackle the difficult tuna/dolphin problem and reduce the dolphin kill. His marine mammal legacy includes numerous scientific papers, articles and books. He has published dozens of articles in magazines and popular books—books that won major awards. Ken's vision for natural sciences—and for life—is with us. Three score and fourteen years from now, marine mammals, students, and scientists will still be benefitting from that vision—will still be benefitting from Ken's vision.

Roger Samuelsen

Just up the coast from here lies Año Nuevo Island, home of an assemblage of thousands of seals, sea lions and elephant seals. Picture a young professor crawling on his belly to within a few inches of these creatures to observe their heart rates. When a seal or sea lion awoke, the professor would simply mimic their sounds and motions by grunting and throwing a little sand over his back. The animal would then go back to sleep. That young professor was Ken Norris back in 1966. And it was that story that first captivated me when I met Ken in January of 1967.

I had just left the practice of law to join the administration of President Clark Kerr, ostensibly to help President Kerr and Vice President Earl Bolton establish a tenth, eleventh, and twelfth campus of the University in the 1970s and 1980s. All that was to change when, three weeks after I joined the University, the Board of Regents fired President Kerr and the thought of additional campuses went out the window. I was devastated with this turn of events and was seriously considering returning to the practice of law when Ken explained that his visit to Año Nuevo was one of a number of visits he had made to prospective sites for a newly established program, then called the Natural Land and Water Reserves System. Ken literally took a leave of absence in the spring of 1966 to tour the state of California, conduct his survey, visit field scientists, determine where they worked and what habitats they felt should be preserved, and write a report. That first meeting with Ken literally changed the course of my career and my life. How many of you here today can relate to that?

As years went on, I came to appreciate even more that the Natural Reserve System would never have come into being were it not for the vision, the creativity, the tenacity and, yes, the charm of Ken Norris.

When asked about the origin of his vision, he liked to tell the story of his thesis project in graduate school. 3.7 miles from the nearest improvement, a Whelan's Drug Store in Palm Springs, and 300 feet from the nearest road, he set up a research plot the size of a football field to study the desert iguana. In the months that followed, he came to know every creosote bush, every accretion dune, and every animal burrow in that plot. He took meticulous notes on the behavior of each iguana he observed. It never occurred to him that his research would be disrupted—remember, he was almost four miles from anything—but one day he discovered to his utter dismay that over half of the football field-sized plot had been leveled and it was not long before a motel had been constructed.

This experience together with similar experiences of others led Ken to realize that a systemwide plan was required—one that went beyond the provincialism of any given campus. He enlisted the support of Starker Leopold of Berkeley, Carl Hubbs of Scripps Institution of Oceanography, and other distinguished scientists from the nine campuses of the University. On June 4, 1963, Ken wrote President Kerr in behalf of these scientists and recommended the establishment of an all-University committee to develop policies concerning natural land holdings and acquisitions within the University system. Among the urgent reasons he gave for establishing the committee were:

The explosive growth of California's human population is destroying natural terrain at an alarming rate, and once destroyed, it cannot be reconstituted.

The University needs to plan carefully both for present staff use and for the future, with regard to these natural areas.

The report of the ad hoc committee led President Kerr and the Board of Regents to establish the system in January of 1965. Today it encompasses thirty-three reserves and over 120,000 acres. It is becoming a more valuable—and indeed an even more indispensable—teaching, research and public service resource with each passing day. And remarkably, it closely resembles in 1998 what Ken Norris and his ad hoc committee envisioned over thirty years ago! President Emeritus Kerr has eloquently paid tribute to Ken's efforts as follows:

Ken Norris had a brilliant idea. The University accepted it immediately and enthusiastically. The faculty committee given charge of the project under the chairmanship of Norris and the staff gave devoted leadership. The University proceeded to develop the best collection of microenvironments among all American universities to the great benefit of biologists and environmentalists in perpetuity.

Beyond "founding" the Natural Reserve System, Ken nurtured its development over the years. He appeared before the Board of Regents, called on countless prospective donors, served on numerous committees and panels, and wrote scores of letters and position papers. And he helped us maintain perspective. I remember one particularly difficult faculty advisory committee meeting. Ken was at the far end of the table scribbling madly on a pad of paper. Afterwards I commented that he seemed to be taking an unusual number of notes. He handed me his so called "notes" and it turned out to be a sketch of the Norris Field Car—a 1926 Dodge Laundry Wagon. There was a bit of Andrew Wyeth in Ken Norris and I will always cherish having this sketch on the wall over my desk.

As a fitting climax to Ken's devotion to the Natural Reserve System, the Packard Foundation granted the Natural Reserve System a $4 million endowment in June of this year. I know current NRS Director Alex Glazer would join me in saying that this gift would not have occurred were it not for the profound respect the Packard family has had for Ken Norris over the years. Ken died knowing that Alex and the Packard Foundation had agreed that this endowment should forever be known as the "Kenneth S. Norris Endowment Fund for the California Environment."

Ironically, my career with the University is ending where I thought it would begin—with the planning and development of a new campus in the San Joaquin Valley. During my last visit with Ken, I told him that, as part of these efforts, Alex Glazer and I were collaborating on identifying and establishing one or more new NRS reserves as integral parts of the UC Merced academic mission and framework. Ken was delighted and reminded me that he has always been the enthusiastic innovator and motivator—that he has had to rely on the likes of Alex and me and, I dare say, many of you within the sound of my voice today, to implement and administer his visions. I can only hope that, as we implement and administer Ken's vision in the San Joaquin Valley and elsewhere, we can do so with half the grace, half the care, half the zest and half the love that so characterized his life and his contributions.

He was a special guy—and a special friend.

William Doyle, UCSC Professor Emeritus of Biology

A dreamer; a doer; a scholar; a stimulating and demanding teacher; a critical thinker; a person of international stature; a mentor; a man consumed with curiosity about nature; a warm and friendly individual; a unique and wonderful person. Ken Norris came to UC Santa Cruz in the fall of 1972 as founding director of the marine sciences program. From 1970-1972, a planning committee had developed a campus plan for such a program and received the go-ahead to work towards its implementation. The campus administration gave approval for a search at the senior (full professor) level for a person who had expertise in marine mammal and terrestrial biology. Ken quickly was identified as a target of excellence appointment.

In addition to having earned an international reputation in marine mammal studies, Ken had broad research interests in terrestrial biology. He also had demonstrated skill and innovation in serving as the founding curator at Marineland of the Pacific, founding scientific director of the Oceanic Institute (Hawaii) and in the creation of the UC Natural Reserve System and Hawaii's Natural Land Reserve System. Ken was also active in significant conservation and natural resource issues. Fortunately for the future success of the Santa Cruz marine program and several other campus activities, Ken was willing to leave UCLA.

Ken served as director from 1972-1975, the formative years of the marine program. Six major accomplishments are described below:

1) Long Marine Laboratory. Marine programs that include marine biology require an on-shore facility with running seawater. Chancellor Dean McHenry and Ken identified a beautiful coastal site about as close to the campus as one could possibly get. Here, faculty and students would be able to carry out studies both at the marine lab and on campus daily, a situation not possible on campuses with remote marine stations. Donald and Marian Younger generously donated this land to the campus. In gratitude, the first research building constructed at this site was named the Donald and Marian Younger Research Building. In December of 1978, the coastal marine station was dedicated and named the Joseph M. Long Marine Laboratory (LML) in recognition of Mr. Long's many years of personal involvement in and financial support of the campus, including the marine program.

The coastal marine station that Ken envisioned has become a reality and is still growing. Faculty, staff and students do, in fact, work and study at the lab and on campus on a daily basis. Interaction with the public, including schools, is fostered through a Marine Discovery educational program. The California Department of Fish and Game has constructed a sea otter and bird oil spill treatment and research facility at the marine lab. Because of the presence of Long Marine Lab, the Southwest Fisheries Science Center of the National Marine Fisheries Service is constructing a research facility on land adjacent to the lab. All of these facilities together provide magnificent research and educational opportunities for UC Santa Cruz faculty, staff and students.

2) Fundraising. From the outset, Ken recognized that the majority of funding for marine station development and many other facilities and activities of the marine program would have to come from sources other than the University of California. Santa Cruz was a new and growing campus and on-campus activities had priority for all available University resources. Undaunted, Ken worked with Gurden Mooser, Assistant Vice Chancellor for University Relations, to develop fundraising strategies and initiate visits with individuals and private foundations from the West to the East Coast. These efforts, which continue to this day, have been immensely successful. To date (November, 1998) over twenty million dollars have been raised from non-University of California sources to develop research and educational facilities at the Long Marine Lab.

3) Coastal Research Vessel. Santa Cruz students, faculty and staff required access to the nearshore coastal water for diverse research and instructional projects. Ken recognized this need and turned his assistant, Dr. Richard W. Pierce, loose to solve this problem. Dick located a surplus Navy Utility Boat in one place and a surplus reconditioned diesel engine in another. With his creative talent for scrounging and fundraising, and a tremendous amount of elbow-grease, Dick put together and outfitted a tough coastal research vessel and had it named the R/V Scammon. This research vessel supported many UC Santa Cruz marine program activities in biology and geology, from San Francisco Bay to Santa Barbara, from 1973 until she was retired in 1986.

4) Organized Research Unit. An Organized Research Unit (ORU) is a special designation that has to be approved by the Regents of the University of California. An ORU is a research and instructional support organization that cuts across departmental lines. The Santa Cruz marine sciences program is interdepartmental. A draft proposal to establish an ORU in marine sciences was developed during 1971-1972. Ken re-worked this proposal and sent it off to the UC President's Office for review and final action by the regents. In

1975, the regents approved establishment of the Center for Coastal Marine Studies. Growth in numbers of people involved in and breadth of the marine program continued and in 1986 the regents approved a name change to the Institute of Marine Sciences. Ken deserves credit for sharpening the proposal and for his patience in shepherding it through many iterations as it moved from campus to the UC President's office.

5) Santa Cruz Predatory Bird Research Group. The Santa Cruz Predatory Bird Research Group (SCPBRG) has earned an outstanding reputation for its work in re-establishing and monitoring Peregrine Falcons and other raptors in California. Ken and veterinarian James Roush initiated this program, which matured wonderfully under the capable leadership of Brian Walton. This soft-funded program developed its office, bird breeding and other facilities on-campus in the Lower Quarry. These facilities are now closed and the program's offices are in the marine lab. Recently, SCPBRG received funding from the state of California to build a research facility at the lab. Why the Long Marine Lab? Pelicans, puffins, and black oystercatchers, for example, are also predatory birds. Ken—what absolutely marvelous foresight!

6) International Recognition. With Ken's arrival came staff for the marine science office and an entourage of researchers, students, technicians, and visitors from around the world. Immediately, marine sciences at UC Santa Cruz achieved international recognition and stature. Coupled with the research of Dr. Burney LeBoeuf and his students, Santa Cruz became known as a center of excellence for research and education on marine mammal issues. The marine science office was an intensely active, noisy, and exciting place—and was known locally as The Zoo. It was. But such a delightful place it was! Everyone was dedicated to building an outstanding marine program for the campus and no one cared about an eight to five work schedule, especially Ken. His enthusiasm was infectious. He attracted extremely capable people and the halls were filled with enthusiasm for research projects. Where else would you see a model of a baby gray whale with a girdle. The goal was to radio-track mother and child using a detachable girdle. Where else would you overhear conversations about time spent in the *Seasick Machine*? The goal was to have the researcher speed under the ocean surface in the company of free-swimming porpoises. Where else would the campus threaten to have

you pay for wages lost because of a malodorous stench created on campus during an attempt to clean the bones of a beached cetacean? Ken wanted the cleaned bones for use in research and instruction. The aroma problem was quickly relocated—up the coast to the Norris Ranch for the Norris family to live with!

Although Ken stepped down as director in 1975 in order to focus his energy and talents in the Environmental Studies program, his influence continued. He was responsible for development at LML of the Bio-acoustics Facility (which has since moved to Hawaii). The dolphin facilities and other outdoor tanks at the marine lab are a result of Ken's interests. His rapport with Mr. Long was extraordinary. There was mutual pleasure in their interactions. I remember Ken's first discussion with Mr. Long about the Big Bang theory of fish stunning by dolphins and his need for a large dolphin tank to test this theory. "All I need is a large bathtub," was Ken's first (and certainly the cheapest) iteration. The final product was a magnificent "bathtub" with underwater viewing ports and no two sides that are parallel. This "bathtub" has since supported a diversity of research activities. What other university has such a marvelous diversity of marine mammal facilities for use by faculty, staff, and graduate and undergraduate students?

Ken always attracted outstanding students—both graduate and undergraduate. He sharpened students' analytical skills and pushed them to develop independence in thinking and work habits, which are two attributes much in demand. I marveled at how he could guide in research so many students at any one time. He made time for them and they loved him. The love was mutual. He loved teaching and interacting with students of all educational levels. He made them think; they made him think.

Ken, thank you. And thank you, the Norris family, for sharing Ken with us.

Shannon M. Brownlee

My name is Shannon Brownlee. I was an undergraduate and a master's student of Ken's. Before I begin, I know many of you are wondering what is going to happen to Ken's last book, *Mountain Time*. Dave Hart and I are editing it to get it ready to send to publishers. We are hoping to finish our work by next spring. Those two announcements aren't going to count against my five minutes, are they, Larry? I'm warning you right now, my talk is seven minutes long.

I'd like to ask all of Ken's former graduate students who are here to please stand up. Could you hurry it up a little? My minutes are ticking away.

What a motley crew. You represent a hodge-podge of biological disciplines. Under Ken, you studied a menagerie of creatures in far-flung habitats, from fringe-toed lizards in the Mojave Desert to right whales off Patagonia. You have gone on to an equally diverse collection of professions—biologists, writers, editors, teachers, artists, psychologists.

The man who could draw in such a varied taxonomic class as you was a rare and extraordinary teacher. That's why so many of you are here today.

There's a concept in physics called basins of attraction. I've always thought of Ken as a basin of attraction, and all of us graduate students as little quarks and electrons, who were roaming around in space until we tumbled into Ken's wonderfully strange and charged world. And you know what happened then. We were off, on the greatest adventure of our lives. Along the way, Ken taught us some very important lessons. But they weren't the lessons you'd ever learn from a normal graduate advisor.

For one thing, you discovered very quickly never to trust a boat built by Ken. He called his first vessel the *Semisubmersible Seasick Machine*. They were all seasick machines. When I was drafted to work on a spinner dolphin project, Ken was building his second boat. I had read his book *The Porpoise Watcher*, and I knew all about the *Semisubmersible Seasick Machine*, and I wanted no part of it. But this boat, Ken swore up and down, as we loaded a ton of lead weights into the keel of a modified Boston whaler, would be much more seaworthy. We shipped her to the Big Island of Hawaii, and christened her the *Maka'ala*, Hawaiian for "Watchful Eye." Well, somebody should have been keeping a watchful eye, because she promptly sank in the first really big rain storm.

The second lesson you learned was, never let your professor touch the equipment. Tape recorders, cameras, computers, spectral analyzers—it was time to panic whenever you saw Ken approaching the "Knurled Knobs" on anything more complicated than a thermometer. This was a man who once said he always delivered talks without slides because he liked to be unencumbered by data. And he never met a statistic he really liked.

The third lesson graduate students learned was getting into a boat with Ken at the helm was a little like getting into a car with Mr. Magoo. Ken navigated with great enthusiasm and very little regard for minor obstacles like pilings and docks and other vessels.

Come to think of it, getting into a car with Ken was like being in the cockpit of a jet—long periods of calm punctuated by moments of sheer terror. This was a man who wrecked three University vehicles on a trip to Baja and who was called into the UCLA motor pool to be informed that he would never again be allowed to check out University property involving four wheels and an internal combustion engine. That was probably wise of them, because in those days, Ken was of the opinion that you could smooth out the ride over washboard roads by driving at sixty miles an hour. Later in life, he came to believe that you could avoid accidents by going under twenty miles an hour on the freeway.

Then there was trying to get Ken to focus on your thesis. You would go up to the house on Smith Grade with an armload of data and an appointment to talk to Ken about how to analyze it. Before you could say standard deviation, you were down at the creek, hauling rocks for a new spring box, or pounding nails into a tree house with Ken shouting instructions from down below.

No wonder so many of us fell under his spell. Silliness was part of Ken's great charm—but it was also central to his genius. All of the fun stuff, the Santa Cruz Geographic Society, the tree houses, the Bunny Club, the hokey-pokey, the outrageous tall tales about things like "Cactomagnetism" (I personally fell hard for that one as a gullible nineteen-year-old), the Society to Inform Animals of their Taxonomic Classification, and the silly songs—all of it made life more fun. It was also part of Ken's creativity.

Ken may have been a stumblebum when it came to electronic equipment, but he possessed one of the most nimble minds I've ever known. Playing was Ken's way of hanging loose intellectually, staying mentally limber. Zooming back and forth between cockamamie engineering projects and practical jokes and science allowed him to come up with some of the most provocative and thoughtful ideas in biology. There's the Big Bang theory, the seven plus or minus two rule of dolphin friendship, dolphins hearing through their jaws, clown fish covering themselves with slime to live among the tentacles of a sea anemone, and why old sand dunes change color.

The list of Ken's accomplishments in science and conservation is truly astonishing. But the lesson I hold most dear from twenty years of knowing Ken, I could have learned from Dr. Seuss. That lesson is this: These things are fun, and fun is good. If you have never done such things, you should. Ken's genius sprang from his sense of wonderment and delight with the natural world. From him I learned that being truly innovative requires having fun.

I also learned from Ken that being an innovator makes you suspect, and that sometimes you have to be stubborn and stick to your guns when the world tells you your ideas are wrong. The world told Ken that he was full of beans a lot. Somehow, that never seemed to bother him.

I think I know why. When I was half way through my graduate course work, I discovered the University wanted me to take the second quarter of organic chemistry. Having nearly flunked the first quarter as an undergraduate, naturally I refused. The heads of the graduate program called a meeting with my advisors, including Ken. It was all very solemn. I sat there, quaking, as I told them I would quit the graduate program if they made me take organic chemistry. Ken never said a word.

At the end of the meeting, the powers that be relented, and said I didn't have to take organic after all. But then I had another worry. As Ken and I were walking out of the building I expected him to really blast me for being such a stubborn young jackass, which I was. Before I could ask him if he was mad, he clapped me on the shoulders and said, "Ha! You didn't let them turn you into a sausage from the university sausage factory."

The collection of former graduate students that I see out there is a group of remarkable people. That's because Ken didn't want to be surrounded by human sausages, or even replicas of himself. He wanted us to be ourselves.

Ken was once quoted in the *New York Times* saying that dolphins and whales were big brains in a sea of dullards. But I don't believe he ever really felt that way about all the lowly little diatoms and fish in the sea. He looked at all creatures with a wide and generous curiosity that also embraced members of his own species. Ken and Phylly, too, accepted us and welcomed us, not in spite of our quirky differences, but because of them. As a result, when you were around them, you felt more like your real self. You felt like your best and brightest self.

And so, every trip with Ken was the greatest adventure of our lives. And every day spent with Ken was all full of joy. And not a single idea that ever came out of Ken's mind was a dull one. In a world full of vanilla, Ken was rocky road. He was sweet, he was lumpy, and he was full of nutty surprises. The planet will be a blander place without him, and I will miss him more than he could ever have imagined.

Stephen R. Gliessman

Ken always used to say that our role as teachers was to help students examine the wellsprings of caring about the natural world and its life. He insisted on balancing our awe and curiosity for nature with our joy of nature.How this worked may be best told by the words of one of our students:

I just wanted to tell you that not too long ago I found myself at Joshua Tree National Park (Yucca brevifolia!!) wandering around amidst the rocks, trees, and bushes. The wildflowers were just beginning to bloom and while I was accompanied by two other people I soon found myself in a world of my own. I'm not sure exactly what it was, for we never visited Joshua Tree on Field Quarter, but I felt the feeling of Field Quarter stronger than I've ever felt it since actually being on it. I don't even know how to begin to describe it except that in addition to noticing the tiny flowers along the trail and feeling everything just slow down, I was transported, mentally, emotionally—somehow back to Field Quarter itself. It's one of those feelings you cannot create but rather it hits you unexpectedly by some stimulus and it hits stronger than thinking of memories or looking at pictures.

I must admit I do not remember all the plants or animals we learned, nor do I remember many scientific names (though there are some, definitely!) but I think while that was a very important part of Field Quarter, equally important was the feeling of mountain time and the desire to learn more about all this great stuff around us. I know that now I do look more carefully at plants and wonder what their names are, and I notice the tiny birds flying about and I try to catch some glimpse of a special feature to look up later.

I think what I got most out of Field Quarter was the desire to learn more and understand more, and to slow down and look around. Equally, it is wonderful to know that no matter how caught up I get in this so called civilized life, I carry with me always a piece of Field Quarter which can always surface and remind me what's important.

And how did Ken teach about the awe as well as the joy of science? I feel some of his own words written on the mountainside during a Field Quarter tell it best:

I want a science that includes us, our unspoken word, the animals, the plants, and the ecology. It has to include us, lest we never reach mountain time. No system that separates us as we really are from our world can be real, or adequately explanatory.

No explanation that omits our camaraderie or our affection for each other will do, for it is the glue that joins us in our quest, and that makes it worth doing.

No explanation that excludes jokes and laughter will do. They are the rapiers that tear away pretense and unmask false explanation.

No explanation that omits music and the exercise of our physical beings will do, for they define our fitness and even the ways we organize our thoughts, our explanations, and our language.

We learn so much from the natural world that envelops us when we are part of it, when it tries in its own way to show us where life comes from.

Our emotional attachment speaks clearly enough of ecological balance, of the silent ticking of mountain time, of the things our science has only defined, not solved. When we slow to mountain time we come closest to the inner peace of our ancient balance, we reach best for bridges between our modern world and all that built us. Those I suspect are the wellsprings of our caring.

And some of my own words written alongside Ken when on Field Quarter—on the last day of our last Field Quarter together just before he retired:

Field Quarter, and teaching in general are about sharing the learning process with our students. As teachers, we never pretend to have all the answers. But we do have experience, and it is the way we share that experience that is so important. Offering views of our world that has grown and evolved over time. And over that time, we have seen the many faces of nature as she shifts her moods from one season to the next. We have seen Calochortus kennedyi show itself only when conditions are right, or returned to find the Deep Springs toad surviving in its little corner of the world. We have watched fennel explode with the removal of grazing animals, and we have watched the edge of Mono Lake contract and expand. I marvel at how you and I got to see the places we take our students shift and change and stay the same, when the students were seeing each place for one moment in time.

What a perspective, and sharing that perspective of time gives power to what each student is experiencing in their own moment in time.

Master of wonder, of seeing, of being in nature where the organism is the authority. Thanks for sharing so much with us and giving us the space we have needed over these years to grow and change. And like Dr. Van Denburgh, always with us on our trips, so will you be with us, always. Thanks for showing us how, for igniting the spirit, but for also showing us how to enjoy and have fun at the same time. It sure beats workin'! I suspect that this spring, as Field Quarter 1999 embarks on the greatest adventure of our lives, that we will be seeing Dr. Van Denburgh in pairs.

Karl S. Pister, Chancellor Emeritus, UC Santa Cruz

I will talk about Ken from two perspectives: first, through the eyes of my brother, Phil, and then from my own experience. Here are Phil's words about Ken:

I did not meet Ken Norris until later in my career yet, as is true of many great teachers, he exerted substantial influence on me through his former UC Santa Cruz students who worked under my direction as employees of the Department of Fish and Game. We also shared a common mentor, the late Carl L. Hubbs, who served as Ken's major professor during his doctoral research at Scripps, and as my close colleague as we worked together in the conservation of Southwestern desert fishes.

It was during the last decade of Ken's life that my real appreciation for Ken began. His influence was instrumental in the creation of two units of the Natural Reserve System on the east side of the Sierra. Inasmuch as I represented jointly the Department of Fish and Game and the University of California in the Owens Valley, I would frequently interact with Ken as he would load his Field Quarter students into the old UCSC blue bus, drive across the Central Valley, cross the Sierra Nevada at Tioga Pass, drop into the Mono Basin, visit the Sierra Nevada Aquatic Research Laboratory on the way south to the White Mountain Research Station, then head up Westgard Pass to the Grandview Campground in the White Mountains. I could always think of a reason to leave my official duties to join Ken and his class in the White Mountains, where I would eagerly share with his students Ken's incredible depth of knowledge and philosophy of nature. It made little difference whether Ken was speaking about the great whales or the inch-long desert pupfishes; his great knowledge encompassed them both.

As a humorous interjection here, the Yosemite toad (Bufo canorus), which Ken and I would often discuss following his trip over Tioga Pass, brings with it a unique identity. The specific name, canorus, sounds exactly like "Ken Norris." During the 1998 meeting of the Board of Governors of the American Society of Ichthyologists and Herpetologists, held in Canada, I mentioned Ken's illness. The herpetologists in attendance agreed that for the duration of the meeting, the Yosemite toad would bear the honorary designation of Bufo Ken Norris!

We will ultimately be judged by the legacy that we pass on to future generations. Ken's legacy is enormous and unending, measured by his students and their contributions, his research publications, his unforgettable smile, and the hospitality that he and Phylly would dispense to those fortunate enough to spend a night with them at their home in the Santa Cruz mountains.

Ken's very fine obituary in the August 31st San Francisco Chronicle, *which summarized in detail his life and career, neglected to mention those simple items by which most will remember him: he was an extraordinarily kind, warm, and generous human being. What more need one ask?*

Although Ken retired the year before I came to the campus, my brother had already prepared me to be ready to meet a remarkable person. I was not disappointed.

Ken Norris made so many contributions and was involved with so many different programs over his nearly forty years in the University, that it is difficult to believe that one individual could have been so pivotal, both for the campus as well as the University of California.

Ken saw the early impacts of DDT on the food chain, and created the Santa Cruz Predatory Bird Research Group, which has played a critical role in bringing the Peregrine Falcons and other predatory birds back from the brink of extinction, a program still thriving today, over twenty-five years later.

Ken, along with Bill Doyle, was a founding father of the Center for Coastal Marine Studies, which has grown into the campus's largest organized research unit, the Institute of Marine Sciences.

Working with founding Chancellor Dean McHenry, Ken felt that a marine program wasn't a real program without a marine lab with seawater and a boat, and he set to work to successfully accomplish both of these projects.

The Marine Lab is now a magnet for marine researchers and other marine programs. The original pools that Ken raised the money for and built remain the core of perhaps the top university research facilities in the world for the study of marine mammals in captivity. And those marine mammals are also at the center of a thriving public education program which attracts thousands of school children every year. Ken was a firm believer in education at all levels.

Ken chaired the environmental studies program for two years in the late 70s and founded and coordinated the extremely popular Natural History Field Quarter. Professor Gliessman just described this field course that, while Ken taught it, took an entire generation of over 400 undergraduates into the natural history of California. Ken also founded the Environmental Field Program with Dick Cooley. They raised hundreds of thousands of dollars from off campus to support those programs for about ten years. This novel and greatly missed program provided support and guidance to undergraduates to complete independent studies of the environment all over the world. These two programs were a major undertaking and commitment for Ken, and they left an indelible impression on the fortunate students. Ken was legendary in his ability to inspire his students.

Finally, Ken was instrumental in arranging for me to take his place on the Board of Directors of MBARI, the Monterey Bay Aquarium Research Institute, enabling continued, close attraction between the campus and the Institute.

Ken has passed on. "If you would seek his monuments, look around you."

Craig F. Schindler,

Former Professor of Environmental Studies, UCSC

I was a junior professor in environmental studies with Ken Norris and many others in the late 1970s and early 1980s. I want to talk about celebrating his impact and the subtitle of my talk is "passing the flame."

First, a Ken story or two. My first experience of Ken was when I was a junior faculty person and going into an environmental studies meeting and there's this guy in blue overalls who looks like a Montana sheep rancher. He says, well he's just come in from shearin' the sheep. And then he mentions, with this grin in his eyes, that he's going to go talk to Dean Adams in a little bit and you can see he's just dressed for the occasion.

Having never taken a biology class in my life and being a little low on the science side, having majored in things like psychology, religion and philosophy, I was shocked when Ken Norris invited me to be a resource person regularly on the Natural History Field Quarter. The first trip I went on that long bus ride with Larry Ford and many others, I was in terror, I really was in terror, that somebody was going to ask me the name of anything. And all of you out there, you knew all those names, you remember, and I'm just there. Ken made a point of telling everybody, "Listen. Don't ask Craig any names. He's along for the reverence for life stuff."

I remember one scene where one of the students got Ken to practice yoga and Ken's there on the ensolite pad and he's got his body like this and he turns to me and he says, "A living pretzel!" And then he says, "I'm just noodling here, just noodling."

And then I remember the time Denny Seymour sprained her ankle and Ken and Larry rigged up this chair. Now, if I was Denny Seymour I'm not sure I'd trust this after hearing about Ken's boats. But they rigged up this chair that was on two poles and the two of them carried her through the Ventana wilderness. And I mean through steep canyons. Remember that, Larry?

Okay. Passing the flame. There are hundreds of us gathered here. And we represent thousands of us from around the world. Isn't this amazing! We're here because we love Ken and because he inspired our minds and as Steve put it, ignited our spirits. As a woman who was a student of his many years ago told me this week, "Ken saw me and my potential and believed in me more than I did at the time." I think that's probably true for lots of us, including me as a young junior faculty person.

Ken, I suggest, was lit. And he has helped to light a flame in all of us. And that's why we're here. He was lit with an irrepressible delight in the natural world. That image of him taking the temperatures of lizards with students gathered all around. Do you remember that scene? With a playful irreverence taking me over to show me the tree house in the redwood tree seventy feet up that he built in his spare time. With an inexhaustible curiosity and wonder before the spider web, the lizard, and the fifty million-year-old songs of whales. With a passion and a grace, and as many speakers have said, with such a generosity sourced so deeply by Phylly's generosity. So that the Norris home is home to countless numbers of us. And with a brilliant scientific mind and a down-home ability to connect with anybody, anybody, however great or humble. And most of all, I would suggest, and this is part of passing his flame, Ken was lit with a tenacious determination and commitment to the stewardship and restoration of our magnificent earth.

Loren Eiseley, the great naturalist, and one of Ken's favorites, says "There're two kinds of scientists. There're the extreme reductionists who are so busy stripping things apart that the tremendous mystery has been reduced to a trifle." And then, he says, "there are the rare few who have a controlled sense of wonder before the universal mystery." And Loren Eiseley says, "before the end of this century we must learn that knowledge without greatness of spirit is not enough." Ken taught us lots of knowledge. But most of all he taught us greatness of spirit. And it is that flame that we can pass on. What does Ken want us to do? Nothing for him. He wants us to pass the flame so that it goes on down through into the next century.

I was talking to Larry yesterday, who has put so much into organizing this, and Larry was recalling a conversation with Ken on the bus coming back from one of these natural history field trips in which Larry asked him, "Ken, what makes a good teacher?" Ken thought about it. He said, "Two things. One," he says, and this is Ken in one of his non-silly moods. Ken says, "one, to teach with love." And love was the word he used. Because the methods don't matter as much as creating a sense of safety for the student so the student can try his or her wings. And the second thing Ken said was, "Get out of the way!" As Shannon pointed out, Ken did not want people to become carbon copies of him. Ken wanted us to be ourselves. And Ken created learning situations like sitting in front of a cactus for five hours or watching a lizard for half a day in which we were to break through our boredom and open up through what he called the "windows to the world." Because Ken believed from experience that once we got through and opened our perception, the ever present festival of wonder that is nature would continue to challenge us and inspire us for the rest of our lives. Ken did that for us.

So we ask you, Ken, how did you do it all? How did you do break-through world class research, create a UC Reserve system, teach the Natural History Field Quarter, read countless numbers of journal pages, work so connectedly with your graduate students and bring such love, laughter, hilarity and God knows what else to your family? How did you do it all? And I think he would say back to us, "Don't worry about it! Do yourself. Do yourself with your own greatness of spirit." And he would tell us, as he showed us again and again. "If you have a vision, if you get an idea, if you see something you can do to help the earth, be bold. Be audacious!" Take the initiative as he did again and again and again, and then remarkable things will happen.

So I close, as a deep privilege to be here with all of you, with this dedication to us passing the flame. Ken, may we in our lives pass the flame that you helped to light in us. Your awe and curiosity before the mystery of life. Your delight and joy in the music of life. Your love and wisdom and celebration of our humanness. And may we pass this flame of stewardship down through the 21st century for the healing and restoration of the earth.

To close, I would like to close the way we closed all the natural history field trips. So maybe I can invite you to stand up and just do this with Ken, okay? I'm going to read the words to the hokey-pokey. You don't have to move. But just stand up for a second. Here we go. But think about these words. Think about these words and think about what they mean in terms of Ken's life. "Put your whole self in. Put your whole self out. Put your whole self in and shake it all about. Do the hokey-pokey and turn yourself around. That's what it's all about." So here's our pledge: We love you. We salute you. And truly, we will pass the flame down through the century. Thanks.

Alisa Fineman, Singer/Songwriter

Song for Ken

We stand on the shoulders
Of those we call our teachers
They shape us, give to us
Help make us better people
You changed our lives, opened our eyes
You believed we mattered
Your secret lived, you said,
In love, in yours we thrived

And reached higher

Oh little fish, now you are big
You have outgrown this pond
You've passed the test, but there's more yet
You're built for moving on

We made camp
You ate spam
We slept beneath the stars
We built trails
You spun tales
Together we went far
We learned more by the river
In the mountains, in the desert
By the ocean, in the redwoods
A million spring wildflowers

Oh little fish, now you are big
You have outgrown this pond
You passed the test, but there's more yet
You're built for moving on

You helped me to see
The world around me
How to look for the story
In every rock and living thing
A sense of place
With passion and grace
You guided our connection
You made it safe
You turned us loose

To find our own direction

Oh little fish, now you are big
You have outgrown this pond
You passed the test, but there's more yet
You're built for moving on

Oh little fish, now we are big
We have outgrown this pond
We passed the test, but there's more yet
We're built for moving on

Some make a splash
Some more, some less
Some take the world by storm
But true success is how you live
And live on in those you leave behind

And you live on in those you leave behind

Dan Warrick, Former Editor, Environmental Field Program

The Flood of Ink

Rain runs my ink, I cannot think
of anything to say.
We got up late this morning, ate,
and then we drove away.
We stopped to see (now let me see)
it started with an ***A****,*
I squashed it in my journal so
it wouldn't get away.

I've got the runs, I'm sick of Munz,[1]
I can't key out that tree.
Dichotomous decisions led me
to *Pinaceae,*
But now I'm stuck in resinous muck
just like the tar baby.
It's all there in my journal just
as plainly as can be.

We joked and laughed and asked that we
be carried far away.
We danced and sang 'til our heads rang,
quite foolish, yes, I'd say.
"Here take a swig, sure make it big,
you'll see the osprey; just
don't spill it on your journal lest
you wash your thoughts away."

[1] Munz, Phillip A., *A California Flora and Supplement.*

We asked our questions, made suggestions
'bout the habitats
of caddis flies and Whippleiis,
'bout lizards and the bats.
Though we found sense in chance events
one question yet stands pat:
Why do we keep our journals? There's
no sense at all to that.

We watched the birds and botched the words,
dismembered countless flowers;
geologized, hypothesized,
scatologized for hours.
We scribbled notes about leaking boats
and how a kind mood sours.
There's life there in my journal and
I thank the holy powers.

California is a lively place,
a slice of nature's pie.
The critters and the plant life
danced before our twinkling eyes.
Again they call, but we've spent all
our m-o-n-e-y,
we'll just reread our journals and
return there by and by.

—Dan Warrick
(Berkeley), biology;
environmental studies

APPENDIX II:

Syllabus and First Instructions

Natural History Field Quarter (1983)

Spring 1983
UCSC
Coordinator: Larry Ford

Environmental Studies 107
Natural History of California
Kenneth S. Norris

Environmental Studies 148
Interpretation and Analysis of California Vegetation
Stephen R. Gliessman

Environmental Studies 168
The California Landscape
K. S. Norris and S. R. Gliessman

The Natural History Field Quarter is designed to be a full-time practical experience. Its purpose is the training of students in the fine art of being good naturalists with the skills and perspectives of science. It will present an overview of the natural history of California, both from the standpoint of human use and intervention in the natural systems and from the view of natural California itself. Exercises, lectures, and experiences are designed to offer steps toward professionalism by exploring and sharpening skills in observation, perception, translation to written or drawn forms, and informed dialogue between colleagues. To provide the best exposure of the students to these things, a departure from standard course format is to be taken. Nearly all instruction will be given in the field. However, there will be scheduled class meetings between trips for lectures and trip planning. A majority of the students' between-trip time will be spent preparing for the next trip—(besides laundry chores)—researching presentation topics or quarter projects in the library, studying class material, or planning menus and purchasing food. All work will be done amidst a cooperative small group of peers living together primitively, closely, and sometimes strenuously.

Five field trips will be from five to twelve days in length. Departures will be from the UCSC Barn Theater. Please make extra efforts to be ready ahead of time. Usually, there will be a long ride in a bus to our wondrous destination, during which time those with the stomach may work on class assignments or read from the traveling library, while others may choose to sleep, inspect the changing landscape, or demand rest and nature stops. Most returns will be in the late evening. It is intended that there will be plenty of time on each trip to make observations, keep journals, and enjoy the country.

Resource people will sometimes be invited to take part in the various trips. These will be carefully chosen people with diverse, provocative, innovative, and knowledgeable viewpoints about the California environment. The instructors have decided that it will be best that no other guests come along.

REQUIREMENTS

Students will be required as their major effort in these classes to keep a journal on each field trip. This will be prepared each evening in the style of a journal, and its contents are expected to vary widely with the student. We hope each individual will bring his own special viewpoints and talents to it. Artists should utilize their special viewpoint of the world, scientists theirs, and so on. These journals are to be kept on three-ringed, lined notebook paper of 6 by 91/2 inch size in a sturdy binder. Black waterproof ink is preferred though not mandatory. It is recommended that a packet of blank paper be included in the binder for sketches, maps, etc. More information in the keeping of journals is to be given in class. Journals will be turned in periodically throughout the quarter for review by the instructors.

Only one book purchase is required and it may be purchased at Kinko's Copies on Cedar Street: Gliessman, S.R., 1982, Professor Papers: A Field Guide to the Vegetation of California.

The following books are recommended. They are considered essential reading for good naturalists:

1. Bakker, Elna, 1971, *An Island Called California.*
2. Barbour and Major, 1977, *Terrestrial Vegetation of California.*
3. Bateson, Gregory, 1979, *Mind and Nature.*
4. Carlquist, Sherwin, 1964, *Island Life.*
5. Cowles, Raymond, T*he Desert Journal.*
6. Darwin, Charles, *Voyage of the Beagle.*
7. Kroeber, Theodora, *Ishi, Last of His Tribe.*
8. McPhee, John, *Encounters with the Archdruid.*
9. Ornduff, Robert, 1974, *California Plant Life.*

Another assignment for these classes will be to complete a "quarter project." This will involve selecting a particular natural history focus for study in the localities and travel routes of the quarter. Records will be kept in the journal and a final paper will be written and presented in seminar form. Ideas will be suggested in class such as morphologic diversity of a species, distribution of a species, flower color, class adaptability to the different regions, etc. We will talk about this and help each student to select a project that will suit individual needs, feelings, and interests. We want to have all students' quarter projects selected and in progress before the end of our first field trip.

The class will be subdivided into a series of presentation groups whose task it will be to examine in detail certain aspects of the countryside through which the group passes. These groups are expected to locate and study written materials about the area prior to departure on the trips and to examine the terrain from their special viewpoints during the trips. They are expected to contribute during the trips and be prepared to present a synopsis to the group at some group gathering during the trip. These presentations should not be introductory or general, but should be relevant to the area, interesting, as in-depth as possible, and restricted to 45 minutes of total time talking for the subgroup. These presentation groups are:

1. Special Topics in Flora and Fauna.

2. Geology, Weather, and Climate.

3. Aboriginal and post-aboriginal history; land use patterns and history, and environmental issues.

FOOD

A fourth group will be a food group for certain trips. (See attached Presentation and Food Groups schedule.) Clean-up will be delegated amongst the three groups not cooking on a rotational basis. This will insure great variability in both our meals and the cleanliness of our pots and pans. The cooking team for each trip is asked to plan the menu, collect the money, and obtain supplies, all prior to leaving, and to prepare all meals on the trip.

Except on backpack hikes (Big Creek and Tuolumne River trips), food will be prepared communally to save valuable time and to enrich the group stew. Experience teaches, if everyone cooks for himself, some may take two hours to make lunch. (A few people, of course, may have special dietary habits.) Food costs will be split equally amongst all participants. All cooking and clean-up gear will be provided, but students must provide their own plates, cups, and utensils. On backpacking trips, students will make their own food arrangements and bring their own stoves and cooking gear. Instruction in the use of camping gear such as Coleman cooking stoves and lanterns and in other camping skills will be provided upon request.

SPECIFIC FIELD TRIPS

Field trip activities and points of focus will encompass the following:

1. Granite Mountains, Mojave Desert—introduction to the field quarter; natural history and vegetation of the desert; observation and hypothesizing.

2. Big Creek, Big Sur (backpacking)—niche hunting, individual species adaptation; natural area preservation.

3. Santa Cruz Island, Channel Islands—island biogeography, isolation and evolution; natural vegetation types.

4. Mattole River, Humboldt County—physical processes; rain, river formation and dynamics, the seashore.

5. Smith River, W. Siskiyou Mountains—plant response to physical factors, ecotypes; endemic species; ecological interference in vegetation.

6.Tuolumne River, Sierra Nevada (backpacking)—microclimates—physical environment; integrative mechanisms.

7. Mono Lake and White Mountains, Sierra-East Side—ecotones and vegetational change; environmental politics; conclusion.

EQUIPMENT

Naturally enough, to make these trips comfortable and to participate in the remainder of the activities, people must take special care to protect themselves in a variety of ways. You are strongly encouraged to utilize the judgement expressed in the following equipment list.

1. Required: ankle-length hiking boots. More than 80% of snake bites are at ankle height or below.

2. Required: snake bite kit, pocket rubber suction. Carry it on all hikes!

3. Warm sleeping bag, pad, and ground cloth.

4. Binoculars. Purchasing advice can be given.

5. Hand lens.

6. Pocket knife.

7. Small pocket notebook and pencil.

8. Clothing. Be prepared to change in camp as conditions warrant. Be prepared for hot or cold; "layering" is effective. Be sure to provide some type of headgear against the sun and cold. Nothing beats wool!

9. Durable raincoat or poncho.

10. Backpack or duffle bag. A backpack will be necessary only for backpacking trips. Day packs or duffle bags will be better for the rest. In the bus, it will be necessary to use soft luggage rather than hard (i.e. backpacks) to fit everything under the seats.

11. Toilet paper.

12. Small canteen or water bottle easily carried.

13. A watch that works so schedules may be kept.

14. A guitar, kazoo, or mandolin or two will not be frowned upon.

15. Personal eating utensils, plates, cups, etc.

16. Field journal.

Special needs for certain trips will be announced before that trip.

OTHER THOUGHTS

Above all else, don't let little nagging things like cuts, chafing, headaches, etc. grow into major problems before telling your leaders. A portable first-aid kit will be along and will include quite a variety of solutions to such problems. Let's watch out for each other.

If any of you have any special medical needs or other problems that might affect you during the trips, be sure to discuss them with your leaders well in advance of leaving, or at the beginning of the quarter.

A rain shelter will be carried sufficient to construct a camp area shelter. Personal equipment of this sort will be appreciated and needed.

Large groups such as this can be unwieldy and troublesome or even dangerous in the rough country if some of the participants fail to abide by the rules of the leaders. People are asked not to take extended hikes alone under any circumstances, and always to file a "flight plan" with the leaders before going off independently of the group. A flight log is provided for this purpose.

As mentioned earlier, these courses involve occasional hard all-day hiking, extended primitive camping, cramped long-distance travel, and close living and studying with a small group for a major portion of the quarter. A serious commitment and a cooperative and spirited attitude will undoubtedly alleviate much soreness, but will also enhance for everyone the joy and learning of this unique opportunity.

Transportation will be by University bus. The use of private cars is not allowed. All driving will be done by trained Class 2 drivers. We ask that you be attentive, cooperative, and appreciative of their difficult and tiring job. No smoking of any kind of drinking of alcohol can be allowed in the bus.

A traveling library (Parnassus) of resource books, maps, and journal articles will be along as will a variety of collection and observation equipment. We ask that everyone make efforts to share. Please return books to the Parnassus and equipment to a central place when not in immediate use. Proper care of such resources will ensure their availability for the entire group, as well as future courses.

Finally, we will be leaving California unspoiled by our passage. We will help by picking up debris from others less thoughtful. We will also be sensitive to the potentially heavy impact of our group upon the natural environments we visit. Special needs, techniques, and backcountry manners will be discussed during class.

Map, trip plans, or other materials will be distributed as we proceed.

For any questions, advice about equipment or some other need, or discussion about the direction of the courses or assignments, please don't hesitate to approach Larry, Ken, or Steve, anytime.

APPENDIX III:

Publications: Kenneth S. Norris

Note: This bibliography was compiled by Daniel P. Costa.

Norris, K. S. 1948. Arboreal habits and feeding of the grid-iron tailed lizard. *Herpetologica*, 4:217-281.

Norris, K. S. 1949. Observations on the habits of the horned lizard, *Phrynosoma M'callii. Copeia* 3:176-180.

Norris, K. S. and R. G. Zweifel. 1950. Observations on the habits of the ornate box turtle, *Terrapene ornata* (Agassiz). *Natural History Miscellaneous Publications,* No. 58.

Lowe, C. H. Jr., and K. S. Norris. 1950. Aggressive behavior in male sidewinders, *Crotalus cerastes*, with a discussion of aggressive behavior and territoriality in snakes. *Natural History Miscellaneous Publications*, No. 66.

Norris, K. S. 1951. The evolution of the iguanid genus *Uma.* M.A. thesis, University of California Los Angeles, 157 pages.

Norris, K. S. and C. H. Lowe Jr. 1951. A study of the osteology and musculature of *Phrynosoma M'callii* pertinent to its systematic status. *Bulletin Chicago Academy Science* 9(7):117-125.

Norris, K. S. 1951. The lizard that swims in the sand. *Natural History* LX(9):404-407.

Norris, K. S. 1953. The ecology of the desert iguana, *Dipsosaurus dorsalis. Ecology* 34(2):265-287.

Reeder, W. G. and K. S. Norris. 1954. Distribution, type locality, and habits of the fish-eating bat, *Pizonyx vivesi. Journal of Mammalogy* 35(l):81-37.

Lowe, C. H. Jr. and K. S. Norris. 1954. Analysis of the herpetofauna of Baja California, Mexico. *Transactions San Diego Society of Natural History,* XII(4):47-64.

Zweifel, R. G. and K. S. Norris. 1955. Contribution to the herpetology of Sonora, Mexico. *American Midland Naturalist* 54(l):230-249.

Lowe, C. H. Jr. and K. S. Norris. 1955. Analysis of the herpetofauna of Baja California, Mexico, III. *Herpetologica* 11:89-96.

Lowe, C. H. Jr. and K. S. Norris. 1955. Measurements and weight of a Pacific Leather back turtle, *Dermochelys coriacea Schlegeli,* captured off San Diego, California. *Copeia* 3:256.

Brown, D. H. and K. S. Norris. 1956. Observations of captive and wild *Cetacea. Journal of Mammalogy* 37(3):120-145.

Norris, K. S. 1957. Second record of the green sturgeon on Southern California. *California Fish & Game* 43(4):317.

Norris, K. S. 1957. Collecting for the world's largest fish bowl. *Natural History* (March):120.

Norris, K. S. and W. N. McFarland. 1958. A new harbor porpoise of the genus *Phocoena* from the Gulf of California. *Journal of Mammalogy* 39(l):22-39.

Norris, K. S. 1958. Facts and tales about killer whales. *Pacific Discovery* XI(l):24-27.

Norris, K. S. 1958. The big one got away. *Pacific Discovery* XI(5):3-9.

Norris, K. S. 1958. The evolution and systematics of the iguanid genus *Uma* and its relation to the evolution of other North American desert reptiles. *Bulletin American Museum Natural History* 114(3):251-326.

McFarland, W. N. and K. S. Norris. 1958. The control of pH by buffers in fish transport. *California Fish & Game* 44(4):291-310.

Davenport, D. and K. S. Norris. 1958. Observations on the symbiosis of the sea anemone *Stoichactis* and the pomacentrid fish, *Amphiprion percula. Biological Bulletin* 115(3)397-410.

Norris, K. S. 1959. The functions of temperature in the ecology of the percoid fish, *Girella nigricans* (Ayres). Ph.D. Dissertation, University of California at Los Angeles.

Norris, K. S. and J. H. Prescott. 1959. Jaw structure and tooth replacement in the Opaleye, *Girella nigricans (*Ayres) and notes on other species. *Copeia* 4:275-283.

Norris, K. S. 1959. Water, pH and tropical fishes. *Tropical Fish Hobbyist* VIII (1):67-69.

Norris, K. S., F. Brocato, F. Calandrino and W. N. McFarland. 1960. A survey of fish transportation methods and equipment. *California Fish and Game* 46(l):5-33.

Norris, K. S. and J. H. Prescott. 1961. Observations on Pacific cetaceans of California and Mexican waters. *University of California Press Publications in Zoology,* 63(4):291-402.

Norris, R. M. and K. S. Norris. 1961. Algodones dunes of southeastern California. *Geological Society of America Bulletin* 72:605-620.

Committee on Marine Mammals. 1961. Standardized methods for measuring and recording data on the smaller cetaceans. K. S. Norris, ed. *Journal of Mammalogy* 42(4):471-476.

McFarland, W. N. and K. S. Norris. 1961. The use of amine buffers in the transportation of fishes. *Annals New York Academy of Science* 92(2):446-456.

Kavanau, J. L. and K. S. Norris. 1961. Behavior studies by capacitance sensing. *Science* 134(3481):730-732.

Norris, K. S., J. H. Prescott, P. V. Asa-Dorian and P. Perkins. 1961. An experimental demonstration of echolocation behavior in the porpoise, *Tursiops truncatus* (Montagu). *Biological Bulletin* 120(3):163-176.

Norris, K. S. 1961. Observations of the Pacific pilot whale, *Globicephala scammoni* in nature. *Science*, Vol. 3, p. 9 (Abstract)

Norris, K. S. and F. E. J. Fry. 1962. Transportation of live fish. Pages 595-608 in G. Borgstrom, ed. *Fish as Food.* Academic Press Inc., New York.

Norris, K. S. 1963. Preparations for radiotelemetry of the body temperature of reptiles. In *Bio-Telemetry*, Pergamon Press, Oxford, London, New York, Paris.

Kielhorn, W. V., K. S. Norris and W. E. Evans. 1963. Bathing behavior of frigate birds, *Condor* 65(3):240-241.

Norris, K. S. 1963. The functions of temperature in the ecology of the percoid fish, *Girella nigricans* (Ayres). *Ecological Monographs* 33:23-62.

Norris, K. S. 1963. A spectrophotometric analysis of color in living reptiles. *Proceedings International Congress of Zoology,* abstract, Washington, D.C., August 20-27.

Norris, K. S. 1964. Some problems of echolocation in cetaceans. Pages 317-336 in *Marine Bio-Acoustics*. Proceedings of a symposium at Bimini, Bahamas, April 1963, Pergamon Press, Oxford, London, New York, Paris.

Norris, K. S. 1963. Environment and a lizard—Desert history is clue to adaptations. *Natural History* LXXII (1):54-59.

Norris, K. S. and W. R. Dawson. 1964 Observations on the water economy and electrolyte excretion of Chuckwallas (*Lacertilia sauromalus*). *Copeia* 4:638-646.

Norris, K. S. and C. H. Lowe. 1964. An analysis of background color-matching in amphibians and reptiles. *Ecology* 45(3):565-580.

Eberhardt, R. L. and K. S. Norris. 1964. Observations of newborn pacific gray whales on Mexican calving grounds. *Journal of Mammalogy* 45(l):88-95.

Norris, K. S. 1965. Trained porpoise released in the open sea. *Science* 147:1048-1050.

Norris, K. S., H. A. Baldwin, and D. J, Samson. 1965. Open ocean diving test with a trained porpoise (*Steno bredanensis*). *Deep-Sea Research and Oceanography* 12:505-509, Pergamon Press Ltd., Great Britain.

Pryor, R. A., K. Pryor and K. S. Norris. 1965. Observations on a pygmy killer whale (*Feresa attenuata Gray*) from Hawaii. *Journal of Mammalogy* 46(3):450-461.

Norris, K. S. 1965. Oceanic coordinate index. *Limnology and Oceanography* 10(4):616.

Norris, K. S. 1965. Trained porpoise released into the open sea. *Science* 147(3661):1048-1050.

Lang, T. G., K. S. Norris. 1966. Swimming speed of a pacific bottlenose porpoise. *Science* 151:588-590.

Norris, K. S., W. E. Evans and R. N. Turner. 1966. Echolocation in an Atlantic bottlenose porpoise during discrimination. Symposium: Les systemes sonars animaux —biologie et bionique. *Biology and Bionics* 1:409-437.

Norris, K. S. 1966. Some observations on the migration and orientation of marine mammals. in R. M. Storm, Ed. *Animal orientation and navigation, proceedings 27th annual biology colloquium*, Oregon State University Press, Corvallis, Oregon.

Turner, R. N. and K. S. Norris. 1966. Discriminative echolocation in a porpoise. *Journal Experimental Analysis of Behavior* 9(5):535-544.

Norris, K. S. 1966. Editor, *Whales, Dolphins and Porpoises,* U.C. Press, Berkeley and Los Angeles, California.

Lowe, C. H., J. W. Wright and K. S. Norris. 1966. Analysis of the herpetofauna of Baja California, Mexico. IV. The Baja California striped whiptail, *Cnemidophorus labialis,* with key to the striped-unspotted whiptails of the Southwest. *Journal Arizona Academy of Science* 4:121-127.

Nishiwaki, M. and K. S. Norris. 1966. A new genus, *Peponocephala* for the odontocete cetacean species, *Electra electra. Scientific Reports Whales Research Institute* 20:95-100.

Norris, K. S. and J. S. Kavanau. 1966. The burrowing of the western shovelnosed snake, *Chionactis occipitalis* Hallowell, and the undersand environment. *Copeia* 4:650-664.

Norris, K. S. and W. E. Evans. 1967. Directionality of echolocation clicks in the rough-toothed porpoise, *Steno bredanensis* (Lesson). Pages 305-316 in *Marine bio-acoustics, Proceedings 2nd Symposium Marine Bioacoustics.* American Museum of Natural History, N.Y. Pergamon Press, Oxford and New York.

Norris, K. S. 1967. Some observations on the migration and orientation of marine mammals. Pages 101-1224 in R. M. Storm ed. *Animal Orientation and Navigation*, Oregon State University Press, Corvallis OR.

Norris, K. S. 1967. Color adaptation in desert reptiles and its thermal relationships. Pages 162-229 in W.W. Milstead, ed. *Lizard Ecology: a Symposium,* held at University of Missouri, June 1965, University of Missouri Press, Columbia.

Norris, K. S. 1967. Aggressive behavior in *Cetacea.* Pages 225-241 in C.D. Clements and D.B. Lindsley, eds. Aggression and defense: neural mechanism and social patterns (*Brain Function*, Vol. 5) UCLA forum in medical science, No. 7, *Proceedings 5th Conference on Brain Function,* 1965, U.C. Press, Berkeley and Los Angeles.

Norris, K. S. 1968. California's natural land and water reserve system. *BioScience* 18(5):415-417.

Norris, K. S. 1968. The evolution of acoustic mechanisms in odontocete cetaceans. Pages 297-324 in E.T. Drake, ed. *Evolution and Environment: a*

Symposium (100th anniversary). Peabody Museum of Natural History, Yale University, Yale University Press, New Haven and London.

Norris, K. S. 1969. The echolocation of marine mammals. Pages 391-423 in H.T. Andersen, ed. *The Biology of Marine Mammals*, Academic Press, Berkeley and Los Angeles.

Norris, K. S. 1969. A review of *The Dolphin, Cousin to Man*, by Robert Stenuit. Pages 147-164 in M. E. McCloskey and J. P. Gilligan, eds. *Quality of life.* Sierra Club, San Francisco,

Porter, W. P. and K. S. Norris. 1969. Lizard reflectivity change and its effect on light transmission through body wall. *Science* 163:482-484.

Norris, K. S. 1970. The third fish. *The New Republic* 162(19):16-18.

Norris, K. S. and K. W. Pryor. 1970. A tagging method for small cetaceans. *Journal of Mammalogy.* 51(3):609-610.

Norris, K. S. 1971. Natural areas—needs and attainment. Pages 17-15 in W.J. Dittrich and J.M. Trappe, eds. *Proceedings symposium northwest science association* 43rd meeting, Salem Oregon, March 1970, A continuing education book, Corvallis, Oregon,

Hubbs, C. L. and K. S. Norris. 1971. Original teeming abundance, supposed extinction, and survival of the Juan Fernandez fur seal. Pages 35-52 in E.H. Burt, ed. *Antarctic Pinnipedia*, Antarctic Research Series, Volume 18.

Norris, K. S., K. J. Dormer, J. Pegg & G. J. Liese 1971. The mechanism of sound production and air recycling in porpoises: a preliminary report. *Proceedings of the eighth annual conference on biological sonar and diving mammals* 1971, pp.1-11.

Norris, K. S. and W. A. Watkins. 1971. Underwater sounds of *Arctocephalus philippii*, the Juan Fernandez fur seal. Pages 169-171 in E.H. Burt, ed. *Antarctic Pinnipedia*, Antarctic Research Series 8.

Norris, K. S. and G. W. Harvey. 1972. A theory for the function of the spermaceti organ of the sperm whale (*Physeter catodon L.*). Pages 397-416 in S.R. Galler, T. Schmidt-Koenig, G. J. Jacobs and R. E. Belleville, eds. *Animal orientation and navigation*, NASA SP-262.

Shehadeh, Z.H., K. S. Norris and C. L. Hubbs. 1972. The grey mullet (*Mugil cephalus L.*): induced breeding and larval rearing research 1970-72. *Oceanic Institute Report* 01-72-76-1.

Norris, K. S. and J. J. Crouch. 1972. Refurbishing a Hawaiian fishpond in a feasibility project for a method of open water fish farming. Oceanic Institute Report No. 01-72-76.

Norris, K. S., W. D. Madden and P. S. Norris. 1972. An experiment in undersea mariculture, in a feasibility pilot project for a method of open water fish farming. *Oceanic Institute Report* No. 0172-78-1, pages 1-21.

Norris, K. S., K. J. Dormer, J. Pegg and F. J. Liese. 1972. The mechanism of sound production and air recycling in porpoises: a preliminary report. Pages 113-130 in *Eighth annual conference of biological sonar and diving mammals,* 1971. Stanford Research Institute.

Norris, K. S., G. W. Harvey, L. A. Burzell and T. D. Krishna Kartha. 1972. Sound production in the freshwater porpoises *Sotalia cf. fluviatilis Gervais* and *Deville* and *Inia geoffrensis Blainville,* in the Rio Negro, Brazil. Pages 251-260 in G. Pilleri, ed. *Investigations on Cetacea.* Volume 5.

Ray, G. C., and K. S. Norris. 1972. Managing marine environments. Pages 190-200 in T*ransactions 37th North American Wildlife Natural Research Conference.* Wildlife Management Institute.

Norris, K. S. and R. L. Gentry. 1974. Capture and harnessing of young California gray whales, *Eschrichtius robustus. Marine Fisheries Review,* 36(4):58-64.

Dohl, R. P., K. S. Norris and I. Kang. 1974. A porpoise hybrid: *Tursiops x Steno. Journal of Mammalogy* 55(l):217-221.

Norris, K. S. 1974. *The Porpoise Watcher.* W.W. Norton & Co., New York. 250pp.

Norris, K. S. 1974. Whale. Pages 805-810 in *Encyclopedia Britannica,* 15th edition, Hemingway Benton Publisher.

Norris, K. S. and G. W. Harvey. 1974. Sound transmission in the porpoise head. *Journal Acoustical Society of America* 56(2):659-664.

Norris, K. S. 1974. To Carl Leavitt Hubbs, a modern pioneer naturalist on the occasion of his eightieth year. *Copeia* 3:581-610.

Schevill W. E., G. C. Ray, K. S. Norris. 1974. *The Whale Problem; A Status Report.* Cambridge, Mass., Harvard University Press. 419 pgs.

Norris, K. S. and W. E. Evans. 1974. New tagging and tracking methods for the study of marine mammal biology and migration. Pages 395-408 in W.E. Schevill, G.D. Ray and K.S. Norris, eds. *The Whale Problem.* Harvard University Press.

Kooyman, G. L., K. S. Norris and R. L. Gentry. 1975. The gray whale's spout: its physical characteristics. *Science* 190:908-910.

Norris, K.S. and C. Szego. 1976. Obituary: Raymond Bridgeman Cowles 1986-1975. *Nature* 261:441.

Norris, K. S. 1977. Tuna sandwiches cost at least 78,000 porpoise lives a year, but there is hope. *Smithsonian* 7(11):44-52.

Norris, K. S., R. Goodman, B. Villa-R. and L. Hobbs. 1977. The behavior of California gray whales (*Eschrichtius robustus*) in southern Baja California, Mexico, *Fishery Bulletin of the United States* 75:159-172.

Norris, K. S., B. J. LeBoeuf, and D. J. Miller. 1978. *A coloring book of sea mammals.* Santa Barbara, Ca., Bellerophon Books.

Norris, K. S. et. al. 1978. PI Marine Mammal and Seabird Survey of the Southern California Bight Area, 1975-76. III(I):1-472, Investigator's reports, *Pinnipedia, Cetacea,* Parasitology. III(II):473-774, Seabirds. III(III):775-1224, Appendices and literature citations. Report to U.S. Bureau of Land Management contract # 08550-CT5-28.

Norris, K. S. 1978. Planning session for the Society of Marine Mammalogists, draft of initial charter. San Diego, CA.

Norris, K. S. 1978. Marine mammals and man. Pages 320-338 in H.P. Brokaw ed. Wildlife and America—*Contributions to an Understanding of American Wildlife and its Conservation.* Council On Environmental Quality, U.S. Fish and Wildlife Service. 532 pages.

Norris, K. S. 1978. Cetacean Biosonar: Part 1: Anatomical and behavioral studies. Pages 215-236 in *Perspectives in Marine Biology* Vol. 2. Academic Press, London.

Pryor, K. and K. S. Norris. 1978. The tuna/porpoise problem: Behavioral aspects. *Oceanus* 21(2):31-37.

Norris, K. S. & R. R. Reeves, eds. 1978. Report on a workshop on problems related to humpback whales (*Megaptera novaeangliae*) in Hawaii. *Final report to the Marine Mammal Commission* No. MMC-77/03. [NTIS PB 280794].

Norris, K. S., W. E. Stuntz, and W. Rogers. 1979. The behavior of porpoises and tuna in the eastern tropical Pacific Yellow fin tuna fishery Preliminary studies. *Final Report to the U.S. Marine Mammal Commission*, 85 pp.

Norris, K. S. 1979. Racing across the desert: Reason takes a wrong turn. *Los Angeles Times* Opinion Column, Pt. VI, pp. 3-4.

Norris, K. S. 1979. Man's impact on the desert—planning for change. Symposium paper Pages 1-10 in *The Fate of the California Desert*, Needles, CA. 1977, Bureau of Land Management.

Norris, K. S. 1979. The natural history of the whale. *Quarterly Review of Biology* 54:346.

Norris, K. S. & J. D. Hall 1979. Development of techniques for estimating trophic impact of marine mammals. *Final report to the Marine Mammal Commission* No. MMC-74/06. [NTIS PB 290399].

Norris, K. S. 1980. Hawaiian humpback whale sanctuary workshop, Ka'anapali and Lahaina, Maui, Hawaii. Dec. 12-14, 1979. Pages 1-19 in Committee report. Publications Office Coastal Zone Management NA79AAA04692.

Norris, K. S. and T. P. Dohl 1980. Behavior of the Hawaiian spinner dolphin, *Stenella longirostris*. *Fishery Bulletin* 77(4):821-849.

Norris, K. S. 1980. Peripheral sound processing in odontocetes. Pages 495-509 in R. G. Busnel and J. F. Fish eds. *Animal sonar systems*, Plenum Publishing.

Norris, K. S. and T. P. Dohl 1980. The structure and function of cetacean schools. Pages 211-261 in L. M. Herman, ed. *Cetacean behavior: mechanisms and processes.* John Wiley and Sons Inc.

Wells, R., B. Würsig and K. S. Norris. 1981. Un reconocimiento de los mamiferos marins en el Alto Golfo de California, Mexico, Pages 1-21 in *Proceedings 5th meeting marine mammals of western Mexico*, La Paz, Baja.

Villa-Ramirez, B., K. S. Norris, G. Nichols, D. Würsig, and K. Miller. 1981. Agrupamientos de ballenas grisas, *Eschrichtius robustus* (Lilljeborg 1861). *Revistas*, University of Mexico 1-45.

Norris, K. S. 1981. Marine Mammals of the Arctic: their sounds and their relation to alterations in the acoustic environment by man-made noise. Pages 304-309 in *Proceedings Congress Arctic Pilot Project*, Petro Canada, Toronto.

Wells, R. S., B. Würsig and K. S. Norris. 1981. A survey of the marine mammals of the upper Gulf of California, Mexico, with an assessment of the status of *Phocoena sinus*. NTIS, BV 81-168791 viii 51 pp.

Connor, R. C., and K. S. Norris. 1982. Are dolphins reciprocal altruists? *American Naturalist* 119:358-374.

Kolb, P. M. and K. S. Norris. 1982. A harbor seal, *Phoca vitulina richardii*, taken from a sablefish trap. California Department of Fish and Game 68(2):123-124.

B. Villa-Ramirez, K. S. Norris, G. Nichols B. Würsig and K. A. Miller. 1983. Lagoon entrance and other aggregations of gray whales (*Eschrichtius robustus*). Pages 259-293 in R. Payne, ed. *Communication and behavior of whales.* Westview Press, Boulder, CO.

Norris, K. S. and B. Mühl. 1983. Can odontocetes debilitate prey with sound? *American Naturalist* 122:84-104.

Weiner R., K. S. Norris and A. Black. 1983. *A plan for a natural areas reserve on the University of California Santa Cruz campus.* Santa Cruz, California Publication No. 12, Environmental Field Program University of California, Santa Cruz.

Norris, K. S. 1984. Review of the sierra club handbook of dolphins and whales, S. Leatherwood and R. Reeves, Sierra Club Books. *Defenders* Mar/Apr:37-38.

Norris, K. S., B. Würsig, R. S. Wells, M. Würsig, S. M. Brownlee, C. Johnson and J. Solow 1985. The behavior of the Hawaiian spinner dolphin, *Stenella longirostris.* NOAA-NMFS-SWFC Administrative Report LJ-85-06C.

Norris, K. S. 1985. Review of animal thinking, D. Griffin, Harvard University Press. *Quarterly Review of Biology* 60:393-394.

Brown M. and K. S. Norris. 1986. *Academic plan for the Campus Natural Areas Reserve. University of California Santa Cruz.* Campus Natural Reserve Committee, University of California Santa Cruz.

Norris, K. S. 1986. Sound production in cetaceans. *Marine Mammal Science* 2(3):233-235.

Norris, K. S. 1986. Contributor to: *Distinguished Teachers on Effective Teaching.* In *New Directions for Teaching and Learning,* No 28. P.G. Beidler, ed. Jossey-Bass, Inc. San Francisco.

Johnson, C. M., and K. S. Norris. 1986. Delphinid social organization and social behavior. Pages 335-346 in R. J. Shusterman, J. A. Thomas and F. G. Wood eds. Dolphin Cognition and Behavior: a Comparative Approach.

Norris, K. S. 1986. In appreciation of Cetaceans. *Whalewatcher* 20(4):14-18.

Norris, K. S. 1986. The animal awareness debate. *Pacific Discovery* 39:13.

Norris, K. S. 1986. Sound production in dolphins. *Marine Mammal Science* 2(3):233-235.

Norris, K. S. 1986. Freezing the desert. Commentary on proposed Cranston Desert Protection Act, Op. Ed. Column, *San Jose Mercury.*

Norris, K. S. 1987. Testimony of K. S. Norris regarding Senate Bill 7, The California Desert Protection Acts. Senate Committee on Parks and Wildlife, Washington, D.C. *Federal Register.*

Norris, K. S. 1987. Commentary on Senate Bill 7, The Desert Protection Act. Op. Ed. Column, *San Jose Mercury.*

Norris, K. S., R. S. Wells & G. K. Silber 1987. Relative Discreteness of Harbor Porpoise Population(s) in North-Central California. Progress report to the Marine Mammal Commission, MMC Contract M3309815-7.

Marten, K., K. S. Norris, P.W.B. Moore and K. A. Englund. 1988. Loud impulse sounds in odontocete predation and social behavior. Pages 567-580 in *Animal Sonar: processes and performance.* P.E. Nachtigal and P.W.B. Moore eds. NATO ASI Series A: Life Sciences Vol 156. Plenum Press, N.Y. London.

Norris, K. S. and C. R. Schilt. 1988. Cooperative societies in three-dimensional space: on the origins of aggregations, flocks, and schools, with special reference to dolphins and fish. *Ethology and Sociobiology* 9:149-179.

Norris, K. S. and E. C. Evans III. 1988. On the evolution of acoustic communication systems in vertebrates. Part I: Historical aspects. Pages 655-669 in P.E. Nachtigall and W. B. Moore eds., *Animal Sonar.* Plenum Pubisher, New York.

Evans III, E. C. and K. S. Norris. 1988. On the evolution of acoustic communication systems in vertebrates. Part II: Cognitive aspects. Pages 671-681 in P.E. Nachtigall and W. B. Moore eds., *Animal sonar.* Plenum Publisher, New York.

Ford, L. D. and K. S. Norris. 1988. The University of California Natural Reserve System: Progress and Prospects. *BioScience* 38(7):463-470.

Goodall, R. N. P., K. S. Norris, A. R. Galeazzi, J. A. Oporto, and I. S. Cameron. 1988. On the Chilean dolphin, *Cephalorhynchus eutropia* (Gray, 1846). Pages 197-257 in R. L. Brownell Jr. and G. P. Donovan eds. *Biology of the Genus Cephalorhynchus.* Reports of the International Whaling Commission, Special Issue No 9, Cambridge, UK.

Ridgway, S. H., K. S. Norris and L. H. Cornell. 1989. Some considerations for those wishing to propagate *Platanistoid* dolphins. Pages 159-167 in W. F. Perrin, R. L. Brownell Jr., K. Zhou, and J. Liu eds. *Biology and Conservation of the river dolphins.* Occasional Papers of the International Union for the Conservation of Nature SSC No. 3.

Ford, L. D. and K. S. Norris. 1989. The University of California Natural Reserve System: Progress and Prospects. *Fremontia* 17(2):11-16.

Silber G. K., R. S. Wells and K. S. Norris. 1990. A preliminary assessment of techniques for catching and radio-tagging harbor porpoises U.S. Marine Mammal Commission. Final report Contract # MM3309815-7. Washington, D.C.

Norris, K. S. 1990. Gill nets and marine mammals. Working paper, IWC conference, La Jolla, CA (SC/090/G46).

Norris, K. S. 1991. *Dolphin Days: the Life and Times of the Spinner Dolphin.* Norton, New York.

Pryor, K. and K. S. Norris 1991. *Dolphin Societies: Discoveries and Puzzles.* University of California Press, Berkeley.

Aroyan, J. L., T. W. Cranford, J. Kent, and K. S. Norris. 1992. Computer modeling of acoustic beam formation in *Delphinus delphis. Journal of the Acoustical Society of America* 92(5): 2539-2545.

Norris, K. S. 1992. Dolphins in crisis. *National Geographic* 182(3):2-35.

Norris, K. S. 1993. *Dolphin Days: The Life & Times of the Spinner Dolphin.* Avon Books, New York.

Leatherwood, S., T. A. Jefferson and K. S. Norris. 1993. Occurrence and sounds of Fraser's dolphins (*Lagenodelphis hosei)* in the Gulf of Mexico. *Texas Journal of Science* 45(4):349-354.

Norris, K. S., B. Würsig, R. S. Wells, M. Würsig. 1994. *The Hawaiian Spinner Dolphin.* University of California Press, Berkeley. 408 pages.

Norris, K. S. 1995. The bowhead whale. *Animal Behaviour* 49(2):558-560.

Backus, R. H., D. Bumpus, B. Lawrence, K. S. Norris, C. E. Ray, G. C. Ray, J. R. Twiss, and W. A. Watkins. 1995. William Edward Schevill, 1906-1994: Memories. *Marine Mammal Science* 11(3): 416-419.

Goodall, R. N. P., K. S. Norris, G. Harris, J.A. Oporto, and H. Castello. 1995. Notes on the biology of the Burmeister's porpoise, *Phocoena spinipinnis* off southern South America. Pages 317-347 in A. Bjorge and G. P. Donovan, eds. *Report of the International Whaling Commission Special Issue, 16. Biology of the phocoenids: A collection of papers.* Cambridge, England, UK, International Whaling Commission.

Goodall, R. N. P., B.Würsig, M. Würsig, G. Harris, and K. S. Norris. 1995. Sightings of Burmeister's porpoise, *Phocoena spinipinnis*, off southern South America. In A. Bjorge and G. P. Donovan, eds. Report of the International Whaling Commission Special Issue, 16. *Biology of the phocoenids: A collection of papers.* Cambridge, England, UK, International Whaling Commission.

Cranford, T. W., M. Amundin, and K. S. Norris. 1996. Functional morphology and homology in the *odontocete* nasal complex: Implications for sound generation. *Journal of Morphology* 228(3):223-285.

Schilt C. R. and K. S. Norris. 1997. Perspectives on sensory integration systems: Problems, opportunities and predictions. Pages 225-244 in J. K. Parish and W. M. Hamner, eds. *Animal groups in three dimensions.* Cambridge University Press, London.

Goodall, R. N. P., K. S. Norris, W. E. Schevill, F. Fraga, R. Praderi, M. A. Iniguez Jr., and J. C. De Haro. 1997. Review and update on the biology of Peale's dolphins, *Lagenorhynchus australis. Report of the International Whaling Commission* 47:777-796.

Goodall, R. N. P., J. C. De Haro, F. Fraga, M. A., Iniguez and K. S. Norris. 1997. Sightings and behaviour of Peale's dolphins, *Lagenorhynchus australis,* with notes on dusky dolphins, *L. obscurus,* off southernmost South America. *Report of the International Whaling Commission* 47:757-775.

Wells, R. S., K. Bassos-Hull, and K. S. Norris. 1998. Experimental return to the wild of two bottlenose dolphins. *Marine Mammal Science* 14(1):51-71.

Norris, K. S. 1998. Cetaceans. Pages 71-91 in *Wild Animals of North America.* National Geographic Society, Washington D.C.

APPENDIX IV:

Environmental Field Program Publications

Andaloro, Louis and Rob Roy Ramey II. *The Relocation of Bighorn Sheep in the Sierra Nevada of California.* Santa Cruz: Environmental Field Program, University of California, Santa Cruz, 1981.

Bickford, Charisse and Paul Rich. *Vegetation and Flora of the Landels-Hill Big Creek Reserve, Monterey County, California.* Santa Cruz: Environmental Field Program, University of California, Santa Cruz, 1979. Second edition, 1984.

Bikle, Anne. *Amphibians of the Landels-Hill Big Creek Reserve, Monterey County, California.* Santa Cruz: Environmental Field Program, University of California, Santa Cruz, 1985.

Carothers, John. Terrestrial *Vertebrates of the Landels-Hill Big Creek Reserve Monterey County, California.* Santa Cruz, Environmental Field Program, University of California, Santa Cruz, 1980.

Defenderfer, Donald C. and Robert B. Walkinshaw. *One Long Summer Day in Alaska: a Documentation of Perspectives in the Wrangell Mountains.* Santa Cruz: Environmental Field Program, University of California Santa Cruz, 1981.

Duncan, Richard B. *Natural and Geologic Hazards: Physical Considerations for Offshore Oil and Gas Development in Norton Sound, Alaska.* Santa Cruz: Environmental Field Program, University of California, Santa Cruz, 1981.

Engles, Eric and Richard D. Norris. (Helen Gibbons and Martha Brown, eds.) *The Natural Features of the Gamboa Point Properties, Monterey County, California.* Santa Cruz: Environmental Field Program, University of California, 1984.

Ferguson, Ava. *Intertidal Plants and Animals of the Landels-Hill Big Creek Reserve, Monterey County, California.* Santa Cruz: Center for Marine Studies, University of California, 1984.

Fleshman, Carolyn and Darrell S. Kaufman. *South Fork Kern River Wildlife Area: Effects of Reservoir Inundation.* Santa Cruz, Environmental Field Program, University of California, Santa Cruz, 1983.

Georgette, Susan E. *In the Rough Land to the South: an Oral History of the Lives and Events at Big Creek, Big Sur, California.* Santa Cruz: Environmental

Field Program, University of California, Santa Cruz, 1981. Second edition, 1982.

Georgette, Susan E. and Ann H. Harvey. *Local Influence and the National Interest: Ten Years of National Park Service Administration in the Stehekin Valley, Washington, a Case Study.* Santa Cruz: Environmental Field Program, University of California, Santa Cruz, 1980.

Josephs, Hugh. *The Effects of Outer Continental Shelf Development on Certain Pinnipeds of the Bering Sea.* Santa Cruz: Environmental Field Program, University of California, 1981.

Lebo, Andrew, Leslie Nitikman, and Charles Salmen. *San Sebastian Marsh: a Resource Survey and Management Plan, Imperial County, California.* Santa Cruz: Environmental Field Program, University of California, Santa Cruz, 1982.

Norris, Richard D., and Martha Brown, ed. *Geology of the Landels-Hill Big Creek Reserve, Monterey County, California.* Santa Cruz, Environmental Field Program, University of California, Santa Cruz, 1985.

Pomeroy, Flora and Martha Brown, ed. *Granite Mountain Spring: an Introduction to the Eastern Mojave Desert, California.* Santa Cruz, University of California, Santa Cruz, 1986.

Stein, Bruce A. and Sheridan F. Warrick, eds. *Granite Mountains Resource Survey: Natural and Cultural Values of the Granite Mountains, Eastern Mojave Desert, California.* Santa Cruz: Environmental Field Program, University of California, Santa Cruz, 1979.

Stone, R. Doug and Valerie A. Sumida, eds. T*he Kingston Range of California: a Resource Survey: Natural and Cultural Values of Kingston Range, Eastern Mojave Desert, Calif.* Santa Cruz: Environmental Field Program, University of California, Santa Cruz, 1983.

Warrick, Sheridan F. and Elizabeth D. Wilcox. *Big River: the Natural History of an Endangered Northern California Estuary.* Santa Cruz: Environmental Field Program, University of California, 1981.

Warrick, Sheridan F., ed. *The Natural History of the UC Santa Cruz Campus,* Santa Cruz: Environmental Field Program, University of California, Santa Cruz, 1982.

Weiner R., K. S. Norris and A. Black. A *Plan for a Natural Areas Reserve on the University of California Santa Cruz Campus.* Santa Cruz: Environmental Field Program, University of California, Santa Cruz, 1983.

Notes on Contributors

SHANNON M. BROWNLEE *first met Ken Norris when she was a UCSC freshman in 1974, and took the Natural History of California field class (as it was originally designated) in 1975. She says of her experience: ". . . after that class, there was no turning back from biology and science for me." She went on to do field work studying turkey vultures in Baja, California, under Norris's direction, and graduated with a B.S. in Biology in 1979. Brownlee joined Norris's research team in Hawaii, studying spinner dolphins from 1979 until 1982, and earned her M.S. in Marine Science from UCSC. Brownlee is a freelance journalist and film-maker specializing in science. For a decade she was the lead science writer for* U.S. News & World Report. *She was a Knight Journalism Fellow at Stanford University in 1992-1993. Her work has appeared in the* Atlantic Monthly *and* The New Republic. *She is featured in The New Science Journalists (Ballantine Books, 1995), an anthology of American science writing. She was a speaker at the Nobel Laureates Symposium on the future of creativity in the age of big science, held in December, 1991, in Stockholm. Of her career she says, "If I've become anybody with an independent mind and the backbone to express it, that's partly Ken's doing."*

LAWRENCE D. FORD *graduated from UCSC with a double B.A. in Biology and Environmental Studies in 1978. At UC Berkeley he earned his M.S. in Range Management in 1986 and his Ph.D. in Wildland Resource Science (Vegetation Ecology and Management) in 1991. At UCSC he worked closely with Ken Norris from 1977 to 1984 as instructor for the Natural History Field Quarter, as coordinator for the Environmental Field Program, and as manager of the Landels-Hill Big Creek Reserve. Later he was a member of the Chancellor's Advisory Committee for the Natural Reserve System (1987-1991); and in 1990 founded the Kenneth S. Norris Fund for UC's Natural Reserve System, where he serves as director. Currently he is Vice President of the Institute for Sustainable Development in San Francisco, developing technical training and consulting programs for community-based ecosystem management.*

STEPHEN R. GLIESSMAN *joined the UCSC faculty in environmental studies in 1981 and has held the Afred E. Heller Professorship of Agroecology since 1983. He taught the Natural History Field Quarter with Ken Norris from 1981 to 1990 and continues teaching the course yearly. Gliessman's research and teaching areas include agroecology, sustainable agriculture and ethnobotany; and California natural history, botany, and ecology. His research is carried out within the framework of agroecology—the application of ecological concepts and principles to the design and management of sustainable agroecosystems, including their economic and social implications.*

RANDALL JARRELL, *who conducted the interviews and edited this volume, received a B.A. in History from San Francisco State University in 1969; an M.A. in U.S. History from the University of California, Santa Cruz in 1978; and an M.A. in Clinical Psychology from the University of San Francisco in 1987. She was appointed as director of the Regional History Project in 1974, and has published oral history volumes documenting Santa Cruz history and the institutional history of UCSC.*

JENNY WARDRIP KELLER, *who illustrated the cover of this volume, graduated from UCSC in 1984 with an independent major in "Natural Science Illustration" and helped to establish UCSC's Science Illustration Program in 1986, where she is a lecturer. She wrote that "the Natural History Field Quarter (as for so many who took part in it) played a pivotal role in shaping the direction of my career. The creation of illustrated field journals during those grand rambles across California combined my lifelong interests in art and the natural sciences, which in turn led to more formal training as a scientific illustrator." She illustrated several of Ken Norris's books, including* The Hawaiian Spinner Dolphin *and* Dolphin Days. *Her work has been published in* Sierra Magazine, Bioscience, Garden, *and* Scientific American.

WILLIAM N. MCFARLAND *attended UCLA where he received his B.A. (1951), M.A. (1953) and Ph.D. in zoology (1953). He became close friends with Ken Norris when they were graduate students, and went with him to Marineland of the Pacific, where he worked from 1954 until 1957 as a chemist and biologist. From 1958 to 1973 McFarland was at the University of Texas; and from 1973 until he retired he was a Professor of Zoology at Cornell University. McFarland's research specialties include fish physiology, comparative physiology and ecology. He now lives at Friday Harbor in Washington state.*

ROBERT M. NORRIS *received his B.A. (1943) and his M.A. (1949) from UC Los Angeles; and his Ph.D. from Scripps Institution of Oceanography (1951). He was a professor of geology at UC Santa Barbara from 1955 until he retired in 1986. His research specialties include geomorphology, especially shoreline processes and desert dunes. Norris was deeply involved in overseeing several of UC's Natural Reserve System sites, and was his brother's intellectual and scientific colleague throughout their professional lives.*

WILLIAM F. PERRIN *received his B.S. in Biology from San Diego State University in 1966 and his Ph.D. in Zoology from U.C. Los Angeles in 1972. His doctoral dissertation, "Variation and Taxonomy of Spotted and Spinner Porpoises (genus Stenella) of the Eastern Tropical Pacific and Hawaii," is considered a landmark work in the field. His research over the years has centered on the population biology (life history, systematics, and ecology), conservation, and management of cetaceans taken incidentally in the tuna purse seine fishery in the eastern tropical Pacific and other fisheries around the world. His research was significant in crafting the Marine Mammal Protection Act of 1972. Currently he is the Senior Scientist at the Southwest Fisheries Science Center of the U.S. National Marine Fisheries Service (NOAA) in La Jolla, California, Adjunct Professor at the Scripps Institution of Oceanography, and editor of the journal Marine Mammal Science.*

IRENE RETI, *who conducted interviews and coordinated the publication of this book, was born in Los Angeles and moved to Santa Cruz in 1978. She received her B.A. in Environmental Studies from UCSC in 1982. She also is the publisher of HerBooks, a small press publisher of creative nonfiction and literary anthologies.*

ROGER J. SAMUELSEN *graduated from UC Berkeley in 1958 and received his J.D. from Boalt Hall School of Law in 1964. He began his University career as Coordinator of Special Projects under UC President Clark Kerr in 1967, when he began working with Ken Norris in developing the fledgling UC Natural Reserve System. He became Director of the NRS in 1974 and during his tenure he continued working closely with Norris as the system expanded to over 30 natural reserves throughout the state, dedicated to teaching and research. He took early retirement from the University in 1991 but has continued on a part-time basis working on the planning of the UC Merced campus in the San Joaquin Valley.*

DONALD J. USNER *received his B.A. from UCSC in Biology and Environmental Studies in 1980 and his M.A. in Geography from the University of New Mexico in 1991. He was a student in the Natural History Field Quarter in 1980 and was a T.A. for Field Quarter in 1984 and 1985. He was the caretaker at Big Creek Reserve from 1982-1986. Usner is a freelance photographer and writer. He has published* Sabino's Map: Life in Chimayó's Old Plaza *(Santa Fe: Museum of New Mexico Press, 1995) and (with Paul Henson)* The Natural History of Big Sur *(Berkeley: University of California Press, 1993). He is a faculty member at Santa Fe Community College and the University of New Mexico and lives in Chimayó, New Mexico, where his family has lived for many generations.*

Ken Norris, Field Quarter 1975. Drawing by Beth Hird

Index

A

B

C

D

E

F

G

H

I

J

K

L

M

N

O

P

R

S

T

U

V

W

Y

Z

CPSIA information can be obtained at www.ICGtesting.com
Printed in the USA
LVOW042210301111

257293LV00002B/48/P